A Testament of Sindh
Ethnic and Religious Extremism
A Perspective

A Testament of Sindh

Ethnic and Religious Extremism
A Perspective

M. S. KOREJO

OXFORD
UNIVERSITY PRESS

... even this will pass ...

To the people of Sindh
Who have lived and loved their land
For thousands of years;
To those who were assimilated
Through the centuries;
To those who are suffering
The pangs of assimilation.

To all the sons of the soil,
Past and present,
From generation to generation,
Of all faiths, castes, and creeds,
Dedicated to make Sindh
A place to live.

PREFACE

The citizens of Sindh, irrespective of their origin, are passing through a traumatic phase. This is evident from their individual and collective behaviour, their inter-community and intra-community relations, their political outlook, their attitude towards local, provincial, and national issues, and last, but not the least, their thinking process. They feel insecure about their socio-economic and political future. Their mode of life, their faith, and their freedom of choice have been subjected to severe stresses and strains.

There have been attempts to analyse these issues with a view to understanding the genesis of the problems, to probe into the dynamics of their causes, and to explore possibilities of softening their impact, if not eliminating them altogether. This book represents my contribution to such attempts.

I felt the need to undertake this exercise while working on my book *G.M. Syed—An Analysis of his Political Perspectives* (OUP 1999). I found a close link between Syed's perspectives and the topics discussed in this book. I recommend that these two books be read in succession, as together the two constitute a political testament of Sindh.

My views and comments are likely to raise a controversy, and if some readers were to have a contrary opinion, I would respect that in the spirit of promoting a culture of tolerance and mutual accommodation. Many friends, both Sindhis and Muhajirs, concerned at the possibility of a strong reaction, advised me to put off the publication of this book till passions cool down and a ray of light appears at the end of the tunnel. But, I feel that such a positive change cannot take place in a vacuum. There has to be a conscious and deliberate effort to light the candle.

I believe that the wounds inflicted on Sindh must be exposed rather than covered up so that their nature can be diagnosed and appropriate remedies applied, to initiate the healing process. As a part of this endeavour, I have sought support from many thinkers and intellectuals, whose thoughts and verdicts have been quoted and reproduced, whose concerns I acknowledge, and to whom I owe deep gratitude.

The use of the word 'Muhajir' is gradually becoming outdated, and this is a welcome development. Even the MQM-A has changed its name from Muhajir to Mutahida. However, newspapers, periodicals, and books still refer to Muhajirs, presumably because of the existence of separate political formations, political agenda, and mode of protest and agitation by influential sections of this community. Certain incidents in Karachi are still being attributed to Muhajirs and not to the citizens of Karachi. For example, the Mutahida chief, Altaf Hussain, recently (June 2000) protested that Muhajirs were being killed in Karachi. Unless members of the community themselves discard this label, the writers would have no option but to refer to them as Muhajirs, without meaning to offend them. Having said that, I apologize for using this word.

Murad Korejo
3 July 2000

INTRODUCTION

Among the problems facing Sindh today, ethnic militarism, sectarianism, fundamentalism, and political terrorism have acquired menacing proportions. Before independence, these problems were neither foreseen nor imagined. There were diverse ethnic groups—Sindhis, Gujratis, Balochis, Kutchis, Marwaris, Punjabis, Pathans, and others—living together in peace and harmony, giving a plural character to the province which enjoyed unity in its diversity. Its capital, Karachi, was cosmopolitan in its outlook, remarkable in its ethnic harmony, and fascinating in its exotic ambience. The rural-urban divide did not exist, and each was considered an extension of the other. Religion played a central role in the life of the people, and yet the degree of inter-religious or inter-sectarian harmony was exemplary. Among the Muslims, there were the Sunnis and the Shiites, among the Shiites were the Ismailis, the Isnaashris, the Bohras, and others. Among the non-Muslims were Hindus, Christians, Zoroastrians, Bahais, Sikhs, and others. By all standards, Sindh was an ideal society and a livable place. People concentrated their energies in constructive pursuits. There was injustice, but there was no tension and disharmony. Karachi enjoyed the reputation of a clean and civilized city, free from ethnic, linguistic, sectarian, or religious tensions. To have lived in or visited Karachi before independence was a source of aesthetic pleasure, spiritual elevation, and a sublime experience.

Today, urban Sindh presents a scene of horror. Ethnic confrontation has reached the dimensions of a mini civil war. There has been talk of the division of Sindh on an ethnic basis. Non-Muslims feel politically alienated. Sectarian intolerance has spread panic among peaceful citizens. The 'killing fields' have expanded to include places of worship. The older generation of

Sindhis is in a state of shock; the younger generation is confused. The future of Karachi is bleak.

How has this situation come about? Has there been any change in the definition, in the outlook, or in the perspective of a Sindhi? How was the demon of ethnicity and sectarianism inflicted upon this land of the Sufis? How and why was peace and harmony shattered? Is this dreadful phenomenon a temporary affair or will it go on forever? Is it an accident of history or is there a design behind it? If there is a design, then who are the players of this gruesome drama? Is there a hidden hand behind the visible players? Is this the price Sindh is paying for joining Pakistan?

The year was 1988. I had gone to Hyderabad to meet the Director of On-Farm Water Management in his office in Latifabad, which was a sprawling new neighbourhood across the railway line. The Director received me with utmost courtesy. He had been good enough to set aside one hour to brief me on his project, which would eventually benefit my own farm in village Murad Korejo. We had barely discussed the project for fifteen minutes, when his office door was flung open by four Muhajir youths. Ignoring the normal courtesies and without waiting to be heard, the young men spoke with authority, made a firm demand to close the office forthwith to enable the entire staff to attend the political rally organized to greet the visiting MQM chief, Altaf Hussain, who was to arrive from somewhere at a certain time. The Director (his name has escaped my mind), himself a Muhajir, visibly taken aback by the interruption and the unusual demand made by the intruders, eventually gathered his wits and tried to pacify the young men by lecturing them on the sanctity of a public office, the decorum to be observed in approaching the head of the department, and the need to maintain discipline among his subordinates, who should not be participating in political rallies during office hours. The young men, without losing their temper, tried to convince the Director that he should appreciate the fact that they had approached him, otherwise the staff members could have left the office without his permission, an act which would have amounted to a greater breach of office discipline. The Director got the message and requested postponement of the office shut-down by half an hour to enable him to complete his business with me and to arrange for the closing formalities. The young men 'granted' his request, left his office, and closed the door behind them.

After their departure, the Director, an expert in his line of work, a conscientious and dedicated officer, and one who was committed to changing the face of rural Sindh with the newly developed irrigation techniques, opened up to me and painted a dark picture, with great pain and anguish: 'If the politics of Sindh is allowed to proceed in this new style adopted by those people who have been given a licence to intimidate, insult, and demolish the established institutions, then God help Sindh.'

The Director's remarks haunted me for a long time as I saw the new political current assuming the dimensions of a flood, engulfing urban Sindh.

A year later, while returning home from a late-night function at a friend's house, near the Quaid's mazar in Karachi, my wife and I were ambushed at 3:00 a.m., on Shara-e-Quaideen, by a group of young Muhajir desperados, armed with automatic weapons. They opened the luggage boot of my car and then let us go unhurt, without offering an apology for their high-handed action. Next morning, I learnt that the entire city was under a siege and search operation, which included all the road inter-sections, news-stands, newspaper delivery vans, motor bikes, bicycles, hawkers, exit points of all bus stations, railway stations, out-going flights, both domestic and international—almost all the conceivable places. The target was *Jang*, a newspaper with a large circulation throughout Pakistan. On that day, not a single copy of the newspaper was permitted to leave the press, as a punishment for publishing news or comment 'derogatory' to the MQM. The message was duly received by the newspaper management which made suitable amendments in its policy. The message was also noted by the citizens of Karachi. On that fateful night, Karachi was under the total control of the MQM, which must have deployed about 20,000 activists to teach a lesson to an errant newspaper, and to set an example to others. The operation was carried out with meticulous planning, absolute thoroughness, and utmost finesse. The law enforcement agencies apparently enjoyed a sound sleep that night, which passed peacefully, without any serious crime being committed—an indication that, given the chance, the MQM could do a better job of policing Karachi, which had earned the notoriety of being the crime capital of Pakistan.[1] The formula applied by the MQM to other 'errant' newspapers and periodicals varied according to the need and nature of the situation.

These were my preliminary encounters with a party which had been founded recently, and was in the process of being nourished and groomed to project the voice of the Muhajir community concentrated in urban Sindh. The main plank on which its structure rested was the deprivation suffered by this community at the hands of the non-Muhajirs; its appeal was addressed to the middle and lower middle classes of the community, and the Muhajir youth formed the core of the party cadres.

Muhajir politics during the last half century has produced a galaxy of startling images. Muhajir politics has followed its own dynamics, whose origin, source of propulsion, and course of movement has very little in common with the political process pursued outside urban Sindh or anywhere else in Pakistan. How they are so different, so far removed from the contemporary political scene, is a question which is difficult to answer.

As far as individuals and groups among the community are concerned, the Muhajirs resemble a rainbow, comprising all colours, shades, levels of intelligence, degrees of tolerance, and capacity to adjust. Among them are intellectuals, top-class lawyers, doctors, economists, journalists, sociologists, scientists, humanists, industrialists, masters in communication skills, artists, artisans, and craftsmen. One also finds heart-warming friends amongst them. At the other end of the spectrum, one finds angry, frustrated men and women, gun-totters, terrorists, secret agents, anarchists, extortionists, and underground operators. Together, they lend an image to

Karachi the like of which rarely exists in any other city. These latter categories have given birth to ethnic militarism and political terrorism, which forms one of the topics of this study. How does one explain this phenomenon? When did it all start, who planned it, who propelled it, who nourished it, and who brought it to the critical stage? Did it all happen openly or was it entirely underground? Why could it not be remedied before it became too late? What were the intelligence agencies doing if the storm was brewing underground?

Did the Muhajirs arrive in Sindh with a planned agenda to cause trouble and destabilize its established edifice? Or, were they driven against the wall, pushed into a corner, and isolated politically, culturally, and economically? Whatever happened, how does one explain the fact that in their journey to isolation, they did not stop to look back and ponder but preferred to reach a point where terrorism became a way of life?

To explain this extraordinary phenomenon, there has been a public debate on the issue for some time. Much has been written, both in Pakistan and abroad, in English as well as in Urdu and Sindhi languages. The subject is now better understood and appreciated. That being the case, what prompted me to write on the subject? I have the following reasons:

• The MQM has been consistent in its denial that it resorted to terrorist and fascist methods to achieve its political goals. This aspect needs to be clearly analysed in order to establish that mere denials will not absolve the MQM of responsibility. People want convincing evidence.

• My personal encounters with terrorism in Hyderabad and Karachi raised a basic question in my mind: when the Sindhis formally identified themselves with Pakistan in 1938, 1943, and 1947, could they have foreseen that they were walking into a terrorist trap, which is what urban Sindh has become under the MQM sweep?

• Dialogue with the MQM has invariably been conducted at the government level or at the ruling party level. Since dialogue is invariably power-oriented, leading to power-sharing coalition agreements, some of these agreements could have been signed under duress. An element of compulsion and greed for power dominates such dialogue at the cost of sincerity and public interest. Was there an alternative?

- The MQM is a party based in Sindh, and its basic goal ought to be peace, harmony, welfare, and progress of Sindh, to enable it to play its rightful role in the federation of Pakistan. Its dialogue should, therefore, focus on Sindh, both urban and rural, and it should be conducted with the people of Sindh, through their party representatives, not for sharing ministerial positions, but for finding short and long-term solutions to the political, economic, and cultural problems of Sindh.

- Dialogue at the grass-roots level between the Sindhi and Muhajir components of Sindh has never been initiated. The language controversy of 1972 closed the door to such a dialogue. The two communities must make a new beginning, establish dialogue through individual and groups contacts, free from past prejudices, rancour, hard feelings, and political affiliations.

- Since 1998, there has been a visible shift in the MQM's perspective in favour of issues pertaining to Sindh. However, there has been no concrete follow-up action apart from press statements and political rhetoric.[2] This aspect needs to be examined.

- I have not come across many Sindhi writers who have analysed the MQM phenomenon from the Sindhi perspective. Sindhis must come forward to fill this gap. I have tried to make my humble contribution to this debate.

- Sindhis and Muhajirs, representing rural and urban Sindh, complement and supplement each other. The two are economically inseparable. Cultural and linguistic diversity can be overcome if both keep their common interests uppermost in their minds. The greatest binding element is the fact that a majority of both communities has a liberal outlook on religion. Muhajirs have generally moved away from the influence of orthodox political leaders. Sindhis are mostly liberal due to the influence of sufism. I have attempted to explore this aspect at some length, in keeping with the religious liberalism of both communities in matters of political creeds and state policies.

- Scores of writers, thinkers, academics, and friends of Sindh have issued appeals to the MQM to shun terrorism and adopt constitutional means to achieve their political goals. I join that chorus to tell them that their fascist methods have ended in chaos and anarchy, and that they must abandon fascism.

- The MQM is a political party without a role model. They have followed methods which have no precedent. Hence, they have lost their bearings and are unable to see the direction clearly. In Jinnah, they have the best role model, and they followed him in their journey from India to Pakistan. They must now be persuaded to follow in his footsteps. If they burned the flag of Pakistan and repudiated the ideology of Pakistan at the Quaid's grave, they must atone for the excesses committed by them against the Quaid and his ideology, and against Sindh and Pakistan.

- The Muhajirs came from India to Pakistan after 1947. Having become Pakistanis, they should have suffered no identity crisis. If they still consider themselves Muhajirs after being in Pakistan for over half a century, then this indicates that they are still going through an identity crisis. They have attempted to overcome the crisis by trying various textbook remedies. Some tried fundamentalism, but in vain. Others tried ethnic militarism, without success. Yet others are trying to create a separate geographical entity (variously called Jinnahpur, Muhajir land, Karachi Suba, etc.) by dividing Sindh, to achieve autonomy (or independence?) and a sense of identity. But, this goal, as explained in the relevant chapter, is beyond their reach, and they are well aware of this. Thus, there continues to be a missing link between the Muhajirs and Pakistan, and in their quest to find it, they have lost their bearings. I am suggesting a way out— the only viable solution. If they adopt a Sindhi identity, they will gain in all respects. Every village, town, and city of Sindh is plural. If Sindh can absorb Arabs, Balochis, Seraikis, Punjabis, Pathans, and others, surely it can absorb the people of Indian origin too. The offer was available in 1947; it is available now. All they need to do is to accept it gracefully and establish their identity. As Sindhis, they will be better Pakistanis, since they will have a base. Despite unity within the MQM, their voice was ignored. Within the framework of Sindh, their voice will carry weight. Besides, it will reinforce the voice of Sindh.

* Sindh is a land of mystics who make no distinction of faith, caste, creed, colour, race, language, and origin. Mystics have a message of peace and love for everyone. That message was conveyed through Shah Latif, and renewed through Shaikh Ayaz. That message enabled Sindhis to receive, absorb, and assimilate immigrants from everywhere, with open arms. That message is as valid today as it ever was. The Muhajirs must listen to it and accept the warm embrace of Sindh in the same spirit, and in a positive frame of mind. G.M. Syed invited them. Hakim Said persuaded them. They were great men. I am a humble man with a feeble voice. But, I feel the urge to join their chorus.

* If ethnic militarism in urban Sindh is not neutralized and pacified by the saner elements and sober leadership in the foreseeable future, there is a distinct possibility that there may emerge an underground, counter-terrorist Sindhi ethnic militant group which may target the Muhajir community and spread through urban Sindh like wildfire. Should that ever happen, a possibility which must be prevented at any cost, it will mark the beginning of the end of a united Sindh. Since Sindhis have to maintain the unity and integrity of Sindh at all costs, they have to restrain themselves and refuse to fall into the trap of MQM terrorism, the call for a UDI (Unilateral Declaration of Independence), and other such ploys.

Another dilemma which baffles Pakistan in general, and Sindh in particular, is whether we are a liberal Muslim state or heading towards theocracy. Before answering this question, one has to resolve the controversy of whether Pakistan is an ideological state or a nation-state, or a mix of both? This controversy has continued for half a century, and is nowhere near a solution.

> Pakistan meant all things to all people. For some it was theology— *Pakistan ka matlab kiya—La'illah illallah,* (What is the meaning of Pakistan? There is only one God). To others it was sociology. Many Muslims, including those who had little time for orthodox practice, were concerned about preserving their culture and language. Yet for others it meant economics, it meant escape from the powerful Hindu commercial and entrepreneurial presence emerging all over India. Yet for others it was an expression of the Hindu-Muslim confrontation that had been taking place for centuries; it was a challenge to those Hindus who believed they could dominate Muslims and impose *Ram Raj* on them. But for everyone Pakistan meant something in terms of their identity. This is what made the movement work. Many scholars trace the Pakistan movement to the 'Two-Nation' theory Sir Syed had espoused which held that 'the Hindus and Muslims of India were separate people and need to live separately'.[3]

These issues have been highlighted in this work to enable readers to find the answers.

It is an interesting phenomenon that the majority of the people of Sindh, both Sindhis and Muhajirs, are by and large secularly oriented. The Sindh-based parties, namely the PPP, the MQM, the Jiye-Sindh, the Sindh National Front, and the Awami Tehrik have practicing Muslims as their members, but they do not mix religion with the business of the state. The ANP (Frontier based) also functions in Sindh among the hundreds of thousands of Pathans who are devout Muslims, but their party has a secular orientation. On the other hand, there are also parties like the JI, the JUP, and the JUI, led by orthodox Muslim scholars who are totally committed to the establishment of an orthodox Islamic state in Pakistan, and these, too, wield considerable influence, particularly in urban Sindh. But, their popularity is restricted to limited pockets and their representation in elected forums has been negligible. The main plank of their campaign was that since Pakistan was created in the name of Islam, it had to be an Islamic state.[4] Prime Minister Liaquat Ali Khan and his team were easily carried away by this logic in their belief that because Islam was a liberal and universal religion, a state based on its injunctions would provide an answer to all the contemporary issues and emerging problems. I have endeavoured to deal with this matter in four chapters in an attempt to project the history and failure of the official policy of Islamization, the use of Islam to capture and perpetuate state power by the mullahs and elected and unelected dictators, and the consequences of these attempts on the people of Sindh for whom this game of power in the name of religion has been a source of disillusionment. Inasmuch as this movement began in the Punjab, a province with majority population, it was bulldozed and thrust on other provinces in general, and on Sindh in particular. The movement manifested itself in many ways, like the passage of the Objectives Resolutions, the anti-Qadiani riots and the proclamation of Martial Law in Lahore, the second round of anti-Qadiani riots culminating in the declaration of Ahmadis as a minority, the rise of the dictator Ziaul Haq in the name of *Nizam-i-Mustafa*, Ziaul Haq's ill-conceived and half-baked attempts to Islamize the legal, economic, and political systems, and non-party elections leading to the weakening of mainstream political parties and the rise of ethnic politics. His orthodox view of Islam weakened the structure, destabilized democracy, shattered the process of national integration, and created a strong lobby in the Punjab to follow in his footsteps. The cummulative effect of all these attempts has fouled the political climate of Sindh, devastated its economy, and divided it politically.

Basically, this book is about Sindh, the people of Sindh—the Sindhis and the Muhajirs, their mental attitudes, idiosyncrasies, political preferences, style of dealing with each other, the elements that unite them, and the issues that divide them. Since Sindh is a part of the federation, and since the people of Sindh are inter-linked with the people of other provinces at the provincial and federal levels, politically, economically, and ideologically, these links, their impact, and their consequences have been discussed and analysed in great detail. The divisive problems include the population census, quota system, ethnic militarism, 'stranded Pakistanis', attempted division of Sindh, failure of the dialogue, etc. But, more important are the factors that unite them—their common perception of the exploitation of Sindh and its resources by the people of non-Sindhi origin, Sindh's share in the waters of the Indus and the national finance commission, the autonomy of Sindh at the provincial, municipal, and district levels, etc. The central theme is that the two communities should mobilize their resources to forge a joint strategy to face common problems, which have assumed threatening proportions, instead of being entangled in acrimony and endless debate on divisive issues.

The reader would observe that the bulk of the material contained in this book has been chosen from secondary sources, namely, printed material, which may create an impression that I had no access to other sources. This calls for an explanation. The subject matter is contemporary in nature and, therefore, it was only natural to place reliance on the material published in newspapers and periodicals, besides scores of books. The press in Pakistan is coming of age and the quality of reporting has much improved. Letters to the editors reflect public opinion, and are hence a valuable source. Senior columnists provide investigative reports, express fearless opinions, and conduct in-depth analysis, and this factor alone has been of great help. As to the interviews with political leaders and workers, I was handicapped by poor health which prevented me from visiting and interviewing them. I thought the absence of this primary source would create an authenticity gap. But, fortunately that has not happened. The views and versions of party leaders and their supporters, as expressed in the assemblies or reflected in the print media, have been faithfully quoted. Readers would agree that our politicians use interviews for personal projection and that their followers sing the same tune as their leaders.

They do not give an independent or a critical assessment of their party policies.

There is also a cult of personality in most of the parties. The prevailing view is that the parties cannot survive without their present leaders. When institutions like political parties are built around personalities, democracy is the first casualty, followed by objectivity. By comparison, the opinions and views expressed by some columnists are highly balanced, objective, and incisive. For this reason, I have drawn heavily upon this source. I found the views and comments of some non-partisan personalities among the Muhajirs, the Sindhis, and the Punjabis very valuable, thoroughly logical, and deeply inspiring, and I have learnt many lessons from their wisdom and frankness.

I am aware that I am touching a sensitive, risky, and controversial subject. My views may be disputed, but so were the views of others expressed before and those that would follow mine. Difference of opinion is a part of this endeavour which must continue for as long as it is needed to rescue society from the dangers that confront it. If we have to survive, we must enter this debate, explore, analyse, and untangle the issues which have been muddled by a plethora of conflicting theories and concepts. We owe it to future generations to counter the forces of extremism, whether ethnic or religious, and to contribute to the creation of a tolerant and stable society.

The issues and events described and analysed mostly pertain to the period beginning with the military *coup* staged by General Ziaul Haq in 1977 and ending with the collapse of the Nawaz Sharif government in October 1999. In the chequered history of Pakistan, punctuated by wars, dismemberment, and turmoil, these twenty-two years stand out in terms of political earthquakes, economic mismanagement, colossal corruption, rise of ethnic issues, proliferation of religious extremism, and general collapse of society. How did these traumatic events originate? Did the previous thirty years lay the foundation? Or, were these developments created by the ruling elites of this crucial period? The first eleven years (1977-88) of the period under review passed under Zia's shadow. These were paraded as the golden period of

Islamic renaissance. Whether such a projection was indeed justified, or was it in reality an era of darkness interspersed with periodic flashes of over-enthusiastic religious bigotry, are questions that need to be probed at length. The subsequent eleven years (1988-99) ushered an era of electoral politics which raised the expectation of a new beginning. In retrospect, one wonders whether this was an extension of Ziaism or a departure from it. There were frequent and premature dismissals of governments and national and provincial assemblies, followed by elections which were manipulated in order to bring about 'positive results'. What kind of positive results, who should be kept out of power, who should be brought in, and who should sift the positive from the negative—the people of Pakistan, or the 'mandated' man sitting in Rawalpindi or Islamabad? This exercise, which was reminiscent of Zia's rule, made it quite clear that the eleven years of electoral politics were, in essence, a parliamentary cloak of Ziaism; that Zia may have physically died in 1988, but his ghost continued to haunt the politics of Pakistan. People often forget that Zia was a diehard fundamentalist who released powerful forces, enlisting the loyalties and support of chosen generals, bureaucrats, and religious groups, who then worked overtime to keep the Zia legacy alive.[5] I have tried to make an assessment of this aspect to provide some clues to those whose legitimate aspirations to see Pakistan take-off were dampened by the slide towards anarchy.

A question may be posed: why look at these issues from a Sindhi perspective and not from a Pakistani one? A valid question indeed. As a matter of fact, what concerns Sindh equally concerns Pakistan, and that is why the involvement at the federal level to tackle these problems has been frequent and substantial. However, the fact is that the superstructure of Pakistan rests on the foundation of four pillars, Sindh being one of them. This pillar has been badly shaken by violent tremors which have weakened its foundations. This is a peculiar phenomenon which has made Sindh vulnerable to many dangers. Hence, the focus has been on Sindh, particularly in relation to ethnic polarization. As to the role of religious fanaticism, although the subject has been enlarged on a wider canvas, its impact on the people of Sindh has assumed a special significance, which has been highlighted.

In presenting this work, I have neither conceived any new ideas nor made any new discoveries. Most of what I have said would be known to readers who keep themselves abreast of the current events and contemporary developments in Sindh and its neighbourhood. Am I, therefore, imposing upon the readers what they already know? Not exactly. I must explain the rationale behind this effort to justify this exercise.

As a humble worker of the Pakistan movement, I owe it to its founder to join the crusade against the political terrorism unleashed on this peaceful land by ethnic militants and religious fanatics. This crusade has been taken up by the print media and in elected forums for some time. But, these attempts have been countered and enfeebled by well organized powerful forces, and consequently, have failed to arouse the national conscience. The national debate has been subdued and overpowered. The state has tried to tackle these issues as a law and order problem and has met with failure. The problem is so deep rooted that no police or army action can solve it on a lasting basis. The lobbies and the parties involved have a deep commitment, strengthened by decades of indoctrination and brainwashing, often under state patronage by rulers like General Zia and his followers.

The solution lies in the re-education of the people through national debate on a massive scale and on a sustained basis, at all levels, in educational institutions, in the print media, in elected forums, through seminars and symposia. History has been distorted and needs to be corrected. Religious seminaries have to be absorbed in the mainstream to revise and expand their curricula to include science, economics, humanities, liberal aspects of religion, and practical courses for gainful employment. Sermons in places of worship must be geared to character building, community service, and sectarian tolerance. The confusion, disharmony, and violence spread by the ethnic and fundamentalist lobbies must be countered on every front so that the concept of Pakistan, as understood and elaborated by its founder, but which has been distorted by opportunists, is re-established. The task is by no means easy. The damage inflicted over decades cannot be undone in a short period of time.

It is a strange paradox that the ethnic and fundamentalist lobbies had nothing in common before independence, and have nothing in common even today. Yet, their strategy and tactics have come to coincide; both follow policies that are divisive and violent, and both are subverting the concept of Pakistan today.

The religious elite had opposed the creation of Pakistan. One of their activists had even attempted to assassinate Jinnah. Now, the same lobby seeks to undermine Jinnah's dream in the name of Islam. On the other hand, the ethnic lobby, which claims to be the progeny of those who created Pakistan, has found a justification to become divisive and violent. They pay lip service to Jinnah, but reject his legacy and rebel against his vision.

I have joined those who have given a call to confront these negative elements. In the process, I have developed a thesis, a case study, and a campaign strategy, and reinforced it with the findings of a large number of writers, thinkers, and intellectuals, presented during the last decade and a half. This combined exercise is presented to the readers to enable them to form their own judgement. If it leads to a broad understanding and agreement on the diagnosis of the malady, it will be my humble contribution to the revival of the spirit of Pakistan.

There is only one way, one guideline to revive that spirit, and that is to follow the legacy of Jinnah. Only then can the people confront and defeat the obscurantist and divisive forces. Such a battle has to be fought with ideas and not with bullets. To restore Jinnah's image of Pakistan, the battle must be launched vigorously, yet peacefully, and within constitutional parameters.

Finally, the reader has to bear with some degree of repetition which became inevitable because the book is not written in the form of a narrative. The nature of the subject matter called for each chapter to be self-contained, going back and forth in time. The ideas and events had, therefore, to overlap in more than one chapter, and occasionally, even within the same chapter, leading to some repetition.

NOTES

1. This story is based on my personal experience.
2. On 1 April 2001, the MQM(A) and the JSQM leaders chalked out a joint-action plan for the restoration of Sindh's share of water from the river Indus. This is a positive development vis-a-vis the MQM's practical involvement in the problems of Sindh as a whole, *Dawn*, 2 April 2001.
3. Akbar S. Ahmad, *Jinnah, Pakistan and Islamic Identity–The Search for Saladin*, Routledge, New York, 1997, pp. 109-10.
4. If this were true, how does one explain the opposition to the creation of Pakistan by the overwhelming majority of Indian Muslim scholars and their powerful political parties, namely, the Jamiatual-Ulama-i-Hind, the Jamat-i-Islami, the Jamiat-ul-Ahrar, and the Khaksars? For details, see relevant chapters.
5. Rafiq Hussain Agha, while commissioner, received audio cassettes, prepared under Gen. Zia's instructions for the training of Haj pilgrims. The cassettes contained an instruction to the effect that persons of a particular sect should not recite such and such verse of the Holy Quran (meant for other sects) as it would mean the immediate dissolution of their marriage. See *Dawn*, 22 June 2000.

1

WHO IS A SINDHI?

Historically, India derived its identity from the Indus—a name which the Europeans gave to the river, locally called Sindhu. The territory known as Sindh, which in ancient times was called Sindhudesh, lay along the Indus and its tributaries, extending from the Arabian Sea in the south to Kashmir in the north. The river, being the uniting factor, a binding element, and a source of interaction among the peoples settled on the Indus system, and also providing an outlet to the sea, gave birth to the Sindhu culture, which despite local variations, had a common thread. The best illustration of this is the shared source of the local languages, namely, Sindhi, Seraiki, Punjabi, and Hindko, which are spoken all along the Indus country. All these languages possess a common vocabulary and several common links which have attained durability despite diversities in the ethnic origin and historical experiences of the regions and the peoples settled along the Indus.

What is known as Sindh today has been an ethnic melting pot since time immemorial. The earliest migration took place with the Aryan invasions while the latest ones followed the creation of Pakistan in 1947. In between the invasions and/or migrations, there came the Arabs, the Persians, the Afghans, the Balochis, and many others. Economic pulls brought the Kutchis, the Gujratis, the Marwaris, the Punjabis, the Pathans, and others.

When the present political boundaries of Sindh were finalized during the British rule, the province became a multi-lingual entity. Ethnically, the Sindhis, or the people living in the province of Sindh, have descended from the Dravidians, the Aryans, the Africans (Shidis, Makranis, etc.), the Arabs (Syeds,

Siddiquis, Farooquis, Alvis, Qureshis, Abbasis, etc.), the Central Asians (Mughals, etc.), the Georgians (Mirzas), the Iranians, the Afghans, the Rajputs (Samats), the Balochis, the Gujratis, the Kutchis, etc.:

> Shar, Magsi, Kulachi, Dodai, Chandio, Jamali, Qaisrani, Jaskani, Gurchani, Shambrani, Leghari, Nutkani, Bhutto, Jakhrani, Rind, Pitafi, Talpur, Jatoi, Bozdar, Mazari, Bijarani, Lund, Lashari, Korai, Bhatti, Mirrani, Parhiar, Almani, Umrani, Gabol, to name a few, as every one knows, are proud names of well known Sindhi tribes. It may come as a shock to many of them that they are not originally Sindhi but parts of Punjabi, Rajput, Jat, Baloch, and Arain tribes.[1]

Linguistically, they speak Sindhi, Urdu, Seraiki, Balochi, Brauhvi, Punjabi, Pashtu, Gujrati, etc. Sindhi has been the official language, but the province is now bilingual due to the increasing population of Urdu speaking people. Sindh has maintained its plural character throughout its history. Even though Sindhi was the official language, other languages were spoken in homes, businesses, and on social occasions. Urban Sindh, Karachi in particular, has always retained its cosmopolitan character and outlook. It has played its part as a commercial and industrial centre and a gateway to the outside world.

For centuries, the Sindhi language was written in the *naskh* script by the majority of the people of Sindh. Even while Farsi (Persian) became the state language and was used in official correspondence by government functionaries, including the *amil* class of Hindus which supplied the bulk of the manpower for government jobs, Sindhi remained the lingua franca at the people's level along with the other local dialects.[2] But, that did not upset the position of Seraiki, Balochi, Brauhvi, etc. in private and social circles. On the language issue, there was complete harmony despite diversity in the ethnic composition of Sindh.

The pre-independence immigrants to Sindh settled here as Sindhis and merged their identity with the locals voluntarily, wholeheartedly, and without any coercion or compulsion.

Irrespective of whether they came as invaders, conquerors, rulers, mercenaries, refugees, travellers, settlers, preachers, divines, holy men, or adventurers, they enjoyed Sindhi hospitality, appreciated Sindhi simplicity, adopted the Sindhi way of life and culture, and identified themselves as Sindhis. Intellectuals and linguists among them found the Sindhi language very rich in vocabulary, much richer than any other language spoken and written in the region.[3] In his monumental work, *Sindh and the Races that Inhabit the Valley of the Indus*, Richard Burton states:

> Sindhi is superior to most of the dialects of Western India in various minor points of refinement and cultivation; as for instance, in the authorized change of terminations of poetical words, the re-duplication of final or penultimate letters to assist the rhyme and many similar signs of elaboration. ... Sindhi is remarkable for a copiousness and variety of words. ... As regards to the literature of the Sindhi tongue, it may safely be asserted that no vernacular dialect in India, at the time of our taking the country, possessed more, and few so much, original composition.[4]

No wonder, even the assimilated immigrants found the Sindhi language and its vast vocabulary rich enough to be adopted as a vehicle for their intellectual expression. The *Risalo* of Shah Abdul Latif Bhitai (1690–1753) has acquired worldwide fame as a universal message of peace and love, and represents the heart and soul of Sindh. It is written in the Sindhi language, using *naskh* script, and employing its rich vocabulary, and drawing upon the vocabulary of sister languages and dialects of the surrounding regions of Kutch, Gujrat, Rajasthan, the Seraiki belt, Lasbella, etc. The *Risalo* made Shah Latif the father of the Sindhi language. It inspired a large number of Sindhis to rise to great literary heights. The latest in the line was Sheikh Mubarak Ayaz, the greatest Sindhi poet of the twentieth century and a literary genius who introduced Shah Latif to the Urdu speaking Sindhis through his versified translation. Another Sindhi scholar, Mirza Kaleech Beg (1853–1929), an immigrant from Georgia, rose to exceptional fame and prominence through his prolific writings in the Sindhi language on a variety of topics. He was a versatile literary genius as an essayist, critic, historian, translator, dramatist, playwright, and above all, a poet and lyricist. In all, he wrote 350 books which are as popular now as they were during his lifetime. Some European and modern Sindhi historians have attributed the talent of Shah Latif and Mirza Kaleech Beg to their foreign origins.[5] By doing so, these scholars ignore the fact that these immigrants or their progeny rose to prominence in an environment conducive to intellectual activity and scholarly pursuit. Their forefathers did not attain any comparable status in their original homes. Talent flowers in a fertile soil; it withers away in a barren soil. Sindh had become famous for literary and intellectual activity. The Holy Quran was first translated into Sindhi in AD 833. In 1699, Thatta had 400 colleges to teach theology, philosophy, and politics. The history of Sindh is replete with towering personalities, both indigenous and immigrant in origin, whose individual and collective contribution to the language and culture of Sindh made Sindh an attractive place even to the immigrants from the great centres of Muslim culture and learning in India, namely Delhi, Lucknow, Hyderabad, and Aligarh.

Among the pre-independence immigrants, the Balochis were most numerous. Their integration with the locals presented many obstacles. First, their language belonged to a different family group of non-Indian origin. Second, their lifestyle was nomadic and pastoral. Third, they lived in a tribal system with its own culture and legal code different in all respects from the settled mode of the Indus people. Lastly, they were warriors who conquered Sindh from the Kalhoras, and their attitude and behaviour towards the locals was shaped by this disposition.

The Talpur Balochis 'appeared in the Kalhora court as their servants, then as their ally and finally as their master'.[6]

The cultural conflict between Sindhis and Balochis clashed strongly against each other during the Talpur regime, ultimately developing into an interesting blend of Balochi, Jat and Hindu element, which was neither purely Balochi in character nor wholly Indian. The degree of culture attained by the Balochis was undoubtedly lower than that attained by the former dynasties.... Those (Baloch), who owing to their wild incursions were disallowed to live even under tents, were destined to be honoured and homaged under magnificent palaces. Instead of riding on mares they rode on ornamental palanquins. Once shepherds of cattle, now shepherded men, at times craved for booty and plunder, now cavilled and coquetted with princely vanities over courses of the most refined and epicurean tastes served in large ornamental dishes of gold and silver, to regale the taste and the eyes. In short the rebels of yesterday were to be the kings of tomorrow.[7]

The Talpur Mirs began gradually to soften the rough edges of Balochi life by introducing fine arts and scholarly pursuits (of the local Sindhis) into the obscure parts of their Kingdom. Sindhi language as well as Sindhi ideas were preponderantly influencing the old Balochi customs and the former was appearing decidedly to win the day. However, the Baloch and Sindhi cultures blended into a happy synthesis. The court language, Persian, was steadily embracing Sindhi.[8]

Two-thirds of the present population of Sindh consists of Balochs.... The Indus Valley has many temptations for an ordinary Baloch. It is a reservoir of inexhaustible wealth and a source of tremendous political strength to the Baloch.... The majority of Balochis consider Sindh as the eye of Hind..... The middle class Baloch prefer to speak Sindhi instead of their mother tongue, deeming it a spark of modernism. .... Their (Balochi) culture, language and customs seem to be gradually dissolving into the Sindhian mode of culture.[9]

Assimilation of the Balochis and the Muhajirs in Sindh presents two interesting case studies, with some similarities and many contrasts. The Balochis were sucked into Sindh under economic pressure which eventually led to their political ambitions. The Muhajirs pulled out of India in the wake of a political upheaval, but the immigration turned into an economic bonanza in the vacuum created by the exodus of Sindhi Hindus. The Balochis, basically a rural people, led an existence which was pastoral and nomadic in character, far behind the Sindhis on the cultural scale. By contrast, the Muhajirs were urbanized, educated, politically conscious, and culturally of a superior mould. Both took full advantage of the opportunities offered by Sindh but both resisted assimilation as they entertained notions of superiority, moving from the status of immigrants or refugees to that of rulers. While the Talpur Baloch became kings and rulers of Sindh, the Muhajirs ruled the greater area of Pakistan on the basis of their political and administrative hold over the newly established state institutions. But, just like the Talpurs collapsed before the superior might of the British invaders, the Muhajirs had to yield ground to superior numbers which eventually moved into positions of power under the rules of the game that prevailed at the time.

The Balochis claim to constitute two-thirds of the population of Sindh, but once they assimilated, their numbers became irrelevant. Consequently, their rise to positions of authority in Sindh has not even been noticed in ethnic terms since provincial elections were introduced in 1937. Mir Bundeh Ali Talpur, Mir Ghulam Ali Talpur, Ghulam Mustafa Jatoi, and Liaqat Jatoi occupied high positions as Sindhis and not as Balochis. They rose to prominence in the mainstream without any Balochi label or Balochi constituency or a Balochi agenda. By contrast, the Muhajirs left the mainstream after their losing political clout, underwent many political somersaults, and finally opted for an isolationist ethnic political formation, called the Muhajir Quomi Movement (MQM), later renamed the Mutahida Quomi Movement (MQM).[10] They have been gradually emerging out of their shell and claim to have opened their ranks to non-Muhajirs, but their actions have to match their pronouncements over an extended period, and they have to re-establish their broken links with rural Sindhis, before they can be taken seriously. Over a period of more than half a century of living in Sindh, they have gradually drifted away from the Sindhis, both socially and politically, and clashed with them on all fronts. Their high level of literacy, instead of enabling them to adopt a conciliatory posture at the grass-root level, has contributed to the widening of the gulf between the two communities. The main thrust of their dialogue has always been to demand their rights, as if rights can be split into Muhajir rights and non-Muhajir rights. They speak about prejudices. History is witness to the fact that they were welcomed by the Sindhis and were provided all the opportunities for their rehabilitation and resettlement. Thereafter, the onus for assimilation was entirely on them and if the Sindhis later developed any prejudices, the responsibility for this rests with the Muhajirs.

The Muhajirs ought to have learnt a few lessons from history. Only a small minority of Muslims migrated from India to Sindh at the time of Partition. The rest of their kith and kin continued to live in India. Despite initial suspicions, created by their support for the partition of India, Indian Muslims readjusted their perspective and re-established their credentials for coexistence as citizens of the nation-state of India.

Nor did the Muhajirs learn any lesson from the multi-ethnic character of the fully assimilated people of Sindh. The Baloch could not convert Sindh into Balochistan because they found Sindh to be a plural and integrated society, and they felt neither a psychological barrier nor any political or economic obstacles in swimming with the Sindhi current. Having lived closely with the Sindhis, they found them to be open and broad-minded which enabled them to overcome their initial hesitation. Besides, being a rural society themselves, the Balochis found rural Sindhis amiable, communicative, and easy to get along with. They did not start any language controversy as they had no illusions about foisting their language upon the Sindhis. They adopted Persian as the court language which did not clash with day-to-day communication, or the literary and intellectual activities of the Sindhis. When Persian was replaced by English as the court language in the mid-nineteenth century, the Balochi community, rather than crying foul, used the change as a window of opportunity and cultivated an intimate relationship with the Sindhis by adopting Sindhi as their official language, whose alphabets had finally been officially declared to be *naskh* script of Arabic.

Just as the notion of Balochi majority became irrelevant after Baloch assimilation, so will be the Muhajir 'majority' after their assimilation.[11] However, while the Balochi assimilation was relatively painless, the Muhajir assimilation has been a painful process. If they rule Sindh while this painful process is on, that will be the saddest day in the history of Sindh, irrespective of whether they are in the majority or minority. But, once integrated, they are welcome to rule Sindh for a thousand years, as no one will notice or count how many they are. And, why not? If a Syed, a Baloch, a Memon, a Pir, a Mir, an Aryan, a Rajput, a Shaikh, a Khuhro, a Soomro, a Pirzado, a Bhutto, a Mirani, a high caste or a low caste can rise to rule Sindh, why not a Muhajir, who is perhaps better qualified, and has assimilated after overcoming psychological barriers.

NOTES

1. Prof. Karar Hussain, 'Islam and Nationalism', *The Muslim*, 2 November 1990. Quoting census reports of 1883 and 1892 by Sir Denzil Ibbetson and E.D. Maclegan, compiled in a book by H.A. Rose.
2. Richard Burton, *Sindh and the Races that Inhabit the Valley of the Indus*, Oxford University Press, in Asia Historical Reprint Series, Karachi 1973, p. 58.
3. Ibid. p. 75.
4. Ibid. p. 75.
5. Sorely, 1940, p. 209, quoted by Sohail Zaheer Lari, *A History of Sindh*, Oxford University Press, 1994, p. 156. The Germans are as proud as the Americans of the achievements of Albert Einstein. But, Georgians and Arabs are not proud of Mirza Kaleech Beg and Shah Latif respectively, while the Sindhis are.
6. Muhamed Sardar Khan Baloch, *History of Baloch Race and Balochistan*, 1958, p. 130.
7. Ibid. p. 129.
8. Ibid. p. 168.
9. Ibid. p. 244.
10. They quit the Muslim League and joined the ranks of fundamentalist parties like the Jamaat-i-Islami and the Jamiat-ul-Ulama-i-Pakistan. Disillusioned, they made inter-ethnic pacts with their co-settlers from the Punjab and Frontier Province under the banner of the Muhajir-Punjabi-

Pathan Front, which was clearly an anti-Sindhi step on the part of the people who voluntarily chose Sindh as their permanent home.

11. At one stage, the MQM claimed that the Muhajir population of Sindh was twenty-two million, and constituted the majority, and that the political and economic share of Muhajirs should be fixed in that proportion. However, the 1998 census has placed the Muhajir population close to seven million. The census has not been accepted, both by the Sindhis and the Muhajirs.

2

GENESIS OF THE MQM

At the time of independence, the Muslim League leadership had given a pledge to the civilized world that the partition of India had no room for the transfer of population, and that the India-based leaders would remain in place to assist the Muslims to recover from the trauma of partition and help them to become loyal citizens of India. (The partition of the Punjab, leading to bloody riots and the two-way migration of population, is not related to this subject, which is confined to the migration from the rest of India to the province of Sindh). When Pakistan came into being, leaders like Choudhry Khaliquzzaman, Raja Sahib of Mahmoodabad, Allama Shabbir Ahmad Usmani, I.I. Chundrigar and others, who were to have remained behind in India, were, in fact, the first to pack up and move to Karachi. This created in the minds of the Indian Muslims a fear of persecution by India, and hopes of a bright future in Pakistan. The Urdu-speaking leadership thus betrayed their own cause, their own ideology, and their own people. The history of the Indo-Muslim nation will not forgive this betrayal, which destabilized millions of Urdu-speaking Muslims, on the one hand, and choked the province of Sindh, on the other.

Hindu suspicion against the Indian Muslims led to discrimination, which in turn led to migration. This vicious circle of suspicion, discrimination, and migration, once created, became a convenient tool for maintaining the tempo of migration.

The Muhajir-dominated government of Pakistan allotted urban and rural evacuee properties to the immigrants, in lieu of their claims of similar properties left behind in India, to rehabilitate them. This property bonanza created an additional incentive whereby migration could be planned, regulated, and programmed. Certain categories of immigrants, like administrators, scientists, financiers, accountants, bankers, jurists, industrialists, and entrepreneurs were encouraged to migrate to Pakistan to fill the vacuum and jump-start the newly created state.

The Muhajirs from the Urdu-Hindi belt of India left behind well-established cultural traditions, nourished and patronized by centuries of Muslim rule. Delhi, Lucknow, Agra, Hyderabad, Bhopal, Rampur, and Aligarh produced eminent scholars, poets, writers, journalists, educationists, and politicians, much admired by the Muslims in the rest of India. During the independence struggle, the preservation of the Indo-Muslim cultural heritage became a burning issue. Any culture, to have a permanent footing, must be rooted in the soil. Similarly, leaders of cultural movements must have a base. When the Muslim leaders decided to migrate to Pakistan, they left their cultural base behind. Their followers were rendered leaderless. While the leaders found refuge in Sindh, their footprints in India were obliterated by the rival culture. Consequently, while the cultural base of Indian Muslims was eroded by the Muslim migration to Sindh, a cultural clash came into being on the soil of Sindh, between the Sindhis and the Muhajirs. This clash, which was entirely unnatural, and politically motivated, has caused deep cracks in Sindhi society and retarded the process of national integration.

Since the Muhajirs were uprooted from their own cultural base in India, it was not unnatural that the heirs to their culture should feel the urge and the compulsion, not only to revive and perpetuate their cultural heritage among their own progeny, which was now physically cut-off from the centres of their heritage, but also to propagate the same among the natives of Sindh. Being the leaders of Pakistan in the formative years, government patronage for the spread of Muhajir culture among the non-Muhajirs was readily available.

In their attempt to spread the Indo-Muslim culture in Sindh, the Muhajirs were also guided by role models in America, Canada, Australia, New Zealand, Brazil, Argentina, Mexico, and elsewhere. Europeans had landed on those vast cultural deserts and were able to establish their cultural superiority without much resistance. The Muhajirs could hardly expect it to be an easy walk-over in Sindh. Their leadership, overflowing with ideological motivation and religious zeal, but lacking in historical perspective and political foresight, failed to impress upon the Muhajirs the need to adopt the Sindhi culture and the Sindhi way of life. They lived in Sindh and spoke of the Pakistani way of life, which in reality meant the Indo-Muslim way of life. A community whose cultural growth and development had taken place over the centuries in India under state patronage, having reached Sindh, lost its bearings, and, once again, relied upon state patronage for the adoption of its culture in Sindh. They could not grasp the reality that Sindhi culture had grown and flourished, not in the palaces of kings, nawabs, and rulers, but at the grass-roots, in the huts, on the sand dunes, on the bare hills, in the fishing boats, on the Indus banks, on the seashore, and under the tree groves. Instead of finding magnificent palaces, impressive mansions, and majestic forts, which had been the abodes of the Indo-Muslim culture, they found the 'unimpressive' ruins of Mohen-jo-daro and some odd-looking places, where the abodes of kings, priests, and the subjects all looked alike, and where palace culture and folk culture were indistinguishable, both rooted deep in the soil, for centuries. Despite the class difference between the *waderas* and the peasants, the culture of Sindh has always been a harmonious whole. After Partition, this cultural bond was further strengthened by the clash with the non-Sindhis.

An adversarial relationship between the Muhajir and Sindhi cultures was thus built in the very origins of the two. That the immigrant Muhajir culture travelled to Sindh on the shoulders of the immigrant rulers of Pakistan further widened the gulf between the two. The manner in which Bengali aspirations were suppressed soon after the creation of Pakistan sent shock waves throughout Sindh. These shock waves were either ignored or remained invisible to the ruling classes and Muhajir intellectuals, and the reasons were many. Firstly, Sindh was overwhelmed by the sheer magnitude of immigration. Secondly, the ideological thrust of the new state had unleashed certain powerful forces, which silenced even the voice of Jinnah (part of his speech of 11 August 1947 was blacked out), let alone the voice of the Sindhis, who bore the brunt of the initial political, administrative, and cultural onslaught.

As long as Pakistan was ruled under dictatorship, both civil and military, the Sindhis remained suppressed politically (Karachi separation, one unit) and culturally (suppression of the Sindhi language by President Ayub Khan). With the advent of electoral politics, while the Sindhis and the liberal groups of the Muhajirs voted for the mainstream party (the PPP in 1970 election), the bulk of the Muhajirs voted for the fundamentalist parties, like the JI and the JUP. When the elected government came into power (1972), the Sindhis tried to restore the position of the Sindhi language, at the provincial level. This was a purely democratic process which met with a strong reaction from the Muhajirs in the shape of language riots. These were pacified by accommodating the demands of the Urdu-speaking people of Sindh. These riots marked a turning point in Sindhi-Muhajir relations, and widened the gulf between the two communities. Taking advantage of this rift, General Ziaul Haq, who had overthrown Bhutto in a military *coup d'etat* in 1977, manipulated the Muhajir youth, weaned them away from the Sindhis, and planted the seeds of ethnic separation among them. He succeeded in reducing them to the level of bystanders during the MRD uprising (1983), which took rural Sindh by storm, and posed a serious challenge to the military regime of Gen. Zia. That the most educated and advanced community of Pakistan should have ignored a genuine grass-root agitation for the restoration of democracy, resulting in large numbers of Sindhis being mowed down by army tanks, constituted a permanent scar on the national credentials of urban Sindh-based parties.[1]

The Muhajir Quomi Movement came into existence in 1984. As an urban Sindh party, it had only two predecessors, the Jamiat-ul-Ulama-i-Pakistan (JUP) and the Muhajir-Punjabi-Pathan Mutahadda Mahaz (MPPMM).[2] Since JUP's membership is confined to religious scholars, and its following spreads over the entire country, it is outside the scope of this discussion. Thus, as an urban Sindh party, the MQM had only one predecessor, namely the MPPMM, which, by its very name, had an ethnic origin, a bitter legacy, an inauspicious beginning, and an ignominious end. For the party to have the MPPMM as a predecessor, and carrying the stigma of Muhajir ethnicity—in the context of Pakistan's ideology—attached to it, should have been an anathema.

During the heyday of the Mahaz, each component used its platform to advance its own ethnic agenda. The Muhajirs executed plans for accelerating immigration from India. The Punjabis consolidated their political and economic clout in Sindh. The Pathans stepped up their immigration and strengthened their hold on selected sectors of the economy. The three partners used the umbrella of the Mahaz to further their respective interests. The uniting triangle of the MPPMM eventually divided the three partners forever.

Thus, the party earned a negative image even before it began to render service to the community it represented. From its very inception, the people of Sindh, with whom the prospective members and supporters of the new party shared land, looked upon it with suspicion and alarm. They saw in its emergence the rebirth of the era of bitterness, hatred, and separation which had been the hallmark of the MPPMM. Was Nawab Muzaffar, the founder of the MPPMM, the source of inspiration for the creation of the MQM? Or, were the seeds of the MQM planted in 1947? The reader may be able to find answers in the pages of this book.

Political parties are formed to promote the political causes of nations or special interest groups within the nation. Formation of a political party is a legitimate political activity in the civilized world. Applying the yardstick, let us examine the basic elements leading to the formation of the MQM.

1. Need for a separate Muhajir political party.
2. Founding principles.

3. The constituency.
4. The manifesto.
5. The strategy for attaining the objectives set forth in the manifesto.

The need for a separate Muhajir political party, comprising of immigrants who (a) came from India following Partition, (b) have been migrating from India during the last half a century, (c) have been migrating from Bangladesh since its secession, and (d) will keep migrating from India and Bangladesh for all times to come, is based on the following assumptions:

   i. The Muhajirs have not been allowed to integrate with the locals.
  ii. The Muhajirs have been termed as 'Muhajirs' by the locals.
 iii. The Muhajirs have been discriminated against socially, economically, culturally, and politically.
 iv. The Muhajirs have been deprived of their legitimate share in the local, provincial, and federal services, and in private sectors.
  v. Since non-Muhajirs in Sindh have organized political platforms, like the Jiye-Sindh Movement (JSM), the Punjabi-Pakhtun Ittehad (PPI), to safeguard their rights, the Muhajirs must do likewise.

Any community or group is entitled to form a political party, but such groups or communities must not invent negative or imaginary grievances to justify their actions. Sindhis have assimilated many ethnic groups, as may be seen in their ethnic mix. But, if immigrants resist assimilation, as has been done by the post-independence Muhajirs, one has to find reasons for their resistance. Could the reason be the Muhajirs' notion of superiority, or their enormous numerical strength?[3] Notions of superiority were held initially by most immigrants in the past as well. The Arabs thought they brought a superior message, and took pride in their lineage. The Afghans excelled in the use of the sword, the Punjabis in their superior farming techniques,

16 A TESTAMENT OF SINDH

the Gujratis in their trading skills, the Balochis in their racial
pride, and so on. But, today all of them are proud to be Sindhis,
because during the initial adjustment, they received nothing but
peace and love, and are now the sons of the soil. The Muhajirs,
on the other hand, are resisting assimilation because they are
not yet sure of their identity. They came as rulers, but that was
a temporary phase. The locals eventually asserted themselves.
The Punjabis moved in to gather the lion's share at the federal
level. Within the Punjab, however, the East Punjabis fully
assimilated themselves with the locals and no one could say
who ruled the Punjab. But, in Sindh, the seeds of a Sindhi-
Muhajir discord existed from the very inception of Pakistan.[4]
Each subsequent step aggravated and widened this gulf. Who
took the wrong steps, who aggravated the discord, who widened
the gulf, and who resisted the assimilation? These questions
became irrelevant when the Muhajirs decided to float a separate
party.

As to the founding principles, the MQM claimed that the
sacrifices of the Muhajirs created Pakistan,[5] that the Muhajirs
and Pakistan are two sides of the same coin,[6] that the Muhajirs
constitute a nationality at par with other nationalities like the
Sindhi, the Balochi, the Punjabi and the Pathan,[7] that census
should indicate their separate ethnic identity, and that the
national identity cards must show the Muhajirs as a nationality.[8]

Muhajirs claim to have created Pakistan[9], but the ideology
of Pakistan finds no place in the founding principles of their
party. The founder of the MQM, Altaf Hussain, repudiated
the ideology of Pakistan and burnt the national flag at the
tomb of the Quaid-i-Azam, Mohammad Ali Jinnah, in 1979.
His followers performed a similar act in 1998. Thus, to claim
that the Muhajirs and Pakistan are two sides of the same
coin is meaningless. Establishment of an ideological state, as
envisaged in the Objectives Resolution introduced by Prime
Minister Liaquat Ali Khan in the Constituent Assembly, is no
longer the goal. On the contrary, the MQM leadership has
condemned the use of Islamic ideology by the parties and the
state as a tool for the exploitation of the Muhajirs. The party

preaches equal rights, but since its ranks were only open to the Muhajirs, equality was confined to the Muhajirs only, and the Muhajirs were to be more equal than others.[10] The constituency of the MQM was restricted to the immigrants from various parts of India (except East Punjab). However, since the bulk of the Muhajirs migrated from the Urdu speaking belt, namely, UP, Bihar, CP, and Hyderabad, Urdu speaking Muhajirs would dominate, particularly, when the Urdu-Sindhi controversy was on top of the agenda. The Muhajir constituency would take the ultimate shape of a Muhajir province, by carving out urban areas of Sindh, to include Karachi, Hyderabad, Nawabshah, Mirpur Khas, Sanghar, and Sukkur.

The proposed Muhajir province would adjoin India to facilitate the movement, to and fro, through Khokhrapar.[11] Transfer of population, ethnic riots, bloodshed, and the human tragedy that would inevitably result from the intended division of Sindh have been taken for granted by its planners. For them, another round of devastation in the subcontinent would be justified if it could create an ethnic Muhajir province spread over half of the province of Sindh, to accommodate millions of more immigrants from India, in fulfillment of the dream that Pakistan was created as a homeland for the Indian Muslims.

As for the manifesto and the strategy to attain the goals set forth in the objectives, the best way to understand them is to observe, study, and analyse the performance of the MQM, which has been dealt with in detail in various chapters.

It is generally believed that the All Pakistan Muhajir Student's Organization (APMSO) gave birth to the MQM. This may be only partly true. A well-run, highly disciplined, and financially rich party, with channels open for regular weapons supply, well-trained cadres in terrorism, complete with an agenda, social services, and propaganda machinery, could not possibly be run with phenomenal success by a band of young Muhajir students. The party has survived repeated crackdowns by the army and shown remarkable resilience. It has an international network with headquarters in London. It has the ability to remain underground for many years and resurface with a bang. It can function under leadership exiled in London with equal, or perhaps an even greater degree of efficiency than if it were based in Karachi.

How can such a party, which has given sleepless nights to major political parties, to the government, the army, and the intelligence agencies, be run by some young people, howsoever dedicated? By all estimates, the party has the following components:

a. A think-tank or a policy planning wing, comprising the best Muhajir brains to plan, guide, and assess the short and long-term strategy, and vary the tactics to meet emerging situations.

b. An executive wing, which conducts the party affairs, organizes election activity and strikes, and carries out propaganda.

c. A finance wing, which collects *bhatta*, varying according to the paying capacity, from a hundred rupees to several lakhs per month. Those who pay voluntarily will not disclose this out of loyalty. Those who pay under duress do not disclose the fact, because their protection, which the state has not been able to provide, is assured by the MQM. Those who cease to pay or refuse to do so run the risk of elimination.

d. A terrorist wing, which is trained in the use of lethal weapons and the art of hit-and-run tactics. It comes into action to spread fear, enforce compliance, eliminate dissidents, confront the police, the rangers, and the army, and terrorize witnesses to frustrate prosecutions and evade convictions. Cases of murder, arson, and other forms of terrorism are pending against the MQM activists. The accused are imprisoned, released on parole under political pressure to then become ministers, arrested again, or allowed to go underground.

The infrastructure of the MQM is foolproof, elaborate, and functioning in top gear. Effective coordination is carried out by a committee, which ensures that all departments work in step. If one cog in the wheel falls out, there is an upheaval and it is corrected at whatever the price. The bloody rivalry and violent clashes to win the turf war between the two rival factions of the MQM has gone on for several years. The crime of dissidence is punishable with death unless the dissident is reformed in the torture chamber.

Altaf Hussain, living in exile, compelled to operate from a headquarters 6000 miles away from 'millions of his deprived followers', has become a symbol of Muhajir alienation and the only hope of Muhajir emancipation. His personality provides a focus; his struggle gives direction, which has caught the imagination of the young Muhajirs, living in sprawling Muhajir localities, isolated from the rest of Sindh. They have been indoctrinated to believe that the bogey of the so-called integration and assimilation, paraded by pseudo-politicians, is a clever ploy to smother the rising political personality of the Muhajirs and to frustrate their ambition to acquire a place of honour and dignity in the promised land.

From its very inception, it adopted a two-track policy to meet the objective realities. By the time it appeared on the scene, Zia's martial law was on the way out and elective politics had been introduced. Non-party elections held by Zia in 1985 had encouraged the formation of groups and movements on an ethnic basis. The MQM leadership seized the opportunity and mobilized the Muhajir constituency for the coming political battles. In the municipal elections held in 1987, its unofficial nominees swept the polls in Karachi. Zia's demise in 1988 opened the gates for party-based elections. The MQM's excellent organization, its popularity among the middle, lower middle, and working classes of the Muhajir community, the commitment of the men and women of the community, and the vast financial resources, enabled it to capture the bulk of urban Sindh constituencies in all the elections held in 1988, 1990, 1993, and 1997. In urban centres where certain constituencies did not have the Muhajirs in a majority, they traded their votes with non-MQM candidates of their choice on the basis of give and take. Only once, in 1993, they erred in their strategy and boycotted the National Assembly elections which had followed an army crackdown on the MQM in 1992. But, they instantly realized their mistake and contested the Provincial Assembly elections held three days later, and regained their political clout at the Sindh provincial level. From 1988 onwards, the MQM has remained the third largest party of Pakistan, with a solid support of the electorate, and an exemplary unity maintained by its elected members, who have been better educated in comparison to many of their counterparts in rural Sindh.

It is amazing that despite its unity and its commitment to the cause of the Muhajirs, and the opportunity of occupying ministerial positions at the federal and provincial levels, very little was achieved for the benefit of the Muhajir community. Coalition partnerships were weakened by accusations and counter-accusations traded by the partners. Agreements were either overloaded with conditions,[12] or were kept secret in order to avoid a Sindhi backlash.[13] Some clauses of the agreement, like the restoration of the 'no-go' areas of Karachi to the MQM (A), were prima facie so absurd, but deep down these exposed the mafia style of political control of Karachi.[14] The MQM (A) employed pressure tactics to use government power and physically clear the no-go areas from the MQM (H) control, but the PML (N) would not oblige in order to keep the MQM (A) on tenterhooks. However, to pacify the restless MQM (A), Prime Minister Nawaz Sharif visited the so-called no-go areas in 1998 and found them normal, like any other area of Karachi. This was a case of one mafia against another, claiming the same turf.

So much about the political achievements and the use of political clout for the betterment or welfare of the Muhajirs. In the realm of street power, the MQM (A) has had some reasonable achievements, if they can be called achievements at all. They include *bhatta* collection, bloody encounters with the Sindhis, the Punjabis, the Pathans, the MQM (H), and government agencies, and the setting up of torture cells, etc. details of which have been given in a separate chapter.

Secrecy is the hallmark of the MQM, and this is considered essential to retain the element of surprise in its actions and dealings. No terrorist group or party can operate without secrecy. A few months after the 1988 agreement with the PPP, it began secret negotiations with the opposition party, the IJI. Torture cells had been functioning secretly until they were exposed by the army in 1992. Weapons were acquired and stored secretly. If and when there was a danger of exposure, the weapons would be surreptitiously thrown in the street so that their real storage location would remain unknown. *Bhatta* collection from rich individuals was a secret operation, and so was the action to kidnap or eliminate them. Disappearance of illegal immigrants from India in the Muhajir localities, and having national identity cards issued to them in collusion with well chosen immigration officials planted in the department, was a clandestine operation which legitimized lakhs of illegal immigrants. Repatriation of the stranded Pakistanis (Biharis) to Mian Channu in the Punjab was a camouflage for their disappearance and eventual reappearance in the revised list of voters in Karachi. Dr Imran Farooq's and Saleem Shazad's disappearance in Karachi in 1992, and reappearance in London in 1999, was a highly clandestine operation of international dimensions. During these seven years, they conducted their party affairs from secret hideouts. Altaf Hussain's disappearance in Karachi, and reappearance in London in 1992 was a clandestine operation meticulously carried out while army action against the MQM was in progress. The top leadership has been able to hoodwink the intelligence agencies, and frustrate all attempts to apprehend them and subject them to the legal process. The MQM has perfected the art and technique of secret and underground operations. In October 1998, Prime Minister Nawaz Sharif called upon the MQM (A) to surrender the culprits allegedly involved in the murder of Hakim Muhammed Said. In retaliation, Altaf Hussain issued instructions that MQM activists should go underground and operate secretly.

Since its creation, the MQM has had brushes with the Jiye-Sindh (JS) (1986), the PPP (1988-89), the PML–N(1990-92 and 1997-98), and once again with the Jiye-Sindh in 1998. Its experience with each party has been unique indeed. The one with the PML (N) ended in disaster in 1992 and 1998. That with the PPP was an exercise in deceit. With the Jiye-Sindh, a party confined within Sindh only, its dealings have been most pleasant, full of rhetoric, and lacking in substance. Ironically, these two parties have irreconcilable differences on the basic issues, namely:

- The MQM stand that the Muhajirs be accepted as a separate nationality is rejected by the JS.
- Repatriation of the stranded Pakistanis is rejected by the JS.
- Division of Sindh is rejected by the JS.

These three issues have never been raised during the dialogue between the JS and the MQM at anytime. Both the parties are aware of each other's divergent position on these issues. With a pre-ponderance of hardliners at the policy making level in the MQM, the possibility of a soft line on the issues is ruled out. That being the case, the agreement between the two, signed in 1998, to fight for the rights of Sindh, is rendered meaningless. Still, the JS leadership considered it worthwhile to sign the agreement because it speaks for the rights of Sindh. Does this give an indication that the MQM's rigidity is gradually turning into flexibility? Change of the party's name from Muhajir to Mutahida is one such indication. Linking of the rights of the Muhajirs to those of Sindh is another. Recent dominance of hardliners in the London headquarter of the MQM is a negative input.[15] But, Altaf Hussain's declaration that Sindh was being ruled as a colony of the Punjab, and his threat of a unilateral declaration of independence and the launching of an armed struggle, sent mixed signals to the Sindhi nationalists.[16] Abdul Khaliq Junejo of the JSM welcomed Altaf's remarks about Punjabi domination, but castigated the MQM for its ethnic and divisive character.[17] Mumtaz Bhutto (SNF) welcomed Altaf's statement, and suggested that:

1. The MQM should abandon its hostile disposition towards rural Sindhis.

2. The word 'Muhajir' should be buried for ever and all urban Sindhis must only be identified as Sindhis.
3. There must be a merger, into one nationalist party, of all urban and rural Sindhis so that a strong movement can be launched for the rights of Sindh.
4. This new nationalist party of Sindh must demand the instant implementation of the promise in the Pakistan resolution that the provinces will be autonomous and sovereign.
5. Devolution of power, as pronounced by General Musharraf, must take place immediately and only those subjects be retained at the centre which are specified in the Pakistan resolution.[18]

Sindhi intellectuals have been pondering on the factors that led to the emergence of the MQM as the representative party of the Muhajirs, its successes at the polls, its encounters with various non-Muhajir communities and government agencies, its power-sharing agreements, and its bitter experiences. Dr Feroz Ahmad has this to say:

…There is nothing wrong about identifying oneself with one's own historically-formed ethno-linguistic group, safeguarding its collective interests, and promoting the language and culture of that group. What is wrong is to nurse ethnic prejudice and hatred. A lot of bad blood has flowed both from the suppression of ethnic diversity and from the expression of ethnic prejudice.[19]

Dr Ahmad suggests the following solutions:

…There are two preliminary solutions towards bridging the ethnic divide. First, all the talk about dividing Sindh must stop, second, there is no need to quibble about the definitions of a nationality, ethnic group or Muhajir. Instead, one must respect the Urdu-speaking people as a distinct ethno-linguistic group and stop demanding the unfeasible cultural assimilation from them.[20]

Sindhi intellectual Abdullah Memon wrote an illuminating series of articles on the subject in 1995. He analysed the problem in depth and finally concluded the series with a dream which reflects his perspective, one shared by most Sindhis:

> It is my dream that one day the MQM will become MSM (Mutahida Sindh Movement), that one day a Sindhi will be elected as an MNA from Liaquatabad on an MQM (MSM) ticket and a Muhajir will get elected as an MNA from Larkana on a PPP ticket. It is my dream that one day the governor, the chief minister and all ministers of Sindh could be Muhajirs. Nobody will find anything unusual or objectionable about this because by then this wretched business of 'us' and 'them' would have been overcome and we shall all be one, single, and unified people of Sindh.[21]

Will this distinction of 'us' and 'them' disappear, and if so, when? Abdullah Memon is a large-hearted Sindhi who has opened his arms to warmly embrace the Muhajirs, in keeping with the Sindhi tradition. He is an idealist and he is in good company. The Muhajirs have also produced great idealists. Hakim Muhammed Said was one.[22] Professor Karrar Hussain was another.[23] Dr Jameel Jalibi is yet another.[24] Who can forget the Banh Beli (helping hand) rural uplift organization set up by Javed Jabbar in the remote Thar desert, which is a unique and substantive step towards rural-urban integration?[25] There are hundreds and thousands more, but their voices have been drowned in the flood of ethnic prejudice. Then there are realists who dig deeper, locate the root of the problem, and offer a frank and candid piece of advice to the MQM. Brig. (retd.) A.R. Siddiqi is one of them:

> ...Originating as a Muhajir activist party, it (MQM) compromised, at the very outset, its credentials as a would-be national party. Under the circumstances, any major deviation from its basically limited manifesto could compromise its character as a Muhajir body. It should also stop and think, in wider national terms, whether it had been a good idea to have launched an exclusive body and thus to set the Muhajirs apart from the rest of the body politic....[26]

Can the future of the MQM be predicted with a reasonable degree of accuracy? Hardly anyone knows the answer. Even the MQM itself, with all the think-tanks at its command, probably has no answer. Yet, one can make some observations on the basis of facts, realities, and experiences. These will be related here to guide the reader to evaluate and find some clues if not the answer itself.

- That the MQM has practiced facism and terrorism as political tools is beyond question. The future of fascist and terrorist parties has been bleak around the world. The MQM has denied the charge of terrorism, but its denials convince nobody. It must disband and banish terrorism which has no place in civilized politics.

- Deprived of terrorist underpinning, will the MQM survive? How will it collect *bhatta* from unwilling donors, once the element of fear generated by terrorism is eliminated? Voluntary donors will represent the committed people among the middle and lower middle classes whose paying capacity is low. The MQM will thus be reduced to a pauper political party, if its scope is confined to the present constituency. If it opens up its membership to non-Muhajirs, it will be hard for it to live down its negative image.

- Possibility of an urban Sindh party comprising the MQM, the non-MQM Muhajirs, the Sindhis, the Punjabis, the Balochis, the Pathans, and others is ruled out. These communities represent diverse political and ethnic groups. For example, the Sindhis owe allegiance to the PPP, the JS, the SNA, the AT, etc. The Punjabis owe allegiance to the PML or the PPI. The Pathans owe allegiance to the ANP or the PPI. The Balochis owe allegiance to the PPP, the BNP, etc. The Muhajir support the MQM, the PPP, etc. Be that as it may, the MQM has little chance, even if it wants to transform itself into a multi-ethnic urban Sindh party. Old and established commitments cannot be sacrificed for the sake of a blind date. Besides, even the thought of forming an urban Sindh party is absurd. Urban and rural Sindh are indivisible politically and economically, and the formation of political parties have to conform to this basic reality.

- Ethnic groups can function for social, cultural, and economic programmes. Their formation as political parties is a divisive and separatist phenomenon. Since the province of Sindh and the State of Pakistan are multi-ethnic, there is ample room for mainstream parties in the country. Struggle for rights within the framework of a mainstream party is the most effective way to demand rights. Existing mainstream parties can be reformed or new parties can be formed for the purpose.

- Since the army takeover in October 1999, some restructuring of the existing parties can be foreseen. Leaders of some of these parties may be eliminated, excluded, or disqualified. Each party, including the MQM, has to adopt a new outlook, re-adjust to new realities, and participate in the process in the new spirit.

- Whether the MQM likes it or not, it has to soften (if not remove) its hardliners at all levels, including the policy-making and the workers level. What exactly are the hardliners doing in the MQM? The common perception is that they are the backbone of terrorism, engaged in *bhatta* collection and making impossible demands. These acts have given a bad image to the MQM in the eyes of those who matter and whose opinions and verdicts carry weight with the people of Pakistan. But, Altaf Hussain cannot dispense with the hardliners, without whom the party would lose its clout, its mass following, its credibility, and its vote bank. Apparently, this dilemma has no solution. When a problem defies a solution, the end result may not be in the best interests of the MQM as a political entity.

- MQM demands include: a) opening of the Khokhrapar border, b) repatriation of stranded Pakistanis, c) declaring Muhajirs as a separate nationality, and d) division of Sindh. Irrespective of the rejection of these demands by the entire Sindhi population, which by itself is a decisive factor, some of these demands impinge on the foreign policy of Pakistan, while others have an impact on the structure of the federation. Inflexibility on the part of the MQM on these demands brings it into direct clash with the federal authority. This clash has gone on for over a decade, but only time will tell who will be the eventual winner.

- MQM threats of a unilateral declaration of independence (UDI), and a resort to arms, have placed the MQM in a position which cannot be defended. That such a party can exist, survive, and operate on the soil of Pakistan raises some serious questions.[27]

- The MQM has been subjected to repeated batterings by the army and law-enforcing agencies. The MQM has also alleged that the army engineered the split within its ranks and midwifed the birth of the MQM (H). There have been accusations of terrorism against it, and counter-accusations against government agencies for carrying out extra-judicial killings and human rights violations. Despite these crackdowns, the MQM has survived and maintained its popularity among its followers. These are unmistakable signs of its resilience, its commitment, its staying power, its organizational solidarity, and its ethnic cohesion. All these plus points ought to have led to some achievements for the betterment of the community. The MQM must subject itself to accountability, and prepare its balance sheet of gains and losses. Its terrorism has led to the collapse of civic life and the economy. It has antagonized the Sindhis, the Punjabis, the Balochis, and the Pathans. It has been responsible for murders, arrests, prosecutions, punishments, and exiles. It's coalition agreements with all the ruling parties ended prematurely and in disaster. Its assumption of ministerial positions was marked with corruption and lack of a sense of responsibility. Its positive attribute of unity in the Muhajir ranks was a negative input to national integration. It wrapped itself into an ethnic cocoon, which rendered its leaders incapable of conducting a dialogue on national issues. Its only spectacular achievement has been the expansion of its ethnic vote bank.

The other positive achievement is its understanding with the Jiye-Sindh. But, this achievement lacks substance, is self-serving, has no direction, and has been induced not by the imperatives of a united Sindh, but by the rejection and condemnation by the mainstream parties, notably the PML (N). Thus, with a few dubious achievements to its credit, and an excess baggage of a negative image, the party stands little chance of survival unless it undergoes drastic structural re-adjustment in keeping with the national ethos.

- Altaf Hussain rode the crest of popularity on the basis of the grievance of second and third generation Muhajirs, who were effectively cut-off from the ideological orientation of their progenitors. He rode it for a decade and a half during which he shared power three times.[28] During these power-sharing opportunities, which should have been utilized for removing grievances, the MQM acted as the opposition, indulged in accusations and counter-accusations, resorted to terrorism, and paralysed Karachi. A strategy of agitation and subversion of its coalition partners was adopted to pacify the terrorists, and to keep them occupied in *bhatta* collection, strikes, and shut-down of industrial and commercial activity. Can Altaf sustain a party on a negative strategy for an extended period? There comes a stage of 'terror fatigue', and signs of this fatigue have begun to show in the shape of a party split, dissidents, change in the name of the party, reconciliation with the JSM, adoption of a British citizenship by Altaf, and an attempt to change the MQM manifesto in view of the change in outlook on Sindhi-Muhajir relations. Can the MQM recover from this fatigue?

- The MQM leadership, on the one hand, and party activists, including the terrorists and *bhatta* collectors, on the other, have a symbiotic relationship with each other, which makes them inseparable. The leaders have been in power thrice, but they have failed to deliver. For their own survival, they have had to go along with the activists, despite pressure from the moderates, from the establishment, and from people in general. If they abandon terrorism, join the mainstream, and switch over to constitutional means, they run the risk of the terrorists' guns being turned on them. How can the activists forego the source which has sustained them for a decade and a half? This is a dilemma facing the leadership. How they solve this problem will determine the future of the MQM.

• Terrorism thrives under dictatorial, despotic, or unscrupulous rule. It is a symptom of a decaying and degenerating society. The regime of General Zia, lasting for eleven years, destabilized the democratic process, rigged the referendum, tampered with the constitution, and created an environment conducive to the growth of ethnic militarism and political terrorism. The MQM was pampered, tolerated, and given a long rope by deceitful politicians like Jam Sadiq Ali and Nawaz Sharif, who wanted its political support to rule Sindh. The long rope eventually became a noose round its own neck.

• It is no longer a secret that the creation of the MQM was not so much to fulfil the aspirations of the Muhajir community of urban Sindh, as it was the brainchild of the establishment, with the sole aim of wiping out the PPP from urban Sindh.[29] Thus, it played into the hands of the powers that be. It was weaned away from the PPP in 1989. When it acquired its own strength, it began to challenge the very establishment that had launched it. In return, it was subjected to repeated crackdowns from 1992 onwards, but it has not learnt any lessons as may be judged from the proliferation of hardliners within its policy-making cadres.

• At the leadership and policy-making level, the MQM is facing a crisis of stupendous proportions. About a dozen top leaders are in exile. Its chairman, Azim Tariq, was murdered in 1992. Dissension at the executive and coordination levels have been too many and too frequent. This is evident by the split in the party in 1992 leading to the formation of the rival MQM (H), the removal of Ajmal Dehlavi as the party's chief negotiator, and the desertion by ex-senator Ishtiaq Azhar, who exposed MQM's involvement in *bhatta* culture and terrorism. All these factors combine to erode the credibility of the MQM (A). These dissensions, rather than mellowing attitudes, have further stiffened the posture of the top leadership. In consequence, public opinion in the entire country, which was partly sympathetic at one time, has turned hostile. To restore its public image, the MQM has to make a complete reversal in its policies, which appears unlikely. If the Muhajir rank and file is still supporting it, it is because of the captive vote bank, coupled with prolonged isolation of the community from the mainstream, induced by ethnic politics. Then, there is the fear of terrorists, which is deep-rooted, and which has been accentuated ever since the activities of the torture cells became known. No Muhajir leader has run the risk of openly challenging the MQM (A). The only challenge was posed by the MQM(H), which was worse, because the latter was even more extremist and separatist in its approach. There is thus a leadership vacuum in the Muhajir community—a leadership which repudiates ethnicity, which is non-fundamentalist and liberal in outlook, and courageous enough to throw a challenge to the MQM philosophy and to bring back the Muhajirs into the national mainstream. The Muhajir community must rise to the occasion and throw up leadership in the vision and the footsteps of Jinnah. They have the talent and the capability to meet the leadership challenge. Among the non-Muhajirs, only Bhutto could have done it, but after his elimination, deep-rooted ethnicity was planted by Zia which cannot be uprooted by a non-Muhajir at this stage.

• The problems of urban Sindh are multi-dimensional: political, economic, social, cultural, inter-ethnic, intra-ethnic, provincial, inter-provincial, national, and international. Their solution calls for a multi-dimensional approach. But, the MQM is mono-ethnic and mono-dimensional in composition and approach, looking at everything from a limited perspective. It has deprived itself of the benefit of knowing or appreciating other peoples' point of view. This restricted perspective is further narrowed to a factional point of view. That explains why there are frequent disagreements, confrontations, accusations, and counter-accusations against non-Muhajir groups, parties, formations, partners, and adversaries. That also explains the genesis of so much frustration, intolerance of dissent, bitterness, turf war, and proliferation of hardliners. Since such attitudes have become part of the faith and creed of the MQM, it is unlikely to change its tune and mend its ways. It appears that the hardliners have either paralysed or dismissed the think-tank. They relied more on their vast manpower, financial resources, and organizational superiority, and less on strategy, which should have been revised and adapted to new situations. These resources brought victory in four successive elections, but the victory at the polls turned into defeat in real life. It is high time the MQM subjected itself to accountability. The hardliners do not have to follow the examples of Tamil Tigers or the Irish Republican Army or other such movements. They are in a peculiar situation, which has no parallel elsewhere. Therefore, the solution must be found in the light of objective realities, within the available framework. In that framework, there is no place for the means and methods followed by the MQM. Will the MQM heed such advice? That seems unlikely, because, if it abandons militarism, it will lose the vital element which sustains its popular support. The two complement and supplement each other, and one cannot survive without the other.

- There is no equivalent of the MQM anywhere else in the world. There are immigrants in many countries, whose stay, job, citizenship, and rights are governed by laws. Nowhere in the world have immigrants ruled the country without first having assimilated. Even in the USA, Canada, and Australia, assimilation is an essential requirement. In the contemporary scene, the MQM is an unnatural phenomenon. The international community would have supported the MQM if it had taken up issues like human rights violations, child labour, discrimination against women and non-Muslims, etc. Discrimination in an Islamic state on the basis of ethnicity cannot exist, and if it does, why should it be against a single community, which is vocal, highly educated, and talented? In any case, there is no ethnic bond between, say, a Upian and a Gujrati; the only common feature being that both are immigrants, and both are doing well, in fact better than their counterparts among the locals. So, what is the justification for establishing a party comprising of immigrants, and how can it justify its continued existence?

The MQM leaders' rationale for fleeing to London or going underground has been that they have been framed in false cases of crimes, which they claim they never committed, and that they have to avoid arrest and prosecution. This explanation lacks courage of conviction. Leaders of other parties have been subjected to arrests and prosecutions. The ANP leaders were tried for sedition while Bhutto ruled, but the trial was discontinued after Bhutto's downfall. Baloch leaders, Marri and Mengal, went into temporary exile but came back to fight their political battle on their turf. Sheikh Mujibur Rahman was put on trial by Ayub Khan for conspiracy, but was released under political pressure. Later, he remained in the forefront while his followers revolted against Pakistan. Bhutto was tried and convicted. G. M. Syed remained in detention for more than a quarter of a century. Leaders never flee the turf and leave the followers to fend for themselves. This may explain the gulf between the followers who resort to terrorism and the leaders who keep disowning terrorism. This gap keeps widening and is bound to show up.

• Altaf Hussain has now admitted that the Punjab created a rift between the Sindhis and the Muhajirs on the language issue. The two communities drifted apart, and this drift culminated in the formation of the anti-Sindh MPPMM, boycott of the MRD, and finally the creation of the MQM, a process which was programmed by General Ziaul Haq. The least that Altaf Hussain can do to atone for his sin of miscalculation, and of playing into the hands of manipulators and instigators who wished to inflict permanent damage to Sindh and the Sindhis—the very people who had welcomed the Muhajirs after the creation of Pakistan, is to tender a public apology, disband the MQM, and join the mainstream to struggle for the restoration of the rights of Sindh in the federation of Pakistan.[30]

The question whether the Muhajirs are in majority (twenty-two million out of thirty million), as claimed by the MQM, or a mere one-fifth of the population of Sindh (six million out of thirty million), as per the latest population statistics, should now become irrelevant, since they are a part and parcel of Sindh's population in their own right, and have been accepted as such. They possess enterpreneurial and managerial skills and have the capacity and talent to contribute to the growth and development of the economy. Rather than waste time and energy on the game of numbers or the pursuit of ethnic objectives, they should concentrate on building bridges of understanding with the locals and merge with them socially, politically, and economically. To be able to do that, they will have to discard the MQM doctrine of isolation and join the mainstream.

NOTES

1. Mahmud Mirza, *Aj Ka Sindh*, Urdu Progressive Publishers, Lahore, 1986, pp. 7-9.
2. Other parties originated elsewhere, the PPP, the PML (N), the PDP, the JI, the NDP, the ANP, the JUI, the BNP, the PML (Q), the PML(Ch), and the PML (J) originated in the Punjab, NWFP or Balochistan. The Jiye Sindh and the SNA are based in rural Sindh. The PML (F) is technically located in Karachi, but its constituency is outside Karachi.
3. For Muhajir notion of superiority, read Dr Jameel Jalibi, *The Identity of Pakistani Culture*, Royal Book Co. Karachi, 1984, p. 90. As for their numerical strength, read the chapter on census.
4. Read Altaf Gauhar's article, 'Thoughts and Afterthoughts—Karachi—a City in Turmoil', *The Nation*, Lahore, 8 April 1994.
5. Shahid Kamrani, *Sindh Ka Manzarnama* (Urdu), Maktaba Fikr-o-Danish, Karachi, 1988, p. 147.
6. Ibid., p. 147.

7. Ibid., p. 149.
8. Ibid., p. 148.
9. This claim tends to distort history. Indian Muslims rendered great sacrifices for Pakistan's creation and are still facing discrimination and misery. The Muhajirs form a miniscule part of that community. Besides, Pakistan could not have come into being without the Sindh Assembly voting for it in 1943, and the Sindhis offering hospitality to the Muhajirs, the Punjab agreeing to partition itself and undergoing the trauma of bloodshed and the refugee problem, the Pathans disregarding the appeal of their acknowledged leader, Abdul Ghaffar Khan, to boycott the referendum, and the Baloch Jirga supporting the call of the Quaid-i-Azam.
10. Since the change of name from Muhajirs' Quomi Movement to Mutahida Quomi Movement in 1992, the membership has been technically opened to non-Muhajirs. However, no concrete steps have been taken to attract non-Muhajirs. The manifesto has not been revised. No contacts have been established at the grass-root level. No non-Muhajirs have been included at the policy-making level, in the think-tank, or at the local/ workers level. No non-Muhajir is permitted to collect *bhatta* which sustains the party. On this score alone, non-Muhajirs are disqualified from membership. Altaf Hussain's marriage to a non-Muhajir girl does not constitute a step in this direction.
11. For details, please read the chapter 'Jinnahpur'.
12. The MQM-PPP agreement of 1988 contained fifty-seven conditions.
13. The MQM-PML (N) agreement of 1989 and 1997 had secret clauses.
14. The MQM demanded that the government should cleanse no-go areas from the MQM (H) and restore them to the MQM (A).
15. See *Dawn*, 1 November 1999. Dr Imran Farooq and Saleem Shahzad comprise the hardliners team in MQM's London secretariat. In addition, Dr Imran Farooq brought the rebels, who had resigned due to the party's alleged softline stance, back into the party's fold. They are Dr Khalid Maqbool Siddiqui, Dr Ishrat-ul-Ibad, Nadeem Nusrat, Muhammad Anwar, Anis Ahmed, Wasey Jalil, Sayed Zulfiqar Haider, and Dr Saghir Ansari.
16. *Dawn*, 28 January 2000.
17. *Dawn*, 30 January 2000.
18. *Dawn*, 29 January 2000.
19. Dr Feroz Ahmad's (Professor of Social Work at Howard University, Washington D.C.) series of articles entitled, 'Ethnic Politics is a Dead-End Street', *Dawn*, 21 November 1995.
20. Ibid., 23 November 1995.
21. Abdullah J. Memon, 'Facing Facts in Sindh – The Dictates of Reason', *Dawn*, 12 November 1995.

22. His deep concern for Sindhi-Muhajir understanding has been described in M.S. Korejo's book: '*G.M. Syed – An Analysis of His Political Perspectives*', OUP Karachi, 1999, pp. 130-1.

23. *Dawn*, 14 April 1995, the Professor interviewed by Maisoon Hussain. Also, see *G.M. Syed* by Korejo, pp. 48-9.

24. Dr Jameel Jalibi and Kazi Quadir (ed.), *The Identity of Pakistani Culture*. Royal Book Co. Karachi, *1984*, p. 90.

25. M.S. Korejo, in his book: *G.M. Syed—An Analysis of his Political Perspectives*, OUP, Karachi, p. 130, mentions the services rendered by Javed Jabbar's 'Banh Beli' (helping hand) rural uplift programme in Thar district.

26. Brig. (retd.) A. R. Siddiqi, 'MQM at the Cross Roads', *Dawn*, 21 February 1992.

27. Read Altaf's declaration issued from London, as published in *Dawn*, 26 January 2000.

28. The three terms came to an abrupt halt due to the slippery style of MQM politics. For details, see chapter 9, 'Dialogue of the Deaf'.

29. Aamir Ahmed Khan, *Herald*, April 2000, pp. 24-5, Gen. (retd.) Mirza Aslam Beg's interview by Ihteshamul Haq in *Herald* of October 1998, pp. 47-8, quoted in chapter on 'Political Terrorism'.

30. This was written in the year 2000. Subsequently, Altaf Hussain has apologized to the Sindhis for his past mistakes (*Dawn*, 9 January 2001), and directed that the party manifesto be revised in keeping with the changed scenario in Sindh (Kunwar Khalid Yunus, *Dawn*, 11 March 2001).

3

POLITICAL TERRORISM—A DEADLY TRIANGLE

The Muhajirs have been the most educated, organized, and urbanized community of Pakistan. Not a trace of terrorism was attributed to them, at least during the first forty years of Pakistan's existence. It was after this period that the MQM took birth in their ranks and became a party which resorted to terrorism as a political weapon. The party membership comprised the middle and lower-middle class Muhajirs. The birth of the MQM marked a watershed between a peaceful and harmonious Karachi and a terrorized Karachi. How does one explain this phenomenon?

Many explanations have been offered. One is that the Muhajir's list of grievances kept piling up for forty years. They were alienated from the mainstream. They had been discriminated against in economic opportunities, job quotas, domicile certificates, civic amenities, fund allocations, autonomy in local and municipal affairs, etc. Political parties like the Muslim League, the JI, the JUP, and the PPP ignored Muhajir grievances. When these reached a saturation point, and all peaceful methods failed, the only option for them was to form a purely Muhajir political party to secure Muhajir rights, nationality, and the division of Sindh by all possible means.

The Muhajir grip on Karachi's economy and resources have been well-known and adequately chronicled. The semi-government and private job market of Karachi is bigger than the entire government of Sindh, and was almost entirely available to them. If there was rivalry between them and the Punjabis and the

Pathans, it was created when they ruled. From 1947 to 1971, and from 1977 to 1988, the Sindhis were a non-entity and they suffered in silence. In any case, formation of an ethnic party to create confrontation is an abnormality, a deviation, and an aberration, apart from being a repudiation of the concept of Pakistan claimed to have been created by Muhajir progenitors. Lastly, the introduction of terrorism as a political weapon was tantamount to throwing a challenge to Jinnah and Liaquat Ali Khan, who were strong advocates of democratic norms, constitutional ethics, and peaceful dialogue.

Karachi has been in the grip of terrorism for over a decade now. This is a phenomenon which is entirely new to this city, which has been the city of peace and harmony throughout its history. Pre-independence Karachi was cosmopolitan, plural, and yet, an integrated city. Each community spoke its own language—Sindhi, Gujrati, Balochi, Punjabi, and Marathi at home, and Urdu as a link language. English, being the language of the rulers and the medium of technical education at higher levels, was spoken by the elite class at the top government level, and in the English language and science classrooms. Newspapers were published in Sindhi, Gujrati, and English. The official language was Sindhi and all, including the British officers, spoke it fluently (I personally heard Governor Hugh Dow speak Sindhi). Inter-ethnic harmony was exemplary. Peace, tolerance, and a spirit of mutual accommodation ruled the city.

The generation which saw pre-independence Karachi is fading away, and so are the memories. The new generation of Karachiites has no links with the Karachi of bygone days. This sort of spiritual alienation has made Karachi a city of strangers, an abode of adversaries, a sort of transit camp whose inmates have little in common and much to quarrel about. These conditions have made Karachi an ideal place for crime, and where there is an erosion of civic sense, an absence of good neighbourliness, a neglect of the environment, and the degeneration of politics into revenge, conflict, devastation, and anarchy.

How has this happened, and why? Why has Karachi been singled out for this exceptional treatment, and why have other cities been spared? What is so special about Karachi? Is Karachi in the grip of terrorism, and if so, what brand of terrorism is it? Is it drug related, gun related, sect related, ethnicity related, politically motivated, or simply a criminal variety? If the problem is examined minutely, one would find all brands of terrorism operating in Karachi, as one may find in any megalopolis elsewhere in the world. However, where Karachi differs from the rest is that here political terrorism dominates over other forms of terrorism. This has become the pattern during the last fifteen years.

An attempt is made here to take up Karachi as a case study, analyse its demographic structure, study its political currents and cross-currents, and see how far political rivalry, economic deprivation, social discrimination, and the absence of grass-roots democracy are related to terrorism. Support for these findings will be sought in the opinions and claims made by various sources, including informed citizens, politicians, governmental functionaries, private individuals, impartial journalists and columnists, editors of prestigious newspapers, etc. There are also judicial findings on the subject which have been chronicled in a separate chapter.

The magnitude of terrorism in Karachi may be gauged from the political upheavals produced by it not only at the provincial level in Sindh, but most significantly, at the federal level. Since 1986, five major clean-up operations have been carried out to flush out the terrorists. In most of these operations, the army was called in to deal with the political terrorists. All operations, whether carried out by the army, by the rangers, or by the police, have produced negative results.

Terrorism in Karachi is neither accidental nor incidental. It has a motivation, a rationale, a pattern, and a method, as well as a plan and a strategy. If it has victimized thousands of people, including important personalities, industrialists, educationists, judges, government functionaries, political activists, witnesses, and ordinary folk, and if it has survived repeated crackdowns, then there has to be a reason for all that. The stakes must be very high, in fact higher than the dismissal of governments, elected assemblies, and indeed democracy itself. Finally, the state itself must be the target if terrorism has acquired dimensions beyond the reach and the resources of the state.

Since April 1985, Karachi has been in the grip of political violence (as opposed to pure and simple criminal activity). It began with ethnic hatred between the Muhajirs and the Pathans over the accidental death of a Muhajir girl caused by a rash Pathan driver. The incident was blown out of proportion, given an ethnic colour, and politicized, leading to the most savage killings between the Muhajirs and the Pathans, leaving permanent scars in its wake. Soon, bloody clashes erupted between the Muhajirs and the Punjabis. By 1988, Sindhis also received their share of battering, and they replied in kind by executing well-planned and co-ordinated murderous attacks against the Muhajirs in Hyderabad. The decade of the 1990s was almost exclusively a war of turf between rival factions of the MQM, which reduced other communities to the status of helpless bystanders. Government agencies which got involved to restore order and sanity got bogged down and burnt their fingers. There was heavy loss of life among policemen, rangers, army personnel, and even judges, who were targetted. Besides, thousands of innocent Muhajir lives have been lost. The carnage is nowhere near an end. The MQM has consistently denied its involvement, but General (retd.) Mirza Aslam Beg, the former chief of army staff (COAS), dismissed those denials:

> The army does not forget such insults. In 1991, an army major and others were kidnapped by the MQM and tortured. It prompted me to take action and Altaf Hussain was forced to publicly hand-over the culprits to the authorities. The MQM workers who tortured the army major were sentenced to rigorous imprisonment for 20 to 25 years.[1]

Despite this devastating evidence, no public apology was offered by the MQM, and no public undertaking was given to renounce terrorism. On the contrary, terrorism was rewarded by making the MQM a partner in the IJI coalition government in 1991-93.

Ironically, this coalition was midwifed by a wing of the army under the same COAS.[2] The motivation for this partnership was to rule Sindh under the minority leadership of Jam Sadiq Ali, with the help of the MQM. This partnership had its windfalls for both the partners. The PML (N) ruled Sindh through Jam Sadiq Ali, and the MQM had a licence to terrorize urban Sindh. Political murders, kidnappings, and extortions of *bhatta* were committed with impunity. Dissidents were tortured and eliminated. Strikes and shut-downs were forced upon industry, business, transport, import, and export. Civic life came to a standstill. The civilian governments in Sindh and Islamabad would not act as their priority was to rule Sindh, even if it was paralysed and devastated. This time it was General Aslam Beg's immediate successor, General Asif Nawaz, who was called upon in May 1992 to strike at the terrorists and bring peace and sanity to Karachi.

The army action began in earnest in June 1992. Widespread arrests were made. Torture chambers were unearthed. The MQM pleaded innocence, and withdrew from the coalition. Its leaders, Azim Tariq, Dr Imran Farooq, and Saleem Shahzad went underground along with thousands of MQM activists.[3] Altaf Hussain fled to London, and has been in exile ever since. Azim Tariq, the MQM chairman, surfaced subsequently and began to soften the MQM attitude, in an attempt to convince his party to abandon terrorism. He was murdered in cold blood, and the culprits have never been traced. The Karachi situation went beyond control. It shook the foundations of the provincial and federal governments of Muzaffar Hussain Shah and Nawaz Sharif respectively. Both had to bow out prematurely in 1993 to make way for new elections.[4]

In the 1993 election, the PPP was voted into power at the centre and in Karachi. The army had to be withdrawn to minimize its involvement, which had gone on for too long. Street violence re-erupted in 1995, which led to the 1995 operation directed by Interior Minister Major-General (retd.) Naseerullah Khan Babar. Babar's action brought peace and sanity, and its positive results were applauded by the print media, columnists,[5] business community, and common citizens. The action was praised by the then President Farooq Laghari.[6]

The MQM condemned the operation and accused the government of human rights violations and extra-judicial killings of MQM activists. Babar refuted the allegation and claimed that sixty terrorists were killed in actual police-terrorist encounters, and as evidence to prove that these were genuine encounters, reported that 195 personnel belonging to the police, rangers, and the army were also killed. In 1996, President Leghari dismissed the PPP government, and one of the charges against it was that of human rights violations during operations to control terrorism in Karachi, a charge which was later confirmed by the Supreme Court of Pakistan. Prior to this, similar operations were launched by various governments in 1986, 1990, and 1992, and subsequently in 1998, with similar allegations of terrorism against the MQM, and counter-allegations by the MQM of extra-judicial killings. As a consequence of this psychological tug-of-war, all the governments of Pakistan since 1985 to 1998 have been branded as oppressive by the MQM, and the MQM branded as a fascist and terrorist party by all the governments since 1986 to 1998. By the same logic, there is no one in Pakistan who can pass a fair and honest judgement on the conduct of any party or any government.

Whether the MQM is resorting to terrorism or successive governments have planned and executed terrorism as an excuse to punish the MQM, the end result is that the province of Sindh has been infected with a virus which has spread into the nerve centre of Sindh with little hope of recovery. Every successive government makes new revelations about the links of the MQM terrorism with foreign agencies. Babar revealed that:

MQM terrorists received training in India and Javed Langra was providing it. Javed's uncle was a member of the BJP and he was running a training camp in Lucknow. When we were in the government, the Indian army helped them set up a code which was used by our army. But due to our interception, they could not decipher these codes.[7] We also arrested 400 terrorists from

Malaysia, Singapore, Sri Lanka and Thailand, but PML (N) government released them. These terrorists were guilty of killing scores of people.[8]

On 28 October 1998, Prime Minister Nawaz Sharif mounted a frontal attack on the MQM (A) and accused it of master-minding the murder of Hakim Mohammad Said in Karachi on 17 October 1998. He called upon the MQM (A) to handover the seven culprits, including MPA Zulfiqar Haider, who had allegedly planned the murder at 'nine-zero' (the Karachi head quarters of the MQM) two days before. This was counter-attacked by Altaf Hussain, who accused the former of murdering Hakim Said, and asked his followers to quit the coalition, go underground, and keep their whereabouts secret from friends and family members.

The MQM's defiant reaction against Prime Minister Nawaz Sharif constituted an open challenge. A large number of well-informed writers came out with their findings. In its editorial of 30 October 1998, *Dawn* Karachi wrote:

...For the Mutahida (MQM-A), the hope, howsoever forlorn, is that it will re-educate its activists and adherents, shed its militant image and enter the political mainstream. Because of some activities of its militants, its very name has to conjure up in some minds the image of a party whose mindset has ranged it against the principles that underline democracy and civil society... The uncomfortable position in which the Mutahida finds itself today can serve as an opportunity for the party to undertake a major overhaul of its policies, operations and organizational structure and turn a new leaf. It has to rein in its militants who in their zeal do more harm than good to the party. Above all, it has to give up the politics of violence and disband its militant wing whose excesses, especially by way of forcible collection of donations, have alienated a large number of people in the MQM's own constituencies. The party, thus, has a moral and political responsibility to acquire a new image that would help it adapt itself better to Sindh's multi-cultural and multi-ethnic reality.[9]

Dawn has been frank and forthright on the issue of terrorism being a part of the MQM's political agenda. Equally forceful was its advice that the MQM must adjust to the multi-cultural and multi-ethnic reality of Sindh as a whole rather than looking at the problem of the Muhajirs and Karachi in isolation from the rest of Sindh. Columnist Irfan Hussain exposed the real face of the MQM:

...Most people have no idea who actually killed Hakim Said. But they are neither surprised nor horrified by the official claim that MQM was behind the murder. Over the years, both factions of MQM have earned a chilling reputation of harbouring vicious killers in their ranks. No protestations of innocence can possibly change this public perception because those of us who live in Karachi have seen these criminals in action... People are fed up with endless strikes (now called under the euphemism of 'mourning days'), car robberies, and hold-ups at gun-point and the unending daily death toll caused by the infighting between the rival factions of the MQM. The criminals responsible for these murderous attacks were sheltered under the MQM umbrella; and as the Mutahida was a coalition partner with the PML, its members were seldom brought to book. Indeed Mr. Nawaz Sharif freed large numbers of alleged terrorists (imprisoned by PPP in 1996) as a price for forming a government in Sindh.

...Boys as young as 13 and 14 roam the streets with automatic weapons. When the security agencies came to these localities, nobody dared to identity these young thugs. So what is the police to do? (MQM has turned the entire new generation of Muhajirs into terrorists. They have made terrorism a way of life. Young recruits can't get a job but with profession of killing they are adequately compensated out of the *bhatta*, in addition to growing up as the saviours of Muhajir culture, politics and working for their ultimate goal).

...To re-establish its credibility among its own constituency, the MQM must show itself able to face the might of the state. It has thrived on its underdog status when out of power, and it would be over-optimistic to assume it has disappeared just because the daily death toll has fallen.

So what next for the MQM? By now it has alienated all the major power groupings in the country. The Muslim League has found it a very prickly partner: throughout the recent marriage of convenience, the MQM has acted as an opposition party while enjoying all the fruits of power. Despite being an ostensible ally, the MQM leadership has sniped constantly at Nawaz Sharif. The PPP tried to crush the party because it did not need it to form a government in Sindh, and attempted to eliminate it through General Babar. To this day, many people, especially in the Punjab, are convinced there is no other way of dealing with this armed and dangerous ethnic group.

The army and many others out of uniform are convinced that the MQM receives arms, money and training from India. Whatever the truth of this allegation, many of the party's words and actions have convinced a large section of Pakistanis that its patriotism is questionable...

Unfortunately, the MQM has been unable to make the transition from a militant band to a mature political party. There has always been a fascist streak that has suppressed dissent. Even worse, its cadres have become so accustomed to collecting *bhatta* or protection money from the individuals and companies that they cannot function as normal political workers any more. This is their only source of income and they cannot live without it. So, if Altaf Hussain were to order them to stop this racket, they simply would not obey.

...If they are to exist and function as a political entity they must renounce their terrorist wing. So far, there has been a symbiotic relationship between the two: the political side of the party has provided cover to the criminal elements while the latter has given muscle to the party that has been out of proportion to its actual parliamentary support. Now if the MQM has to continue as a player in the national power game, the nexus between the political and the armed wing must be broken.

The irony is that the decade-long mayhem in Karachi has frightened away billions of dollars in investments, thus further reducing jobs. This, in fact, is the MQM's lasting contribution to the solution of the Muhajirs problem...[10]

Amina Jilani is a frank, fearless, and hard-hitting columnist. Writing in her weekly column, 'Jaywalker', in the Sunday Magazine of *Dawn* Karachi, she said:

…But with his fantastic luck, the Mian (PM Nawaz Sharif) can never quite get anything quite right. He fluffed up the Karachi move by choosing to appoint a man… Ghaus Ali Shah … His name is associated with the formation and the rise of MQM, a party steeped in militancy since its very inception. How can we forget that at one of its opening public meetings, for the first time in 40 years, members of a political party publicly and blatantly showed us their mettle by brandishing their guns above their heads, the administration meekly standing by. Who were those thousands of gun-toting Muhajir young men heralding the debut of their party in presence and under the patronage of their supreme leaders? They were not the terrorist wing of men but the MQM itself, as proudly owned and embraced by Altaf.

…One additional great relief is the removal from our hair of the so-called Minister for Provincial Coordination, who contributed mightily to mayhem with his perpetual flitting, like Peter Pan, between Karachi and London, doing deals, organizing pay offs…

…The MQM is a tough nut to crack, and old habits die hard. The leader in London, though he may have lost the love and respect of many of his followers who voted for his party, here in Sindh, still commands the obedience of his party members, activists and others. It is highly unlikely that he will be in any way willing to change his policies and his *modus operandi*? His troops cannot act independently, they truly are but slaves to his thoughts.[11]

Pakistan's leading intellectual, humanist, and pacifist, Eqbal Ahmed (d. 1999), had a keen and perceptive mind, and whenever he analysed a situation, he did it thoroughly and with sincerity of purpose. He spoke the minds of devoted Pakistanis, whom he inspired with his high sense of values and fairness of judgement. He wrote a piercing piece:

...A decade ago, two ranking MQM leaders had asked how I viewed their party and its future. MQM will have a bright future, I had said, if it can rid itself of three cults: the cult of personality, the cult of violence, and the cult of victimhood. A decade later, it is clear that this party has become so decisively ensnared in the deadly triangle that only an outside force can disentangle it.

But that demands from Pakistan's ruling establishment, which invokes Islam so often and opportunistically, the knowledge and wisdom of the *ahl-al-hall wa-al-aqd* of bygone days. It is wrong to make the MQM the sole target because Karachi suffers from other sources of violence and crime, including organized mafia, religious zealots, the break away faction of MQM and elements even of the forces of law and order. It will take even handed integrity, time, intelligence work and organizations to sort these out.[12]

Eqbal Ahmed missed out the cult of *bhatta* which sustains the MQM at the international, national, and local levels. He saw MQM terrorism in the overall context of all kinds of terrorism. But, each brand of terrorism has sprouted from its own seed and nourished by its own diet. Other forms of terrorism did not even exist, and at any rate, did not pose any real danger when MQM terrorism started in 1985, and began to grow and flourish. It was propelled by its own philosophy of ethnicity. Thus, while other forms of terrorism may be crushed by the long arm of the law, MQM terrorism, motivated as it is by a political philosophy, can only be countered by a political weapon of a superior philosophy. The MQM terrorists have been brainwashed with an overdose of ethnic passion, and they need prolonged treatment, consisting of re-education, to make them see the futility of the MQM philosophy and the damage it has done to the national economy, national integration, and to the cause of the Muhajir community.

As far as governments go, they seldom separate one form of terrorism from another. Crime or violence, once it rules, loses its brand name, and cannot be distinguished, whether it is purely criminal, drug-related, poverty-related, sect-related, or MQM-related. In a clean-up operation, everyone in the line of fire gets blown up, including the innocent bystander. Just as terrorists do not always target their enemies, so the police do not always isolate the terrorists of a particular brand.

Eqbal Ahmed felt that the MQM is unable to come out of its deadly triangle. In his judgement, the MQM lacks the ability to extricate itself, and advocates that an outside agency should help it to do so. No government, since 1985 till 1998, has proved capable of doing it. The author feels that the task calls for a process of re-education, and no government can do it, nor can it be done by any other community, be it the Sindhis, the Punjabis, the Pathans, or the Balochis. The people who are qualified to do it are the Muhajirs themselves; but, those Muhajirs who have the ability to undertake the re-education process are unable to do so because they have been politically marginalized by the meteoric rise of the MQM. The Muhajirs possess the talent, the intellect, and the ability to provide the right kind of leadership. They have provided superior leadership to Pakistan. Now, they should make a new beginning with the misguided Muhajir youth, guide their energies into the right channels, encourage their assimilation with the locals, and integrate them with the national mainstream, which by no means is an easy task.

M. H. Askari is a senior journalist, highly respected for his knowledgeable and balanced columns on the subject of political terrorism in Karachi. He said:

In a wide ranging interview to a panel of Karachi-based journalists, reported by a Karachi Urdu *Daily Jang*, in four installments, Altaf Hussain has conceded that because of the official policy to deprive MQM of its due share in political power in areas such as Karachi where the party has repeatedly demonstrated its electoral strength, a section of its activists has been driven out of the fold of the party discipline and has resorted to desperate methods. A great deal of militancy which Karachi has witnessed in the recent years has been the result of in-fighting between the Haqiqi faction and the MQM (A) and their bid for the control of the turf has turned many areas into 'no-go' areas...

A large section of the people tend to place credence in the alleged implication of MQM in Hakim Said's murder. This is basically because in the recent years a great many killings have taken place... with which MQM's activists and their adversaries were reportedly connected. If the MQM leadership were to make a categorical declaration condemning militancy and showing readiness to cooperate with efforts to deweaponize Karachi they would perhaps succeed in redeeming their reputation.

While some MQM leaders themselves in their private conversations acknowledge the involvement of their activists in the militancy, they believe that it is the result of their consistently having been deprived of their due share in political and economic power, and to a great extent, the massive unemployment which has resulted from the economic policies of various governments designed to protect vested interests.

MQM insiders maintain that when the MQM-PML (N) coalition was formed in Sindh, the MQM was assured that the Chief Minister and the Governor would both be MQM nominees...

What the MQM erred in the past was in identifying itself too much with what is perceived as national aspirations by endorsing the centre's policies with little or no concern for the aspirations of the people of Sindh...[13]

Governor of Sindh, Major-General (retd.) Moinuddin Haider, who was assigned the delicate job of combating political terrorism in Karachi and restoring peace and sanity in the chaotic city, following the dismissal of Chief Minister Liaqat Jatoi, made his own independent and unbiased assessment of the role of the MQM in the following words:

The fact that MQM, a coalition partner of the government, was using weapons and terrorism as part of its party policy, seemed to me to be a serious dichotomy. One can understand criminals and mafias, but the bullet and the ballot do not go together.

If the MQM-PML coalition agreement (1997) stipulated that the governor and chief minister of Sindh would be MQM nominees, as was claimed by the MQM after the coalition's breakdown in October 1998, two questions begged for answers: Firstly, why was the agreement kept secret if the motives were honest? Secondly, when the agreement in respect of the governor and the chief minister was not honoured, why did the MQM acquiesce and accept junior positions for almost two years? Were they compensated? What was the trade-off? Let us hear from one of the MQM insiders, Ishtiaq Azhar, former senator and former convenor of the MQM Rabita (co-ordination) Committee:

...Soon MNAs, MPAs and other MQM parliamentarians will also enter the picture (of being exposed) after they are accused of massive corruption. Chaudhry Nisar, who is considered to be MQM sympathizer, carried 24 files with him when he went to London. When they were shown to Altaf Hussain, he (Altaf) admitted that he knew about 10 cases of corruption within his party. If that is so, why didn't the party leadership look into the cases? In fact, the party condoned the corruption of its ministers and parliamentarians.

...When the party was re-structured, corruption crept in. I told Altaf Hussain that MQM was never accused of corruption even during the previous operations, but that now corruption had become the rule and his ministers, MNAs and MPAs were all involved.

Hakim Said himself told me that he had documentary evidence that 600 million rupees collected as illegal *chanda* (donations) were sent to London. I wrote a letter to Chaudhry Nisar, asking him to confirm this information from Hakim Said. If he now denies receiving the letter, it would mean that Altaf Hussain was also involved, and that funds were indeed transferred to London.[14]

These chilling disclosures, read with the accusations made by MNA Ejaz Shafi on the floor of the National Assembly to the effect that the government had paid crores of rupees to Altaf Hussain, complete the story of the MQM-PML agreement,

whereby the PML ruled Sindh as a minority group while the
MQM reaped the windfall, which included lucrative ministerial
appointments, crores of rupees as *bhatta*, unchecked terrorism,
frequent strikes, political anarchy, social unrest, and economic
collapse. If the game is so dangerous, and the player so determined
and consistent for more than a decade, what could be the goal?

On the floor of the National Assembly, the treasury benches
made a candid confession that in their greed to rule Sindh as a
minority party, they blundered into forming a coalition with the
MQM, a terrorist party, which collected *bhatta* for its survival
and for running its London outfit. MNA Khwaja Asif (PML)
claimed that during the presidential election in 1993, he was a
witness to the MQM demand of five million sterling from
Farooq Leghari and Waseem Sajjad in exchange for MQM votes.
Ejaz Shafi repeated his earlier allegation.[15]

There is one Sindhi whose depth of feeling and sorrow on
account of the events in Karachi has touched the hearts and
minds of his readers. In his book in Sindhi entitled *Zikr Zindan
Jo* (The Story of a Prison), author Maula Baksh Chandio, who
is not a diehard extremist but a simple rural man, unspoiled by
the complications of urban politics, has made some very
poignant observations on the contemporary scene in Karachi:

> The seeds sown by Gen. Zia have sprouted and borne fruit. It has
> yielded a rich crop of ethnic hatred. The harvest of ethnic hatred
> has been reaped for years, and new crops of hatred are sprouting all
> the time... He planted ethnic and sectarian hatred on a permanent
> basis in the name of Islam to perpetuate his rule. This hatred has
> reached a point of no return.

> Sindh, the land of mystics and peaceful people, rose in revolt against
> the dictator Zia in 1983 (MRD), which exposed Zia's basic
> weakness at the national and international levels. As a revenge, Zia
> created ethnic hatred in Sindh, and destabilized it for ever.

> Ethnic hatred was created and encouraged under government
> patronage. Such hatred has no parallel in Pakistan's history. Before
> Zia, there was no ethnic party and no ethnic hatred. Yes, there were

ethnic affinities but they never turned into hatred and bitterness. Each party before Zia had a mix of all ethnic groups. Under Zia, ethnic polarization became a fact of life, and developed into Hitlerite fascism.

Present ethnic policies did not take birth by accident. Nor was it caused by the absence of any basic amenities of life to the Karachiites. If lethal weapons were a pre-requisite for civic amenities, then the original Karachiites would have all been terrorists for the simple reason that they don't have any civic facility; they don't have a peaceful existence in the villages and even in the graveyards of their forefathers... Ethnic politics constitute a dangerous conspiracy against Sindh and the people of Sindh.

Immigrants take time to assimilate. They had different backgrounds. It was natural that the immigrants, who included educated elites, thinkers, and those who rendered sacrifices for the creation of Pakistan, considered it their right to occupy positions of authority and superiority. This mindset kept the immigrants aloof from the locals and their physical presence in Sindh did not develop into a spiritual bond with Sindh. However, time would have healed the gap. But, the vested interests in the Muhajir leadership, short-sighted local politicians, and ideologically misguided self-styled leaders fanned the fires of ethnic hatred which has set Sindh on fire and destabilized the province for ever.[16]

In victimizing various sections of the community, the MQM had been particularly rough with the press. In fact, the press was targetted in such a crude and uncouth manner that it would surprise even a dictator. Sultan Ahmed, a senior journalist who has been a witness to the treatment meted out to the press by democrats, dictators, ruling parties, opposition parties, terrorists, and peace lovers, during his long journalistic career, has written:

...Major newspapers in Karachi were under pressure from the MQM elements not only not to publish news uncomplimentary or unfavourable to MQM... The pressure exerted on the *Jang* and *Dawn* and the threats to the *Herald* and *Newsline* are too well known... The attacks on the weekly *Takbeer* and threats to its editor, Mr Salahuddin, which made him shift to Lahore... The *Jang* incurred the wrath of MQM by publishing two photographs of the marriage of Dr Farooq Sattar, the then Mayor of Karachi... Bundles of newspaper were destroyed as they came out of the press and they were prevented from reaching most of its readers. The attacks on *Dawn* by the MQM elements... is also known. The individual journalists were also victims of intimidatory telephone calls from MQM activists at their houses and offices... The manner in which they attacked Zafar Abbas of *Herald* and BBC, and his brother, and injured them seriously, had received wide publicity... on 17 March 1991, armed men, about 15 in number, stormed the offices of *Takbeer*, ransacked it and set it ablaze... The hard fact is that the MQM's attitude towards the press had been undemocratic, intimidatory and dictatorial and, at times, violent to obtain favourable results. Any amount of denying from the top now will not wash that away.[17]

These frank observations by a professional journalist received total support from all quarters, representing all ethnic groups. Here is the verdict of Zafar Iqbal, a highly respected Urdu-speaking intellectual, whose opinions carry immense weight. 'There is little doubt that intimidation and physical force had been adopted by the strong-arm sections of the MQM as a way of life. This is witnessed by their bashing of the press, whom they successfully intimidated temporarily, while alienating them on a more permanent basis.'[18]

How to analyse the MQM terrorism? Can it be called an uprising, an insurgency, a civil war, or a revolution? If it was plain and simple terrorism, politically motivated, then it was conducted in a style which sent out different signals to different groups at different times. Some considered it a reaction of an aggrieved, deprived, and victimized people, who were driven against the wall and had no option except to resort to confrontation, becoming violent when provoked. Others think that an urban society, if not given its due rights, and suppressed for long, gives vent to its emotions with anger, in the form of violence. Yet others claim that urban violence is a manifestation of self-defence against police excesses, including extra-judicial killings. But, there are many who think that it is plain and simple terrorism conducted in a planned manner by the MQM for attaining a political goal which can only be achieved through terrorism.

It is worth considering how history will judge MQM terrorism. Pakistan was achieved under the leadership of mature, non-violent democrats like Jinnah, Liaquat Ali Khan, Sardar Abdur Rab Nishtar, Shaheed Suhrawardy, Khwaja Nazimuddin, and many others who strongly believed in adopting constitutional methods even under the gravest provocations. Resort to violence was completely ruled out under all circumstances. Even those leaders who opposed Jinnah, namely Abdul Ghaffar Khan, G.M. Syed, and others, conducted themselves and their parties in an exemplary manner within legal and constitutional bounds.

The MQM leadership has its own explanation. In this respect, the surfacing of top MQM leaders, Dr Imran Farooq and Salim Shahzad in London on 9 September 1999, after remaining underground since 1992, and the case of seven MQM dissidents, who quit the MQM on 1 August 1999, become relevant. Their explanation for remaining underground for seven years is that they were implicated in false cases. In that case, they should have submitted themselves to a judicial trial, and there were bright chances of their acquittal because no witnesses would have deposed against them, and fake witnesses would have been demolished under judicial scrutiny. If they could escape to London in 1999, they could have done the same in 1992 as well. Did they have a role to play from their hideout in Karachi? What role could that be, except to ensure that the terrorist wing of the MQM did not come under the influence of the moderates, and also to ensure that the leadership, which was turning moderate, was eliminated so that the MQM philosophy was not eroded.[19]

The seven dissidents were: Muhammad Anwar, chief organizer; Dr Khalid Maqbool Siddiqui, deputy convenor of the coordination committee and MNA; Zulfiqar Haider, advocate and MPA; Dr Saghir Ansari, MPA; Anis Ahmad, advocate and member of the coordination committee; Wasey Jaleel; Dr Ishratul Ibad, former provincial minister and party organizer in the UK. Their explanation was that the MQM had taken a soft line with a government which had killed 15,000 MQM activists, and was trying and punishing MQM activists in 'kangaroo courts'. The higher judiciary was unable to take *suo moto* action to stop the killings. The dissidents blamed all that on the failure of the MQM policies of conciliation through coalition agreements with the PPP and the PML (N). They alleged that all attempts to secure Muhajir rights by operating within democratic parameters and the constitution had failed. 'We have tried through five elections but each time the experience has been worse, you are trying to plant the tree of democracy and constitutional rule in a barren land. When we cannot get justice through courts, then what other course is left to us (except terrorism)?' In view of the threatened split in the party, it was decided to hold a referendum on the issue and go by the majority verdict.[20]

Sensing the dangers inherent in the persistent militancy in the ranks of the MQM, the daily *Dawn* administered a warning:

...Structured on lines which are anything but democratic, the party (MQM) has never been without a large number of militants in its ranks. Involved in murders and extortions of money, these elements have given MQM (A) an image that has come to stick. No wonder, every government since 1988, has after a brief honeymoon, come down hard on its armed activists, whom the establishment suspects of working at the behest of the party high command. It is also no coincidence that some of the MQM's top functionaries have been accused of involvement in murders. Another problem with the MQM has been the absence of well defined clear-cut aims which its friends and detractors both could understand and use as a point of reference. Mr. Altaf Hussain no less has contributed to this absence of clarity by loose talk which has ranged from fifth nationality to a revolution of 98 per cent of the population against the exploiting elites numbering two per cent... MQM has to demonstrate practically that it believes in the rule of law and in the ventilation of grievances within the legal and constitutional framework, and is, thus, abjuring the politics of violence by purging its ranks of armed militants, adventurers, hoodlums and hotheads who have hitched themselves to MQM's bandwagon. Being the representatives of an ethnic minority, the MQM should know that it is only in a democracy and by constitutional means, that the rights of all communities and regions can be secured in a multi-cultural and multi-ethnic society...[21]

The justification for terrorism given by the hardliners deceives nobody. Terrorism was adopted as a political weapon from the very beginning of MQM's creation. Terrorism and *bhatta* collection are a source of nourishment for the party. The MQM leaders have confessed to this. The judiciary has given a verdict to that effect. Every Muhajir, Sindhi, and Pakistani knows the truth. The hardliners do not have to give justifications which nobody believes.

Columnist Tariq Niazi has tried to balance his verdict on MQM terrorism. He has described five clean-up operations against the MQM: the first under Junejo (1985-88), the second under Benazir Bhutto (1988-90), the third under Nawaz Sharif (1990-93), the fourth under Benazir (1993-96), and the fifth under Nawaz Sharif (1997-98). During all these operations, the state of violence has moved in an inverted 'u' curve: weak in the beginning, strong in the middle, and again weak in the end. The beginning and the end violence curves have time and again proved ineffective. The middle curve, though short-lived, always produced an impact, but it could not be sustained longer than a few months.

...MQM has never proclaimed violence as its strategy for political action. It stands apart from such political outfits that embrace violence as a political creed: Irish Republican Army, Ulster Unionist Party, ETA of Basques of Spain, Black Panthers (USA), Oromo Liberation Front (Ethiopia), Polisario Front (Morocco), Abu Sayyaf Front (Philippines), Kurdistan Workers' Party (Turkey), Mujahideen-i-Khalq (Iran), Gamma Islamia (Egypt), Islamic Salvation Front (Algeria), Hizb-i-Jihad (Lebanon), Hamas

(Palestine) and such others. Unlike these militant groups, the MQM believes in elective polities and wants to lead the under classes of Sindh out of deprivation and misery through political and economic improvement. Regardless of its proclaimed platform, though, MQM has not been accepted as a legitimate political voice of the 20 million Muhajirs.

...Its protest politics, complete with strikes, pen downs, tool downs, shut downs, and massive rallies as well its alliances with the ruling elite since the mid-eighties have been attempts at legitimizing itself as a power claimant. Yet, rival power claimants have been pushing them out of their way to power.

Continued violence could well be a part of this battle for political legitimacy. Ironically, violence has furthered de-legitimization of MQM's claim to power. The average Muhajir who hoped his voice would be heard in high places, couldn't assess party leaders who are always at war and in battle fatigues.

...Violence weakened Muhajir unity on the one hand and strengthened Muhajir rivals on the other ... the MQM needs to step back and search its soul ... it is time to call off this madness, and to get on with the hard part of getting elected: delivering goods.

The present crop of MQM leaders do not represent an ideal community of urban Sindhis ... If they want to be remembered as community builders, they should have two goals to work for democratic governance and service to the community. Right now they are far from those goals. For realizing such goals they need to put down their guns and pick up spades and shovels on behalf of those nameless and faceless millions who have honoured them with their vote, year after year, election after election.[22]

A brief account of the hell that broke on Karachi on 6 and 7 October 1998 is given here as a sample of the suffering which the city has undergone for fifteen years. On 5 October 1998, four MQM (Mutahida) activists were shot dead. Among them were Amir Zaki, a member of the organizing committee, Abdul Qadeer, and Mustafa, all three targetted near the Sindh Madressah. The fourth activist, Muhammad Shahid, was targetted in Sector 11 J of New Karachi.[23] Apparently, the shooting was inspired by political rivalry, and this mode of eliminating foes of rival factions had become a pattern. The citizens had been conditioned to hear news of such heinous crimes committed by rival political factions on a daily basis. But, they were shaken by the manner in which the protest against such killings was registered.

In the Central District of Karachi, shopkeepers were forced to shut down their business. The MQM workers indulged in heavy aerial firing to create panic in preparation for what was to follow the next day. On 6 October, the MQM (A) gave a call to observe a day of mourning on 7 October and to protest against the killing of its workers. The mourning was to be peaceful and non-violent. 6 October was devoted to preparing the city for the mourning:

> Pitched battles were fought by rival groups in Liaqatabad and adjoining areas. The Central District reverberated with gunfire from dawn to late night. An Assistant Sub-Inspector of police and a constable were ambushed and killed in Defence Phase-II. Panic and tension spread throughout the city, as young men spread out into the entire metropolitan area to kill people, burn tyres, passenger vehicles and private cars. Car burning was done with relish in purely residential districts like Clifton and Defence. City streets were deserted, shops were closed, business establishments were shut down. People could not buy essential food stuffs for the second day in a row. At the end of the day, the casualty count was eleven people killed and fifty vehicles set on fire.[24]

On 7 October, the day of 'peaceful mourning', metropolitan Karachi wore a deserted look. The entire business, industrial, and economic activities remained suspended. Districts Central, East, and West shook with heavy gunfire. Police and Rangers' mobile patrols were fired upon in many localities in New Karachi, Nazimabad, and other localities. At the end of the day, fifteen people were hurt (mostly policemen who patrolled the deserted streets), and twenty-four vehicles, including Edhi ambulances, oil tankers, buses, trucks, mini-buses, private cars, and jeeps were set ablaze. Karachi was cut-off from the rest of the world. Flight schedules were upset. Inland transport to and from the city came to a halt. Offices of the provincial and federal governments were deserted. The entire industry, including the steel mills, Sindh industrial trading estate, Korangi industrial area, Karachi port, Port Qasim, oil refineries, and the export processing zone industrial area were paralysed. All educational institutions were closed. Examinations scheduled for the day could not be held. Hospitals could not perform surgical operations; out-patient departments were deserted. Karachi wore the look of a ghost city, with one exception: the MQM (Haqiqi)-controlled Lines area was open for shopping.[25]

The MQM (A) strike and its preparatory activity must have resulted in a loss of five billion rupees (my estimate). The terrorism and violence sent shock waves through homes, business establishments, and industry. The citizens were in a state of panic, remained confined to their homes, and out of fear could not utter a word of condemnation. The strike was considered a success, and shut down of the entire economic activity was declared as a demonstration of sympathy and a spontaneous show of solidarity with the aggrieved party. At the time of the strike, the MQM (A) was ruling as a coalition partner.

During the crackdown of November 1998 against the MQM (A) by Prime Minister Nawaz Sharif, the history of torture cells, originally discovered in 1992, was repeated, and hit the headlines. *Dawn* staff reporter said on 11 November 1998:

CIA Police raided a torture cell run by MQM (A) in Gharibabad. The cell was unearthed on the lead given by two workers of MQM (A) who were arrested on 10 October 1998 after a shoot-out in the locality. SSP Manzoor Ahmad Moghal giving details said that Mazharuddin son of Qamaruddin and Abdul Waheed son of Mulla Amin had been arrested with two Kalashnikovs and two TT pistols and hundreds of live rounds. The same CIA party later unearthed the torture cell set up in a two-room house near gol park in the same vicinity.

Several gunny bags, axes, ropes, chopper, knives, daggers, pieces of ropes, nooses and flags of MQM (A) were recovered from the cell. During the preliminary interrogation the suspected confessed to having killed at least four people, including two constables, after torturing them.

Head Constable Sher Khan of District East Police and Constable Mammood Siddiqui of Sharifabad Police were allegedly tortured and killed in this cell, he confessed.

Replying to questions, suspect Mazharuddin who was presented during the briefing, said that he along with Waheed was on guard duty in the area on the instruction of Bobby, a joint unit in-charge in Gharibabad, when police arrested them.

The suspect who appeared to be in his early twenties said that his gang was involved in kidnapping people for extortion. Those who did not pay the money were killed at the torture cell. He and other workers of his unit were being paid Rs. 200 each per month by the party and he committed shop robberies to generate money.[26]

Political terrorism is now a fact of life in Karachi. Since 1984, the year in which the MQM made its debut on the political stage of Sindh, about 1000 persons have been killed on an average in the city of Karachi every year. Since 1995 (upto October 1998), nearly 3000 lives were lost in acts of politically motivated violence.[27] Nearly 10 per cent of the victims belonged to the MQM (A), 9 per cent to the police, 8 per cent to the MQM (H), while the remaining 68 per cent had no known political or sectarian affiliation.[28]

Crime detection, prosecution, and punishment in individually committed crimes is relatively easy. In organized crime, committed in mafia style, mystery surrounds the entire crime landscape. 'No criminal in the world will hesitate to commit a crime if he is convinced that he will never be convicted even if he is actually apprehended,' says Jamil Yousuf of the Citizen-Police Liaison Committee (CPLC) Karachi. 'Today, conviction rate in Karachi is barely one per cent, and crimes are committed repeatedly because the criminals get away with it.'[29]

Thousands of MQM terrorists were apprehended red-handed, with substantial evidence, including lethal weapons, witnesses, and confessions, but none were convicted. Confessions were retracted, and witnesses were eliminated or turned hostile because of fear. Then there were complaints of human rights violations agitated at local, national, and international levels under a well-orchestrated campaign financed lavishly with the crores of rupees of *bhatta* recovered from urban Sindh. Secret agreements were made, and underground deals were cut with ulterior motives on both sides. The deals were exposed, and the crime wave escalated. Dissidents were murdered, non-payers of *bhatta* were eliminated, opponents were crushed, and the vicious cycle continued.

After the 1997 elections, a secret agreement for coalition between the PML-N and the MQM (A) was finalized in London, from where the MQM chief, Altaf Hussain, directs the MQM. When, in October 1998, the coalition agreement went up in flames amid allegations and counter-allegations of breach of terms, the MQM threatened to expose the secret deal. Besides, the MQM (A) accused the PML government of master-minding the murder of Hakim Said and all other murders to implicate their party. If this line of argument is to be believed, then one has to believe the following unlikely contentions:

a. That various governments at the centre and in Sindh, belonging to various parties and coalitions, since 1988, namely the PPP-MQM (1988-89), the IJI-MQM (1990-93), the PPP-PML Chathha group (1993-96), and the PML (N)-MQM (A) (1997-98) must have planned and executed mafia style political terrorism in Karachi, in which almost all the ruling parties of Pakistan, cumulatively representing the overwhelming majority of the people, must have conspired to victimize and eliminate the MQM (A) which held an overwhelming mandate of urban Sindh.

b. That since MQM (A) victims constituted only a small percentage of the total number of victims, the governments must have organized a massacre to kill not only innocent people, but also its own functionaries, among whom were judges, police officials, rangers, and army personnel.

c. That murdered personalities like Azim Tariq, Senator Mohsin Siddiqui, chief editor of *Takbeer*, Salahuddin, and ex-Governor Hakim Said must also be believed to have been on the hit list of various governments.

Accompanying the massacres were the inevitable consequences in the from of strikes, shut downs, and wheel jams, losses in production to the tune of rupees two billion per strike, economic collapse, suspension of financial, commercial, export and import activity, erosion of the tax base, and destruction of civic life in the largest city of Pakistan.

When things exceeded limits, every government targetted the MQM, arrested thousands of its activists, then released them, inducted them in coalitions, and the cycle began all over again.

Who stands to gain and who stands to lose out of this state of anarchy? If the government and the MQM had worked in harmony, both would have gained as both would have jointly prevented chaos. But, there has been disharmony, disagreement, death, and destruction ever since 1988. The consequences have been total chaos.

This state of anarchy was alleged by the MQM to have been created by its coalition partners, from 1988 to 1998. But, the MQM failed to explain what political gains would have accrued to the senior coalition partners by creating anarchy? They were dismissed, and they lost the very power they had gained from the coalition with the MQM. This was in addition to the immense loss of human lives, the vast majority of whom were pro-government or neutral people. To assess gains and losses in terms of human blood and misery is a cruel business. But, such being the yardstick of the political balance sheet in Karachi, one has to live with the inhuman outcome of the power games played on the soil of Sindh under the directives received from London.

The question is, could the outcome of chaos and anarchy not be foreseen? If so, could not the coalition partners work in harmony, and harvest the mutual benefits of the coalition agreements? The bitter truth is that they did foresee the consequences, and could have harvested the mutual benefit, but they had no intention of doing so. Each had its own agenda—

the senior partner to rule, and the junior partner to consolidate, regroup, and strike back to get closer to the final goal.

Who financed the expensive game of terrorism? It needed elaborate organization and planning, sophisticated communication network, acquisition of weapons and ammunition and its storage, training, treatment of the injured, public funerals, public relations, travelling, legal defence, buying of witnesses, looking after the widows and orphans, and other known and unknown items of expenditure. Many sources of financing remain secret. However, some sources have been directly and indirectly revealed. According to the press release of a law enforcing agency, the annual collection of *bhatta* by the MQM amounted to Rs 765 million. This was based on the monthly collection of Rs 100 from small shopkeepers, Rs 200-500 from big shops, Rs 10,000 from each big industry, Rs 5000 from each small industrial unit, Rs 100-200 from small and middle class homes, Rs 100 from each mini-bus, taxi, and rickshaw, and Rs 50 from each hawker. These details were revealed in a confessional statement of an MQM activist, Mubashir Ahmad alias Razo, a cousin of the MQM MNA Aminul Haq. He also confessed to having tortured a number of persons, for not giving *bhatta*, in the torture cell run by Suhail Akbar. He also confessed to having killed Syed Ali of Martin quarters under instructions from Suhail Akbar. Mubashir was as ASI in the Sindh Police, a job he had obtained on the recommendation of the MQM vice-chairman, Salim Shahzad.[30]

In 1992, there was a split in the party ranks of the MQM. The MQM blamed it on the army which had cracked down on the party to combat terrorism in Karachi. The substance of the allegation against the army, whether true or not, is not as important as the fact that there were serious differences among the top leadership of the MQM over certain basic policy matters, their formulation, and implementation. No outside agency, including the army, could penetrate into the secret circle of the MQM leadership, let alone plant any such discord within the party. Basically, the disagreements within the organization were home-grown, and once the differences became irreconcilable, they created an opening for certain outside agencies to play some part. But, to blame an outside agency for engineering the cracks within the MQM is tantamount to confessing the fragility of the structure and the inflexibility of the top leadership to accommodate dissent and diversity of opinions within the party, or even within the inner circle.

The dissidents, Afaq Ahmad Khan, Aamir Ahmad, Badar Iqbal, Kamran Rizvi, and others, sensing that their dissent would not be tolerated and their punishment would not be less than death,[31] had to leave the country to save their lives. They returned and formed the rival MQM eventually. This splinter faction of the MQM was named Haqiqi (true to the original mandate), and in keeping with the intent and significance of the chosen name, the party adopted a hard line, much harder and more extreme than that of the parent body. For example, on the issue of Jinnahpur, it abandoned the hide-and-seek and double-faced posture of the MQM (A), and declared openly, without mincing words, that its goal was to divide Sindh and create a separate homeland for the Muhajirs.[32] Its terrorism, however, is confined to targetting the Muhajirs of the opposing group. It tries to even out the score with the MQM (A), as both factions kill each other's activists. Since it has not yet been able to win any seat in an elected forum, it tries to make up the deficiency by seizing physical control of the area from which the MQM (A) candidates were last elected. Thus, in the period 1997-99, some elected members of the MQM (A) could not even enter their own constituencies.[34] In *bhatta* collection and kidnapping, it tried to beat the parent body. In this connection, the classic case of Karachi's prominent industrialist, Mukhtar Sumar, is worth noting.

Mukhtar Sumar, 46, owner of Farooq Textile Mills, Korangi, recounted a series of events due to which he had to remain in hiding for a fortnight. MQM (H) leaders began issuing threats when he resisted frequent demands for cash which were progressively becoming larger and more frequent. These threats would be conveyed by Afaq Ahmad Khan or his colleagues, Nazim, Raees, Abid, and Mahmood:

Three months back, we received a demand to donate 3000 metres of cloth for banners. We refused, but to defuse the matter we offered 1000 metres. The MQM (H) then threatened to buy the cloth from the market on our mill's account. At gunpoint, they robbed 1200 metres of cloth worth Rs 60,000. I contacted Senator Kamal Azfar to approach Chief Minister Abdullah Shah. I also met Minister Nisar Khuhro. In the same month, the chief of the MQM (H) demanded Rs 200,000 for distribution among the poor. I declined. On 4 February 1995, Deputy Manager Ahmad Ali was asked by the Haqiqis to meet Afaq Ahmad at the 'White House', the MQM (H) headquarters. There, he was threatened by Afaq Ahmad and Badar Iqbal. Ahmad Ali was terrified to see four bodies brought to the 'White House' for identification. Afaq identified three and said that the fourth was not the one he wanted killed, and that they should kill the 'real man'. Thereafter, we got threatenig phone calls from Haqiqi men, Mansoor, Feroze, and Shoaib. On 27 February 1995, five unidentified men fired at the mill gate and then we received a phone call to pay up or we would be taught a lesson.

Sumar contacted Senator Kamal Azfar who put him in touch with Qaim Ali Shah. No help came. Then he moved out of his house, and as a precaution dispersed his family. Sumar contacted the intelligence agencies, believing that the Haqiqi was the creation of the army, but he was surprised at their inaction. Sumar alleged that the Haqiqis had a hold in Landhi and Korangi, and were extorting money from the industries, including small businessmen and their employees. People were afraid to come out. 'I decided to risk my life and business as my faith and religion do not teach me to remain silent. The police were silent spectators... This is political terrorism, opposition terrorism, agency terrorism, and religious terrorism.' The MQM (H) instigated, planned, and executed a robbery since Sumar had not given in to their extortion. Sharafi police station accepted the robbery report, but refused to register the FIR against Afaq Ahmed Khan and his party. 'I had no other course of action left but to come out publicly and let the people know the facts—facts which prove that the local administration supports these criminals and is not willing to assist the people of this unfortunate city.'[34]

Sumar's frank, forthright, and fearless disclosure was a serious indictment against the MQM (H), the government, and the society as a whole which had been reduced to the level of a silent spectator. He approached the president and the prime minister, besides all the relevant authorities in Karachi. Since the authorities failed to come to the rescue of Mr. Sumar, and take the culprits to task, the inference that the MQM (H) could have been the creation of the agencies carries some weight.

Industrialist Mukhtar Sumar was not the only extortion victim. There were thousands, some equally rich, and equally fearless, some even more so. Why was he the only one to speak out? The industrialists were not the only target. There were bankers, traders, shopkeepers, pushcart owners, the salaried class, and the working class. Then there were politicians, and religious leaders, doctors, teachers, mullahs, young people, senior citizens, and many others in the sprawling city of Karachi.

How does one assess this phenomenon? Why do the people of Karachi act the way they do? Why do they revolt when they should sit back and think of a better alternative?[35] Why do they suffer in silence when they should be rising in revolt against MQM terrorism? Why was the voice of Mukhtar Sumar drowned in deafening silence? Had there been a thousand such protests, it would have driven the MQM out of existence. If urban Sindh can be kept in chains through terrorism, how does it differ from rural Sindh where the powerful feudals control the minds of the peasants? In the rest of Pakistan, urban centres provide leadership to the rural folks in the political, economic, and cultural fields. In Sindh, the biggest urban centre presents a picture of terror, disharmony, torture, turmoil, and anarchy. This is the city of Karachi, the capital of Sindh, yet trying to be alien to Sindh politically, economically, and culturally, the city held hostage by terrorism, the city in search of peace, and the city at war with itself.

Even if the situation changes for the better, future generations will always remember with dismay that the MQM had two faces:

the democratic face and the terrorist face, a visible face and an invisible face, a conciliatory face and a violent face. Neither Sindh, nor Pakistan, will be able to recover from the trauma of urban terror in Sindh for a very long time. Here was a party created on the soil of the sufis which terrorized the city and reduced the educated elites of that community to the level of helpless bystanders. The party had the courage to enter into a dialogue with its adversaries. Had it resorted to terrorism after the failure of the dialogue, it might have had some meaning, though it could not have been justified even then. To everyone's amazement, it resorted to violence immediately after celebrating the signing of the coalition agreements which enabled it to enter into a ruling partnership and occupy ministerial positions. This pattern of public behaviour was adopted not once, but repeatedly, as frequently as the coalition agreements were signed, between 1988 and 1998.

NOTES

1. *Herald*, October 1998, pp. 46-7, Interview of Gen. (retd.) Mirza Aslam Beg by Ihteshamul Haq.
2. The army had played a leading role in putting together the Islamic Jamhoori Ittehad (IJI) and its subsequent coalition with the MQM.
3. Azim Tariq surfaced later in 1992, and was murdered. Dr. Imran Farooq and Saleem Shahzad surfaced in London in 1999, and being hardliners, resumed the top leadership of the party in the party headquarters which is now located in London.
4. President Ghulam Ishaq Khan dismissed the government in 1992, but the Supreme Court set aside the dismissal and restored the government. However, the president and the prime minister could not pull on together, and through the intervention of the COAS, Gen. Abdul Waheed Kakar, both quit their positions, paving the way for new elections in 1993.
5. Columnist Ayaz Amir condemned MQM terrorism and paid compliments to General Babar in his column, 'Karachi: Has the tide turned?', *Dawn*, 26 February 1996.
6. *Herald*, Nov-Dec 1998, p. 44a.
7. Ibid., p. 44b.
8. Ibid.
9. *Dawn*, 30 October 1998.

10. Irfan Hussain, 'Back to the Barricades', *Dawn*, 7 November 1998.
11. Amina Jilani's column, Jay Walker, 'Luck vs. Loyalty', *Dawn*, 8 November 1998.
12. Eqbal Ahmad, 'The Governor's Challenge', *Dawn*, 10 November 1998.
13. M.H. Askari's column in *Dawn* of 18 November 1998.
14. Maj. Gen. (retd.) Moinuddin Haider, governor of Sindh's comment on the MQM.
15. *Herald* of Nov-Dec. 1998, p. 45, interview of the late ex-senator and former convenor of the MQM co-ordination committee by Idrees Bakhtiar.
16. Read revealing and sensitive disclosures about the MQM-PML (N)'s coalition's objectives, and bribes made by MNAs of the treasury benches, including Khwaja Asif (PML-N) and Ejaz Shafi (PML-N) in *Dawn*, 30 December 1998.
17. Maula Baksh Chandio, *Zikr Zindan Jo* in Sindhi (The Story of a Prison), Mehran Publications, pp. 12-13. The author was imprisoned for his participation in the MRD. The prison experience matured him into a political thinker and analyst of a fine calibre, as can be judged from his book (quoted extracts translated by me).
18. Sultan Ahmed, 'MQM and the Press', *Dawn*, 17 September 1992.
19. Zafar Iqbal, 'Provincialism and Muhajir Dilemma', *Dawn*, 26 September 1992.
20. Azim Tariq surfaced in 1992. He turned moderate, and was murdered.
21. *Dawn*, 6 August 1999.
22. *Dawn*, editorial extracts, 5 August 1999.
23. Tariq Niazi, 'History of Karachi Violence', *Dawn*, 28 November 1998.
24. News item, *Dawn*, 6 October 1998.
25. *Dawn*, 7 October 1998.
26. New item, *Dawn*, 8 October 1998.
27. *Dawn*, 11 November 1998.
28. *Herald*, October 1998.
29. *Herald*, October 1998.
30. Ibid.
31. *Dawn*, 22 October 1999. Such press releases by government agencies were invariably denied by the MQM. Although the MQM denied charges of terrorism and *bhatta* collection, both cases were proved against MQM activists in the court of law. The MQM's involvement in these activities is a matter of common knowledge. Even non-Muhajirs like the Memons, the Bohras, the Khojas, and non-MQM Muhajirs paid the *bhatta*, out of fear, and became unwilling partners in terrorism, murders, and other heinous crimes.
32. Dissident Azim Tariq, chairman of MQM (A), met with a similar fate. His murderer remains untraced.
33. Read MQM (H) leader Kamran Rizvi's declaration in Daily *Jang* of 8 November 1998.

34. The MQM (A) declared such areas (Malir, Landhi, and Korangi) as 'no-go' areas. They pressed Prime Minister Nawaz Sharif and Chief Minister Liaqat Jatoi to get these areas rescued from the MQM (H), and restore them to the MQM (A). But, both Sharif and Jatoi claimed that during their visits to the so-called 'no-go' areas, they found no trace of occupation by the MQM (H). Thus, on the political chess board, the 'no-go' areas were reduced to being pawns, to be played around by the contestants, the PML (N) and the MQM (A).
35. Extortion victim speaks out. Extracts, *Dawn*, 4 May 1995.
36. They revolted against Z. A. Bhutto's election rigging in 1977, and invited martial law and Zia's despotic rule of eleven years.

4

POLITICAL TERRORISM— JUDICIAL VERDICTS

The crime rate had escalated during the decade of the 1990s. To the usual crimes were added those which were politically and religiously motivated. Political crimes like kidnappings, murders, revenge killings, encounters with law-enforcing agencies, and battle-for-turf became a common phenomenon in Karachi, while sectarian killings started in the Punjab and spilled over into Karachi. By the year 1998, the situation had gone out of control. The politically motivated murder of Hakim Muhammad Said, and large scale sectarian killings in places of worship, shocked the people. To begin with, the government set up military courts to conduct speedy trials. Under a Supreme Court judgment, military courts were later disbanded and replaced by civilian Anti-Terrorist Courts (ATCs), presided over by Additional Session Judges, who were selected and appointed by the Chief Justices of the High Courts, on the basis of their merit, professional competence, and integrity. However, before disbandment, military courts had sentenced three men to be hanged as a result of summary trials, which shook the conscience of the civilized world. Irrespective of the merits of the cases that were tried by the military courts, the accused had the constitutional right to a fair trial which was denied to them.

The ATCs were subordinate to the High Court which supervised their work and heard appeals against their judgments. They were to function as single-judge courts, conduct the trials on a day-to-day basis, and complete each trial within seven working days. Both the defence and the prosecution had the right to challenge the verdict before the appellate bench, which comprised two High Court judges. The appellate bench was also required to decide the appeal within seven working days. A second challenge could be made in the Supreme Court which was expected to settle the final appeal as soon as possible. The right of appeal in the country's superior courts provided sufficient check against any possibilities of unfair practice or miscarriage of justice.

The establishment of the ATCs was welcomed by people of all the provinces terrorized by gangs of criminals of all varieties, including political, sectarian, or professional, the only exception being the MQM (A), which raised a hue and cry against them and branded them as 'kangaroo courts'. They accused them of conspiring to hang hundreds of MQM activists without a fair trial, as a part of the vendetta against the MQM. Had the courts been illegally established, or if the judges were not sufficiently qualified, or if they entertained any prejudice, the MQM was free to seek remedy from the superior courts.

Before the ATCs came into being, heinous crimes committed by terrorist gangs were tried under ordinary law in normal courts. As lamented by Jamil Yousuf, Chairman of the Citizen-Police-Liaison Committee, the rate of conviction was barely one per cent.[1] The creation of these speedy trial courts was greeted with relief by the people.[2]

Since the emergence of the MQM, politicians owing allegiance to it seldom volunteered to separate crime from politics. Murders, kidnappings, encounters, revenge killings, gun culture, *bhatta* collections, and rioting had become a way of life in Karachi. There had been repeated police/rangers/army crackdowns in 1989-90, 1992-93, 1995-96, and 1998-99. There were allegations of extra-judicial killings, attacks on police stations, human rights violations, etc. The fallout of this terrorism had destabilized successive governments in Karachi and Islamabad. Cases were pending in law courts for a decade or so due to pressure of work and an accumulated backlog.

Once the ATC verdicts began to be announced in the second quarter of 1999, convicting some accused, acquitting others, and after appeals were decided, either confirming or reducing the sentences or acquitting the accused, the fairness and transparency of the judicial system began to be recognized throughout the country with the exception of the MQM. Cases of terrorism were not confined to MQM activists or the Muhajirs. The Sindhis, the Punjabis, and the Pathans in Sindh and the Punjab were also tried in these courts for similar offences. However, while no protests and agitations were voiced by other communities, the MQM spared no effort in condemning the verdicts. Thus, there had been no miscarriage of justice as far as the non-MQM parties, groups, or individuals were concerned. As for the MQM, it did not accept the creation of the ATCs, it did not accept their verdicts, and it did not voice its appreciation even in cases of acquittals, or light sentences.

Criticism against these courts began to be voiced by human rights groups when deposed Prime Minister Nawaz Sharif was made to appear before one such court as an accused person in the plane hijacking case in late 1999 and early 2000. Ironically, ATCs were the creation of Nawaz Sharif himself. It was argued that in its present form, the anti-terrorist law infringed on civil liberties and due process of law.[3] However, the criticism was countered by Nawaz Sharif himself when he reposed full confidence in the ATC during his trial.

During one year of their functioning, from May 1999 to April 2000, the ATCs decided 265 cases of heinous crimes, including eighty murder cases, involving the killing of 126 persons. 105 cases were registered in Karachi East, fifty-seven in Karachi Central, forty-nine in Karachi South, thirty-two cases in Karachi West, and twelve cases in Malir. Out of these, forty accused in twenty-two cases in Karachi Central, sixteen accused in eleven cases in Karachi South, twenty-three accused in sixteen murder cases in Karachi West, and eleven accused in seven cases in Malir were awarded capital punishment. Other verdicts included thirty-seven cases of car and motorcycle lifting and thirteen cases of kidnapping. More than eighty cases of unlicensed arms and more than twelve rape cases were also decided.[4] There was a large number of acquittals at the trial or the appellate stage.

This data does not include cases pertaining to the rest of the country, including the Punjab.

The list placed in the appendix gives details of each case tried by various ATCs in Karachi, including the verdict of the appellate court given up to the time of compilation of the list.[5] It is up to the reader to judge whether these verdicts were given by the so-called kangaroo courts, as alleged by the MQM, or by highly qualified, professionally competent, and unbiased judges. That some of their verdicts were set aside by the High Court is a normal judicial process and was, in fact, reassuring to the accused persons, and to the people at large, that there had been no miscarriage of justice. The rejection of these verdicts by the MQM is politically motivated.

Political terrorism in Karachi had been the subject of controversy for a long time. Everyone knew that it was sponsored by the MQM, whose denials convinced no one. The normal judicial process could not cope with the magnitude of terrorism which was conducted in mafia style. Credible witnesses, evidence, and testimony were not forthcoming because of the terror spread by the mafia. The ATCs generated confidence, and helped in presentation of the cases in an environment free from fear. By giving fair verdicts, compatible with the magnitude of the crime, the judiciary scored a triumph, and restored the self-respect of the people. Judicial scrutiny has exposed the real face of the terrorist mafia which had reduced a civilized city to a collection of ten million dummies. A large number of judicial verdicts given by the ATCs pertain to politically motivated crimes in Karachi.

An analysis of these judicial verdicts is risky. The judgments may be questioned by jurists in forums like superior courts. Even in the cases of acquittals, any analysis would be unfair. Many cases were old, in fact as old as a decade. Some witnesses had disappeared from Karachi, and some had died. Some cases were poorly and half-heartedly prepared, as remarked by the judges. Some witnesses must have been fake since they fared badly under cross-examination. Genuine witnesses were reportedly tampered with. In a number of cases, the judges took the police to task for submitting incomplete cases. Yet, in other cases, the prosecution failed to produce incriminating evidence.

The poor performance of the police was due to many factors. Corruption played its part. The majority of policemen were non-locals who had superficial knowledge of local conditions. Their interest and loyalty to Karachi affairs were further diluted by their transfer back to their home provinces during the decade. Local police officials would have delivered better because of their commitment, but the issue of their appointment—normally a non-issue—had assumed a contentious political dimension, each party having it own agenda. Whatever the case, had the law enforcement agencies been staffed by the locals, it would have softened attitudes, reduced confrontation, improved the quality of investigation, opened the doors of conciliation, and obviated the need for creating ATCs. Basically, everything was linked to the denial of autonomy. Local issues were dealt with at the federal level. The ruling parties, the PPP as well as the PML (N), tried to tackle the Karachi situation from Islamabad, through interior ministers, who in turn relied upon agencies like the police, the rangers, and the army, whose personnel were predominantly non-locals. Some of these may have done a fine job, but they could not inspire confidence. Hence, there were frequent confrontations, leading to encounters, killings, prosecutions, and the need for speedy trials.

Appeals were invariably made against convictions, and the appellate court verdicts, reversing, reducing or upholding sentences, restored confidence. After the first year, most trials were conducted by the District Judges or Additional District and Sessions Judges. The large number of acquittals sent positive signals to the concerned parties, particularly the accused, who had suffered prolonged detentions as under-trial prisoners.

The MQM got the message that law courts, though slow and handicapped, provide a more soothing remedy than settling scores through unlawful means. Government agencies got the message that false cases, built on concocted evidence, invariably rebound, and that, without proper investigation, and complete documentation based on credible evidence, no case would stand in a court of law.

Were the ATCs really necessary? The MQM cried foul at the time of their creation. Nawaz Sharif justified their creation on the basis of the large number of pending cases pertaining to heinous crimes, which could not be disposed off in reasonable time due to a shortage of judges. But, with the benefit of hindsight now available, one can venture to make some observations.

To create extra positions of judges to clear the backlog of pending cases should have been a normal function of the government. But, the manner in which the decision was taken clearly demonstrated its political motivation, calculated to drop a political bombshell. This became obvious from the setting up of the military courts which were later disbanded by the Supreme Court. However, before being disbanded, they had already sentenced three young men to the gallows. Irrespective of the fact whether these men were innocent or guilty, they were entitled to a fair trial by a normal court.

Trial of cases by judges, whether in the ATCs or in the normal courts, helped to move at least one contentious issue from the political platform to the courts of law, which was a positive development. The ATCs were more inclined to convictions, but the High Court restored the balance. In the first year ending April 2000, the cases decided numbered 265. That much disposal could have been achieved by appointing extra judges without making so much capital out of it.

Subjecting MQM activists to fair trials could not be questioned. But, subjecting the MQM to a media trial after it quit the coalition with the PML (N) was a different issue. It was done in keeping with the pattern set in the country. Condemnation of opponents and incarceration of the dissidents had become a rule. The main parties, namely, the PPP, the PML (N) and the MQM excelled in this exercise, but the MQM, being either the junior partner or an opponent, was often at the receiving end.

In a democratic society, contentious issues are resolved within the framework of the constitution through established institutions, and an independent judiciary is one of these. Unfortunately, Pakistan has not had the good fortune of letting democracy strike roots and grow. The people, including the citizens of Karachi, must have patience and wait for better times.

That the MQM resorted to fascism is not in doubt. The cases and the judicial verdicts resulted from political confrontation. Could this confrontation have been kept within manageable limits? The answer is yes, through a political dialogue at the peoples' level. The dialogue did take place, but mostly for the sake of the short-term goal of power-sharing, with the PPP (1988) and the PML (N) (1997). Since these dialogues did not take place at the grass-roots level, they ended abruptly. All the concerned parties harvested bitterness and confrontation, followed by police and army crackdowns, arrests and prosecutions.

The missing link in the dialogue was ignored by all the three parties because it needed patience and willingness for a give-and-take approach. In a refreshing contrast, before the power game had begun in the mid-1980s, and after it was over in 1998, the MQM either responded to, or initiated a dialogue with its rural Sindhi counterparts, the Jiye-Sindh Movement. Both the MQM and the JSM were rooted in Sindh, but that is where the similarity ended. While the MQM represented Urdu-speaking urban Sindhis, spoke for Muhajir rights, and entertained the ambition to get into the power structure, the JSM spoke for the rights of entire Sindh and despite its Sindhi base, lacked electoral support. At one stage, Altaf Hussain almost walked into the arms of G.M. Syed and ethnic harmony became the hallmark of Syed-Altaf meetings. Once again, in 1998, having broken links with the PML (N), the MQM leaders re-established the dialogue with the JSM. As if to greet the second phase of the MQM-JSM dialogue, there has been relative calm in inter-ethnic relations.

The moral of these developments is that if the two Sindhi parties, one urban and the other rural, came closer without any motive of using each other as a stepping stone for capturing power, but with the common agenda for the restoration of the rights of Sindh as a whole, then that would help in cooling down tempers, end fascism, and make the ATCs redundant. Such a dialogue needs to be established on a permanent basis, and should not be broken by occasional irritants. In fact, irritants would indicate weaknesses in the dialogue and should, therefore, be removed.

NOTES

1. *Herald*, October 1998.
2. Ibid.
3. *Dawn*, 26 November 1999. New York based Human Rights Watch (Asia) urged Pakistan to amend the anti-terrorist law so that the trial of Nawaz Sharif could be conducted according to international fair trial standards.
4. *Dawn*, 15 May 2000, Report by Tahir Siddiqi.
5. Details collected from *Dawn* and *Jang* (Karachi), as and when the verdicts were announced.

5

CENSUS MERRY-GO-ROUND

The population of the world is growing at a varying pace. The growth of population has assumed importance in relation to the availability and the development of resources—food, water, energy, and goods. However, in the context of Sindh, the growth of population is seen more as a political tug-of-war than anything else. This is a unique situation which cannot be explained except in terms of the power game played by the people who migrated to Sindh after independence. This peculiar phenomenon has created a commotion not only in the socio-cultural and political life of Sindh, but its fallout has shaken the rest of Pakistan as well. Before independence, the ethnic composition of the population in Sindh was a non-issue. People from multiple ethnic backgrounds and different religions resided in the province. According to the Government of India Act of 1935, the ratio of Muslims and Hindus in Sindh was 75:25, but their representation in service and the provincial assembly was 60:40. This weightage was given to the non-Muslims in lieu of the weightage accorded to the Muslims in UP, etc.

Sindh was the first province in the subcontinent where a modern census was conducted in 1856. The census exercise had always been smooth before the creation of Pakistan. The trends are shown in the following table:

Year	Population	Growth Rate
1901	3,071,000	
1911	3,336,000	0.90
1921	3,034,000	− 0.90
1931	3,586,000	1.80
1941	4,804,000	2.91
1951	6,128,000	1.84
1961	8,367,000	3.15
1972	14,156,000	4.57
1981	19,029,000	3.56
1998	29,991,000	2.71

Source:
1. Statistics for the year 1901–1972 quoted from Mushtaqur Rehman, *Land and Life in Sindh,* Ferozesons (Pvt.) Ltd., Lahore, p. 90
2. Statistics for the years 1981 and 1998 are figures released by the government as published by *Dawn,* 9 July 1998.

Since 1972, there has been a tug-of-war over the issue of census in Sindh. The controversy has roots in the immigration to Sindh after the creation of Pakistan. Immigration is a global phenomenon, an on-going process, and is generally the result of wars, conquests, persecution, famines, economic compulsions, political upheavals, etc. Immigration into Sindh took place as a result of the partition of India in 1947. Up to a point, this influx was inevitable. Firstly, the exodus of the Hindus had created a vacuum which had to be filled. The central government employees who had opted for Pakistan came to the capital (then at Karachi) as a matter of right. Besides, the new country needed expertise in business, industry, and finance. That was followed by the influx of immigrants on account of the attraction created by new economic opportunities. Subsequently, the influx assumed the dimension of a flood with no end in sight. The people of Sindh, who had generously responded to the refugee problem as a national obligation, began to suspect the bona fides of the problem.[1] To all appearance, the problem had assumed the dimension of an 'occupation army'. Sindhis were thrown off balance, as noted by Altaf Gauhar:

When I next came to Karachi in 1956, as District Magistrate, it had already become a Muhajir city. Messrs Hashim Raza, who was the administrator of Karachi under Prime Minister Liaquat Ali Khan, and his brother Kazim Raza, the Inspector General of Police, had taken enormous pains to ensure rehabilitation of hundreds of thousands of refugees from the UP. These rehabilitation plans were followed even more vigorously by A.T. Naqvi when he became the Chief Commissioner of Karachi. All the municipal shops and even the pavements along Bunder Road were allotted to the refugees. Mr Liaquat Ali Khan who had no political base wanted to turn Karachi into his constituency. But an even more sinister plan was to give Sindh a more 'national' outlook by changing the composition of its population. I learnt about this plan from Chaudhry Muhammad Ali himself.[2] After the Round Table Conference called by Ayub Khan in March 1969, when I was talking to him about the unhappiness of the Sindhis about the 'outsiders' in their province, he asked me not to worry because 'his government in the 1950s had foreseen the problem and had planned the induction of Muhajirs into Karachi and Sindh to forestall Sindhi nationalism.'[3] By the time the allotment of evacuee properties was done the main towns of Sindh had come under the domination of the Muhajirs. But more was to follow. With the completion of G.M. Barrage, vast tracts of barren lands became cultivable. Instead of giving these lands to the landless Sindhis they were allotted to senior military and civil officers almost all of whom were non-Sindhis. The alienation of Sindh as Zahid Hussain had predicted, was now a bitter and unalterable fact of life.[4]

I remember a memorandum written by Mr Zahid Hussain in 1948, when he was acting as Finance Minister in the absence of Mr Ghulam Muhammad. The proposal of shifting the capital to Gadap, between Malir and Hyderabad, came up to him and he wrote that the take-over of Karachi by the central government had not only disrupted the provincial government of Sindh but had robbed the Sindhis of their only port town, their principal cultural centre. If Karachi was not restored to the Sindhis they would be deeply frustrated and their development would be retarded resulting in their alienation from the mainstream of national politics. Taking away Karachi from Sindh was like robbing the French of the city of Paris.[5]

The origin of the present state of political turmoil in Sindh, in all its manifestations, which include the emergence of ethnic and sectarian parties, political terrorism, economic collapse, strikes and wheel jams, flight of capital, closure of thousands of industrial units, lawlessness, and the storm raised over the question of census can directly be attributed to the pioneers of Pakistan, who descended upon Sindh, duly inspired by an ideology, and determined to use Islamic rhetoric to dominate Sindh. The emergence of the Muhajir Qaumi Movement (MQM) is the culmination of the movement which started in 1947 to subdue Sindh and counter any uprising of the local population:

> Today the province of Sindh stands culturally and economically divided. The urban areas are dominated by the Muhajirs, the rural areas are populated by the Sindhis. The discriminatory economic and political policies followed by successive federal governments, with the assistance and support of *wadera* politicians, have caused deep political fissures which will not be easily healed. The Muhajirs, now organized into a major political force under the Muhajir Qaumi Movement (MQM), won't give up Karachi and without Karachi the province of Sindh will remain bottled up. The 'pundits' say that one day the Sindhis and the Muhajirs will learn to live together. But between now and the promised day they are more likely to obliterate one another. The Muhajirs must recognize the fact that Sindh belongs to the Sindhis and reconcile themselves to their position as settlers which gives them all the rights of a citizen but not the right to dominate... The Muhajir plans to carve an 'Urdu Desh' out of Sindh will only deepen the present divide and could become a threat to the security of the country.[6]

Viewed in this perspective, the furore over the census can be easily understood. Democracy being a game of numbers, the larger the number, the bigger the share in the cake. That explains the repeated claims made by the MQM that the Muhajirs form the majority in Sindh (and, therefore, should rule Sindh). Such claims were based on the estimates of the immigration which continued with increased tempo even after the Liaquat-Nehru Pact.[7] But, pact or no pact, the immigration was to continue, as planned, to beat back the threatened 'Sindhi nationalism and enlarge and expand the Muhajir constituency', by offering all kinds of incentives, including the allotment of evacuee properties.[8]

The first major quarrel over the census surfaced in 1972 when Karachi's population was disputed. Official figures showed Karachi's population to be 3.5 million. It was alleged that this figure was 12.5 per cent less than the actual population, and that Z.A. Bhutto's government (1972-77) had ordered rural Sindh's population to be increased by 12.5 per cent. In protest, a Karachi leader, Mirza Jawad Beg, challenged the census figures, but he was sent to jail on 16 May 1973, allegedly to silence him.[9] It was also alleged that the census of 1972 was inflated in favour of rural Sindh (Sukkur Division 509,000, Hyderabad Division 5,454,000, Karachi Division 3,515,000). Besides, the increases over the 1961 figures were allegedly unconvincing: (Badin 364 per cent, Kandhkot 155 per cent, Mehar 209 per cent, Sakrand 200 per cent, Sujawal 200 per cent, Ghotki 117 per cent, Dadu 148 per cent, Jati 107 per cent, Hala 99 per cent, Tando Muhammad Khan 72 per cent).[10] The protesters disregarded the vagaries of census in a rural area where accessibility was difficult and the people were not previously census-conscious. Besides, floods and population mobility disrupted the census exercise. Finally, there was a gross absence of a sense of commitment on the part of the enumerators. But, these facts assume a different meaning when there is an unhealthy competition between two desperately divided communities, among whom the seed of division and separation was planted soon after the creation of Pakistan.

The 1981 census kept up the same trends as were visible in 1972, for the same reason, each of the two contending parties sticking to its own position. But, the dust raised was uncalled for because the rural population was shown as 56.7 per cent and the urban population as 43.3 per cent, which was both reasonable and convincing. Nevertheless, the controversy raised over the 1981 census involved alleged doctoring of the census of Sindh at the highest level. Ansar Hasan Burney stated in his article, 'Sindh demands an early census', published in *Dawn* of 4 February 1995, that Dr Mahboobul Haq, finance and planning minister in the Ziaul Haq regime, revealed the tampering of the 1981 census, which was done in consultation with General Fazle Haq (NWFP) and General Jilani (Punjab), to the detriment of the Sindh province. Protests were reportedly made by the Sindh government and the mayor of Karachi, Abdul Sattar Afghani. Afghani claimed that Karachi's population in 1972 was 5.7 million, and at 6 per cent growth, it should have been 6.7 million in 1981 instead of stagnating at 5.6 million.[11] General Abbasi (the then Sindh governor) did not protest as he did not feel so strongly about it. Columnist M. Ziauddin called it an immoral act on the part of Pakistan's ruling generals against the province of Sindh, whose share in the national resources stood curtailed to the detriment of its population.[12] However, these objections and protests were overruled by Syed Munir Hussain, the former federal secretary for information and broadcasting, in his letter dated 13 February 1995 addressed to *Dawn*. He claimed that he had supervised the census himself in his capacity as the then federal secretary, statistics division, that the census was fair and transparent, and that the revelation attributed to Dr Mahboobul Haq had no basis. Whatever the truth, the fact remains that the census of Sindh created ripples not only in rural and urban Sindh, but its effect were also felt in the Punjab, the NWFP, and at the federal level. This should have induced a measure of realization among the people of rural and urban Sindh, who should have reached an understanding on this sensitive issue in the interest of Sindh as a whole. But, such hopes did not materialize and the rural-urban confrontation further escalated, as will be seen later.

The next census was due in 1991. This was when the MQM held complete sway over Sindh's urban population, and was in a position to paralyse the administration, which it actually did, thereby compelling the army to crack down and bring order out of chaos in Karachi in the following year. The government was able to start the 1991 census on schedule, but could hardly complete the first stage, namely, the house census, when it was compelled to discontinue by the volatile situation in urban Sindh. The house census indicated the number of inmates in each household; the results for rural Sindh, which were dubbed as inflated, showed an increase over the previous census as follows: Nawshahro Feroze by 711 per cent, Larkana 397 per cent, Jacobabad 288 per cent, Sukkur 265 per cent, Shikarpur 272 per cent, Dadu 257 per cent, Sanghar 315 per cent, Thatta 199 per cent, Tharparkar 196 per cent, and Hyderabad 135 per cent.[13] These alleged inflations needed to be verified, and corrected if necessary, but the government of the IJI, headed by Nawaz Sharif at the centre and Jam Sadiq Ali in the province of Sindh, was entirely at the mercy of its coalition partner, the MQM, under whose pressure the entire census exercise was called off and could not be held for the next seven years. It became apparent that census had become a life-and-death struggle for the MQM, and in consequence, for Sindh as also for the Punjab because ultimately, the census quarrel in Sindh hurts the Punjab whose share in the pool gets diminished.

In 1998, the government of the PML (N) mustered enough courage once again and finally held the overdue census according to which the population of Sindh was shown as 29.991 million, out of which 51.1 per cent was rural, 48.9 per cent urban, the increase over the 1981 census was 10.962 million, and the annual growth rate was 2.71 per cent, as opposed to the previous growth rate of 3.56 per cent. Karachi's population stood at 9.256 million. The census did not indicate the number of Sindhis and Muhajirs separately—an issue which had been a source of much bitterness in the past. But, the two communities must have estimated their numerical strength out of the data released already. For example, if the total population of Sindh is about 30 million, the rural-urban ratio stands at 50:50. The rural component is entirely Sindhi. In urban Sindh, including Karachi, Hyderabad, Sukkur, Larkana, Nawabshah, and all the district and *taluka* towns, in which, out of 15 million, the Muhjair component could not be more than 50 per cent, i.e. about 7.5 million. This also stands to reason, because, out of Karachi's 9.256 million, 54.3 per cent is Urdu speaking,

13.6 per cent Punjabi speaking, 8.7 per cent Pushto speaking, and 6.3 per cent Sindhi speaking, according to the 1981 census. This proportion could not have changed to make any significant difference.[14] In cities other than Karachi, the proportion of Muhajirs may be less. Hence, it would be safe to estimate that the size of the Muhajir population was 7.5 million, or 25 per cent of Sindh's population. Subsequently, authentic data has been released by the statistical division of the government of Pakistan, as published in the *Daily Jang*, Karachi of 28 July 2000, according to which the latest population composition of Sindh is as follows:

Total Population	30.4 million
Rural	15.6 million
Urban	15.8 million
Sindhi speaking	59.75 per cent or 18.164 million
Urdu speaking	21.05 per cent or 6.39 million
Punjabi speaking	7.00 per cent or 2.12 million
Pustho speaking	4.90 per cent or 1.48 million
Balochi speaking	2.11 per cent or 0.64 million
Seraiki speaking	1.00 per cent or 0.30 million

When Altaf Hussain declares that the Muhajir population is over twenty million, he poses a standing challenge to the official statistics. To his followers, his word is gospel truth. Consequently, they get frustrated when their inflated expections remain unfulfilled. Such frustration is manifested in political terrorism, failure of Sindhi-Muhajir dialogue, confrontation, and animosity.

The 1998 census was rejected by the PPP, the PPP (SB), the Awami Tehrik, the STPP, the Sindh Sagar Party, the JSQM, and the JUI, besides the Sindhi press. Sindhis complain that they have been undercounted by ten million.[15] The MQM was quoted as claiming the Muhajirs to be twenty million,[16] Wali Khan claiming the Pathans to be six million, the Punjabis claim to be three and a half million, and the Balochis claiming to be two million.[17] On that basis, the non-Sindhis add up to a figure of 31.5 million, which exceeds the total population of Sindh (29.9 million according to 1998 census). These claims, whether genuine or inflated, wipe out the entire population of Sindhis from Sindh. On their part, Sindhis claim to be forty million.[18] They protested against illegal immigrants, numbering two and a half million, who, in addition to the immigrants from other provinces, were an unbearable burden on the resources of Sindh.[19]

The racket of the Karachi population explosion has been exposed repeatedly by the newspapers. In 1992, one M. Naim was arrested in Karachi for issuing thousands of Pakistani ID cards to Indian nationals at Rs 2000 per card. Under this racket, millions of Indians became Pakistanis, enlarging the MQM vote bank. The opposition party (PPP) moved an adjournment motion on this issue but was voted out amid shouts by the MQM members, who encouraged the racket to go on.[20] The racket of illegal immigration continued underground. In 1999, it was once again exposed in the press. Thousands of passports were issued to illegal immigrants from India and elsewhere.[21] Thus, when Altaf claimed his followers to number twenty million, he relied upon guess-estimates based on these rackets. The census of Sindh has been reduced to a rat race.

The census dilemma in Sindh has had an inevitable political fallout. By inflating their numbers, the Muhajirs are sending dangerous signals to the Punjab, which might like to see the population of Sindh restricted to a reasonable limit so that it does not threaten their majority. If this be the case, then the unhealthy competition between the Sindhis and the Muhajirs has done permanent damage to both. This trend, showing Sindh catching up with the Punjab, is already visible from the census figures of 1998. In 1951, while the Punjab had 60.8 per cent of Pakistan's population, Sindh had 17.9 per cent. The figures have changed in 1998; while the Punjab has gone down to 55.6 per cent, Sindh has gone up to 23 per cent.[22] If this trend continues, Sindh may catch up with the Punjab by the middle of the twenty-first century. Who will benefit from this population bonanza? The Sindhis, whose claim is 5000 years old? The Muhajirs, who gave their blood and tears for the creation of Pakistan, and who used all methods, fair and foul, to catch up in the rat race? Or someone else who may be waiting in the wings to reap the harvest?

Prior to the 1998 census, the Sindhis and the Muhajirs traded charges and counter-charges for inflating their respective populations. If there was any truth in such allegations, the blame must be laid squarely at the doorsteps of the authors of the ethnic divide, who have been active since 1947 to prevent the assimilation of the Muhajirs with the Sindhis.

Be that as it may, it is fair to say that while the Punjab settled down to business soon after going through the trauma of partition, Sindh continues to groan under the mounting pressure of immigrants, which is growing in magnitude and complexity even half a century since the British quit India. As Muhajir ethnicity grows and multiplies, it sets into motion a chain reaction of inter-ethnic hatred in urban Sindh. Born under the Zia regime, and nourished under illusions of ruling Sindh, either wholly or in part, the ethnic worm has grown into a monster. The monster, once let loose, could not be tamed even by the democratic elections of 1988, 1990, 1993, and 1997. But, the census of 1998 made a dent in the MQM's calculations, at least on the surface, and prompted them to re-think their strategy, change their tune, and re-establish dialogue with the Jiye-Sindh, which had been initiated by G.M. Syed a decade earlier, but scrapped unceremoniously soon thereafter. Thanks to the 1998 census, the spirit of G.M. Syed has been revived. MQM leadership began to talk in terms of mother Sindh, Sindhi rights, Sindh's autonomy, and Sindh being ruled as a colony of the Punjab. Whether this marks a permanent change of attitude, or is merely a temporary change of tactic, only time will tell. So far, no concrete steps have been taken to signify any change in the policy.

NOTES

1. The matter has been dealt with in detail in M.S. Korejo's book, *G.M. Syed—An Analysis of his Political Perspectives*, Oxford University Press, Karachi, 1999.

2. Chaudhry Muhammad Ali was the secretary-general of Pakistan and a close confidant of Liaquat Ali Khan. Later, he became prime minister, in which capacity he knew all the intricate details of the plans and designs in respect of Sindh.

3. Altaf Gauhar, *Ayub Khan, Pakistan's First Military Ruler*, Sang-e-Meel Publications, Lahore, 1993, p. 467.

4. Altaf Gauhar, 'Thoughts and After Thoughts, Karachi—a City in Turmoil', *The Nation*, Lahore and Islamabad, 8 April 1994.

5. Ibid.

6. Ibid.

7. The pact was signed on 8 April 1950 in Delhi to ensure full protection to minorities by both countries so that further migration should stop. See Choudry Muhammad Ali, *The Emergence of Pakistan*, Research Society of Pakistan, Lahore, 1973, p. 274.

8. Mushtaq-ur-Rahman, *Land and Life in Sindh*, Ferozesons Lahore, p. 90.

9. Ibid., p. 90.

10. Ibid., p. 90.

11. Ansarul Hasan Burney 'Sindh Demands an Early Census', *Dawn*, 4 February 1995.

12. Read M. Ziauddin's article, 'Distortion of Demographic Picture and Price Inflation', in *Dawn*, 4 February 1995.

13. Mushtaqur Rahman, *Land and Life in Sindh*, Ferozesons, Lahore, p. 90.

14. Ibid., p. 71.

15. Sindhi Daily, *Kavish*, 10 July 1998.

16. *Dawn*, in its issue of 30 December 1994, quoted Altaf Hussain as having claimed in the human rights constitutional petition submitted to the Supreme Court, that the population of the Muhajirs was twenty million.

17. Sindhi Daily, *Jago* of 10 July 1998.

18. Ibid.

19. Sindhi Daily, *Awami Awaz* of 10 July 1998.

20. *The News*, Karachi, 28 October 1992, *Nation*, Islamabad, 28 October 1992.

21. *Jang*, Karachi, 25 June 1999.

22. *Dawn, Economic and Business Review*, 23 November 1998, article 'Census '98 Figures about Sindh under reported', by S.H. Zaidi.

6

QUOTA SYSTEM

The quota system is a hot topic. Almost every day there is an opinion expressed in the newspapers for or against the system. Most of the opinions are based on personal observations and half-baked data, and do not take into account the history of the quota system and the rationale for its present status. Many of the views are influenced by the genuine frustrations of persons adversely affected by the system. Others are based on principle, that merit should be the criterion for all selections to curb the evil of nepotism, favouritism, and inefficiency. It is often forgotten that the creation of Pakistan itself was the product of the quota system. Indian Muslims wanted a share in the political power in proportion to their numbers which was granted to them in the shape of separate electorates.[1] After the creation of Pakistan, this system was considered indispensable for the survival of the ideology. In spite of being aware that the quota system was un-Islamic, it was favoured even by an orthodox Muslim ruler like General Ziaul Haq. The territory of Pakistan was carved out on the principle of Muslim majority area (quota) from the Hindu majority area. Before independence, the Muslims of minority provinces of UP received an enhanced quota (weightage) in representation, and the price was paid by Sindh, which had to surrender its Muslim quota from 75 per cent, based on the population ratio, to 60 per cent.

The allotment of farmland to the refugees from UP under the refugee rehabilitation scheme also followed the quota system. Each claimant filed his claim on the basis of his holding in India. Since the quota claim filed exceeded the land available, the foreign office requested High Commissioner A.K. Brohi to have the claims verified by using his personal rapport with Prime Minister Jawahar Lal Nehru. On receipt of the verification, President Ayub Khan fixed a ceiling (quota) of 300 acres per claimant. This was resented by the refugee lobby, and a delegation of their leaders and lawyers called on Foreign Minister Manzur Qadir to seek an explanation. Qadir informed the delegates, one of whom was Manzar-e-Alam, that according to the verification carried out under Nehru's orders,[2] all claims were found to be inflated, except one, namely, that of Raja Sahib of Mahmoodabad, and that the minimum inflation was three times the actual holding, while the maximum was limitless. As a compromise, General Ayub Khan fixed a ceiling (quota) of 300 acres per claim, which he considered fair and equitable.[3]

Despite separate electorates and efforts to uplift the Muslims and bring them at par with the Hindus, the Muslims were way behind and did not feel confident enough to compete with the Hindus in the economic, administrative, and political fields. The disparity had its origins in the Muslims rejecting the British system of education, whereas the Hindus grabbed all the opportunities presented by the British rule. Aggravated by communal intolerance, the gap could not be narrowed because the British were in a hurry to leave India at the end of the Second World War.

Similarly, the disparity between urban and rural Sindh was deep-rooted due to the feudal character of the rural society and neglect of rural uplift by the British rulers. After independence, this gap had to be narrowed by maintaining a balance in the development strategy for the rural and urban areas. This did not happen. On the contrary, rural agriculture financed urban industry resulting in the net transfer of resources from rural to urban areas. Consequently, Karachi developed faster in infrastructure, quality of education, trade, industry, and economic opportunities. The rural-urban gap remains as it was in 1947, hence the quota system continues.

Since the quota system had become the guiding principle, the refugee influx into Sindh was also expected to follow the same principle. Consequently, if the non-Muslim exodus from Sindh was to the tune of 1.3 million, the refugee influx was to be limited to this figure (quota) to avoid socio-economic disharmony and ethnic upheavals. When this figure was exceeded, the obvious inference was that it was designed to increase the numbers and expand the Muhajir constituency to boost up the share (quota) of Muhajir representation in the economic, administrative, and political structure of Sindh.

On the basis of the above mentioned strategy, a dominant Muhajir constituency emerged in urban Sindh in the form of the MQM in 1984. Preparatory to the 1988 elections, all the party leaders were given an opportunity to present their party manifesto on television. The main thrust of Altaf Hussain's presentation was that the Muhajirs were denied their legitimate share (quota) in the services, economic opportunities, and political representation. He was well armed with facts and figures to substantiate his claims.

In 1994, the MQM issued a memorandum of demands asking for the Muhajir share (quota) in jobs, political appointments, educational opportunities, etc. on the basis of its population, claimed by it to be 50 per cent of the total population of Sindh.[4] To make up the shortages, it was demanded that the following actions be taken:

1. Special recruitment of Muhajirs on an emergency basis to make up for the deficiency (in quota) in all services, including police.
2. Positions of the governor and the chief minister be rotated between the Sindhis and the Muhajirs (50:50 quota).
3. Urban Sindh to receive funds in proportion (quota) to its population.
4. Immediate repatriation of stranded Pakistanis (to increase the Muhajir quota).
5. Representation in the National Assembly, the Senate, and the Provincial Assembly to be on the basis of quota.
6. Admissions in colleges on the basis of quota.
7. A census be carried out by an impartial body[5] (to increase Muhajir quota), because the census figures of 1961, 1972, and 1981 were doctored to reduce the Muhajir population by half.

The memorandum gave a comprehensive list of jobs in which the Muhajirs had either nil representation or below quota representation, as of March 1994. These covered the entire range of political, administrative, and military appointments, from the high position of the president of the country down to the level of a police constable. These demands were based on two fallacies: firstly, the Muhajirs did not constitute 50 per cent, but 25 per cent of the population of Sindh. Secondly, they assumed that the urban quota was entirely the Muhajir quota, which was not correct. Urban Sindh includes all the cities and towns, where Muhajirs will number roughly 50 per cent. Even in the territory of 'Jinnahpur', which the Muhajir's want to create by dividing Sindh, they may manage to have a 'razor thin' majority, as estimated by Feroz Ahmad.

According to Major-General (retd.) Nasserullah Khan Babar, 'Muhajirs received many favours and were appointed to attractive positions in the civil service. In 1989-90 (the PPP regime), there were 600 Urdu-speaking people at the grade 22 (highest grade) level. They dominated the Karachi Port Trust, Port Qasim, and nationalized banks, and held 100 per cent of the jobs in these organizations. Under these circumstances, they should not have had any grievances. They had no reason to feel hurt.'[6]

Prior to independence, the quota tug-of-war in Sindh took place between the Muslims and the Hindus. Since the Muslims could not fill their quota with Sindhi-Muslims, they opened the jobs to Muslims from elsewhere in India. Most of the non-Sindhi Muslims who filled the Sindhi-Muslim quota were from the UP and the Punjab. Thus, a fraternity of Sindhi and non-Sindhi Muslims developed in almost every department. There was no rivalry, no language controversy,[7] no cultural domination, and no pretensions to superiority. After independence, the spirit of fellowship and fraternity lasted for as long as the Muhajir influx was manageable. When immigration assumed the magnitude of a flood, it spread panic, a feeling of insecurity, and a sense of political, economic, and cultural domination. Thus, a post-independence quota was imposed as a safeguard of a Muslim of one kind against a Muslim of another kind. The tug-of-war had started, and its victory depended on numbers, which explains the Muhajir preoccupation with increasing its population and concentrating it in Sindh, ever since the creation of Pakistan.

As a matter of principle, open competition should have been enforced from 1947, but the objective conditions of Sindh, with a glaring disparity between the urban and rural Sindh, made it impracticable to adopt the merit system. To uplift the rural regions and bring them at par with urban Sindh, a massive development programme was to be initiated by diverting resources from the urban to rural Sindh. Rather than doing that, the resources moved in the reverse direction—the industry of Karachi was financed from the foreign exchange earned by rurally produced cotton and other commodities. Thus, there was a net transfer of resources from the rural to urban areas, and this distortion still persists.

The quota system has been open to objection on many grounds. In 1992, the Federal Shariat Court declared it un-Islamic. In 1997, the Supreme Court held it to be unconstitutional. But, ignoring the court verdicts, the parliament passed the sixteenth amendment in 1999, extending the quota system for another twenty years (from 1993 to 2013). Earlier, the quota system had been sanctioned in 1973 for ten years, and further extended for another ten years. In 1993, the then PPP government introduced a bill for further extension, but it could not be adopted for lack of the two-third majority needed for passing the bill. Since then, the issue had been dormant. The fact that the sixteenth amendment was passed in 1999, despite the contrary position taken by the judiciary, with the support of the ruling party (PML-N), the opposition (PPP), and all other groups and independents, except the MQM, gave an indication of the true state of disparity between provinces, and between the rural and urban centres, a situation which could not be gauged by judicial forums which go by the letter of the law. MQM Senator Aftab Shaikh opposed the amendment as a matter of principle.[8] So did MQM Senator Jamiluddin Aali. But, while Aftab Shaikh was the odd man out by taking an untenable position against the ground realities of Pakistan as represented by the mainstream parties, Aali, mindful of the poor educational standards in rural areas, proposed that centres of excellence be set up in backward areas to at least ensure that those who compete for the services from those areas have the right qualifications to join the country's highest administrative service.[9] PPP Senator Raza Rabbani supported the amendment in keeping with the national consensus. The passage of the amendment brought into sharp focus the rural-urban divide prevailing in the country, and the negative attitude of the MQM towards the backward and deprived sections of the Sindhi society.

It has been argued on behalf of the MQM that the rural quota did not benefit the poor sections of population, since the opportunities offered by the rural quota were grabbed by the scions of landlords and other influentials to obtain lucrative positions for themselves. Thus, they acquired a vested interest in the quota system, and sought its perpetuation at all costs. Assuming that this assertion is correct, how has this situation been created? Landlords and influentials are products of the system, which they themselves did not create. If they have a vested interest, so does every other group, within its own sphere of influence. But, the rural influentials do educate their boys in centres of good education in the cities. Since the system has failed to provide good quality education and centres of excellence in the rural areas, students of poor sections remain backward and, therefore, have little chance to utilize the rural quota. The solution lies in improving the quality of education, creation of centres of excellence, and making them accessible to the poorer sections of the rural population, rather than abolition of the quota system. If the system has remained stagnant, and the cities have gone far ahead, leaving the rural areas in a state of decay, the fault lies with the rulers who, with a few exceptions, have been either city-based, or in an army uniform.

Within Sindh, the urban population consists of the Muhajirs, and many other ethnic and religious communities. Together, they rule Sindh in all fields of trade, commerce, and industry,

94 A TESTAMENT OF SINDH

on the basis of their superior education and leadership qualities. They are the cream of intellectual elites. They occupy almost the entire urban job market in the private, semi-public, and public sectors.

In comparison, this urban job market is many times bigger than the size of the government services. Besides, there is a relationship of mutual enrichment among the urban Sindh elites, and this vast potential is used to create urban elitism, urban wealth, higher institutions of learning, and an intellectual ambience. Rural Sindh, still at the primitive stage, looks at this contrast with bewilderment and envy.

Rural Sindhi youth pleaded with the PPP for government jobs during its rule in 1972-77, 1988-90, and 1993-96, for want of a better alternative.

Moved by their concern for human rights, the MQM leadership wholeheartedly participated in the cyclone relief work in the rural areas of Thatta and Badin districts, following the devastation caused in May 1999. This was probably the first time that the MQM saw the pitiable conditions of rural Sindh, the suffering of the affected people, the devastation caused by the calamity, and the magnitude of loss of life and property. They found that the government had failed to warn the people in advance and the relief work was inadequate. They complained that the flood affectees in the affluent Punjab were better compensated than the devastated rural Sindhis. They also found that the areas affected were backward and primitive, with no infrastructure, no escape routes, and nothing to fall back upon.

Within Sindh, all non-Sindhi communities have built-in socio-economic and political leverages. The MQM looks after the Muhajir interests, fights for their cause, and can paralyse Karachi to press for its demands. Its propaganda machinery within and outside Pakistan is unbeatable, and its financial resources are vast. The Punjabi settlers control the economy—they own industry, trade, commerce, export, import, finance, etc. They have a powerful political home base in the Punjab. Pathans monopolize the transport business and construction activity. Their politics in urban Sindh are an extension of ANP politics in the Frontier province, from where they receive inspiration. For the Sindhis, the quota system is the last refuge, which they believe is the only source left for them to fall back upon, when all other resources are controlled by non-Sindhis, and when successive governments have failed to bring them at par with other communities for the last half a century.

The quota system is divisive and un-Islamic. This is true. Anything that divides one section of population from another is un-Islamic. Ethnic separation is un-Islamic too, but it has been forced upon Sindh. Cultural and language-based superiority is un-Islamic too. Extortion of *bhatta*, political terrorism, denial of basic facilities of health care, education, infrastructure, etc. are also un-Islamic. Why single out the quota system for being un-Islamic, when it has at least some positive attribute, that of providing opportunities to the deprived people?

It has been argued that since 1973, rural Sindh has been provided an infrastructure, and, therefore, the quota system is no longer justified.[10] Those who make this assertion have probably never visited rural Sindh. They should consult great Muhajir minds like (Late) Hakim Said, Abdul Sattar Edhi, Javed Jabbar, and others, who know the reality of rural Sindh and the primitive conditions existing there.

It is true that rural Sindhis have started to become visible in a few places in the socio-economic spheres. But, they are far behind their urban counterparts, who have gone ahead much faster due to better opportunities available to them. Rural Sindhis are more visible in politics, but judging from the results, their impact has been minimal. The country has been run by the generals and the bureaucrats for most of the time. Then, it has been run by the urban elites, industrialists, and businessmen, whose priorities include motorways, airports, urban housing, urban ring-roads, and expressways, at the cost of rural uplift. To enrich themselves, they earned billions of rupees out of state subsidies on exports. They tailored import-export policies to enrich the industrialist lobby, irrespective of the damage done to the rural economy. For example, in 1999, the PML (N) government imported two million bales of cotton, which caused the prices of local cotton to crash by 50 per cent. In the last half a century, there have been three elected rural-based prime ministers, all from Sindh, and ironically, all of them were dismissed and disgraced by the generals, fundamentalists, and their fellow travellers.[11] The rural-based elected prime ministers favoured balanced development, for urban and rural areas, unlike their urban counterparts.

The quota system is neither an ideal nor a permanent solution, but it is a necessary evil which must be endured. If rural Sindh has suffered for half a century, let urban Sindh share some of the suffering as a part of its debt obligation to Sindh. The storm raised on the quota system by a section of urban Sindhis is grossly exaggerated and disproportionate to the adverse consequences of the system, and the fact that such an attitude hurts the vital interests of the rural counterparts has been a negative input to national integration. Conversely, had integration taken place, or at least initiated during the last half a century, the quota system would have gradually been phased out. There is no doubt that the system is a curse and an insult to a civilized society. But, no one will call this society civilized when the disparity between the urban and rural population is much wider today than it was in 1947.

NOTES

1. Demand for separate electorates was made before the Viceroy, Lord Minto, by a Muslim leaders' deputation led by Agha Khan III, in 1906. In Jinnnah's 14 points, Muslims demanded one-third quota representation in the Central Legislature, even though Muslims were one-fourth in population. The resiling of this demand led to the demand for partition.
2. Verification was not total but limited to 33 per cent, which was a substantial sample.
3. The source of this information is Mr Azizullah Sheikh, Bar-at-Law, of the Sindh High Court, who was a member of the delegation which called on Manzur Qadir. He related this to the author on 1 December 1999.
4. A memorandum demanding 50 per cent quota on the basis of 50 per cent share in the population of Sindh was published on behalf of the MQM in the *News International*, Karachi on 5 June 1994.

5. Census due in 1991 was abandoned half way due to allegations of rigging. Finally, it was carried out by the army in 1998, and the results showed that the MQM claim of 50 per cent Muhajir population of Sindh was grossly exaggerated.
6. *The Herald*, November-December 1998, p. 446.
7. Non-Sindhi Muslims learnt to speak fluent Sindhi as a part of their service requirement. There were hundreds of non-Sindhi Muslims in Sindh services and along with their families they constituted an influential section of the population. They did not call themselves Muhajirs and were fully assimilated as Sindhis.
8. By opposing the quota system, the MQM ignored the realities of rural Sindh, refused to participate in rural uplift, and confined its focus to the Urdu-speaking people, who were already far ahead educationally and economically.
9. 'The Day of Harmony', *Dawn*, 4 June 1999, by Ziauddin.
10. Read Dr Mehdi Masood's letter in *Dawn*, 3 May 1999.
11. Z.A. Bhutto was overthrown by General Ziaul Haq in 1977, who was supported by the religious lobby. Muhammad Khan Junejo was dismissed by General Ziaul Haq in 1988. Benazir Bhutto was dismissed by President Ghulam Ishaq Khan in 1990 and Farooq Leghari in 1996.

7

'STRANDED PAKISTANIS'

The term 'stranded Pakistanis' has been coined as a consequence of the unfortunate separation of East Pakistan and the creation of Bangladesh in 1971. It is applied to the group of people who migrated from the Indian state of Bihar to the former East Pakistan, and were stranded there following the creation of Bangladesh. The term itself has become controversial. The Muhajirs of Sindh insist on calling this group of people 'stranded Pakistanis'. On the other hand, Sindhis, whatever their political affiliation, insist on calling them Biharis. These two views, mutually antagonistic as they are, continue to be in vogue. Which view will ultimately prevail, is left to be determined by future events. The term used by the people of the Punjab, Frontier, or Balochistan is irrelevant, because, irrespective of where (in Pakistan) these people are initially repatriated, Sindhis know that their ultimate destination is going to be Sindh.[1]

Before arriving at the correct nomenclature, free of rancour or emotion, but based on factual history, one has to examine various dimensions of the problem. There is a political, legal, ideological, religious, humanitarian, and an ethnic dimension to the whole issue.

To place events in their correct historical perspective, it needs to be recalled that Muslims of the (pre-independence) Indian state of Bihar became victims of some murderous communal riots in 1946. These riots were a manifestation of the Hindu resentment at the Muslim's espousal of the Pakistan movement, and their vote for the creation of a Muslim homeland. To escape murder, rape, loot, and arson, waves of Bihari Muslims migrated to what was then East Bengal because this was a territory demanded by the Muslims to be part of Pakistan. Some even came to pre-independence Karachi, where a Bihar Colony was established even before Pakistan came into being.

After independence, more refugees migrated to East Pakistan, resulting in the concentration of the Bihari community which grew to 1.5 million by the year 1971.[2] This community did not integrate with the locals and kept their separate ethnic, linguistic, and social identity. In doing so, they followed in the footsteps of their counterparts in Sindh.

In 1971, East Pakistan separated from West Pakistan and became Bangladesh. During the upheaval, 1.5 million Biharis, who had refused to integrate with the locals, faced the moment of truth. Three lakhs were driven back to India, five lakhs were exterminated by the Mukti Bahini, and five lakhs arrived in Pakistan at different intervals via Nepal. The remaining 2.5 lakhs are languishing in camps in Bangladesh.[3] After a dialogue, the transfer of certain categories of population was allowed. Pakistan accepted the central government employees, their families, divided families, hardship cases, etc. The remaining Biharis had to stay back as citizens of Bangladesh which would continue to remain Muslim Bengal forever, irrespective of whether it was called Pakistan or Bangladesh or by any other name. It is a republic, and its constitution is liberal enough to accommodate diverse elements. If Bengali is the official language of Bangladesh, it enjoyed the same status before 1971. It is a rich language and to learn it should be a matter of pride for all citizens, including the Biharis. But, this is a position that the Biharis do not accept, just as their counterparts in Sindh do not accept the supremacy or even equality of any language other than Urdu.

Legally speaking, all permanent residents of the former East Pakistan, who were Pakistani citizens, became the citizens of Bangladesh on the day of the latter's recognition by Pakistan in February 1974. Those who escaped to Pakistan or were allowed into Pakistan under various categories do not create legal entitlement for those ethnic non-Bengalis who were left behind.

The mutual non-acceptability between them and the government of Bangladesh was motivated by considerations other than legal.

Ideologically, the Biharis feel that their claim to repatriation is based on the two-nation theory. They assert that they created Pakistan on the basis of that theory, and their desire to migrate from India was rooted in the birth of the ideological state which came into being on the basis of their vote. This is a highly controversial issue. Firstly, the crux of the ideology was the two-nation theory, which aimed at the creation of a state as a homeland for the Indian Muslims. This theory passed into limbo when the proposed partition of India completely ruled out the transfer of population. The emergence of a nation-state of Pakistan on the territorial base of Muslim majority areas of India signalled an end to the two-nation theory for the purpose of migration. The Liaquat-Nehru pact was further evidence that the theory was no longer valid for the purpose of migration from one country to another. In 1971, the state of Pakistan, as conceived in the Lahore Resolution of 1940, split into two states. The people living in each of the two states, *ipso facto*, became citizens of that state, irrespective of their ethnic, linguistic, or ideological orientation. Thus, the Muhajirs of Sindh continued to be the citizens of Pakistan and the Biharis of the the former East Pakistan became the citizens of Bangladesh. If some transfer of population did take place, the basis for such transfer was not ideological, but functional. Had the two-nation theory been operative after the partition of 1947, Prime Minister Liaquat Ali Khan would not have closed the doors to Indian Muslims under the Liaquat-Nehru pact. Nor would the nation-state of Bangladesh have emerged in 1971. If the term ideological state refers to a Muslim majority state, then Bangladesh is as much a Muslim majority state as Pakistan; both were created under the same impulse in 1947, and both share equal responsibility to give citizenship rights to the Muhajirs who were displaced from India.

The fact that the Biharis fought against the Mukti Bahini on behalf of the Pakistan Army, does not qualify them for Pakistani citizenship, or disqualify them for Bangladesh citizenship. When there is a civil war, people do support one side or the other. When one side wins, the losing side does not have to emigrate. It has to accept the reality of the defeat and reconcile to the fact of being loyal citizens of that state. A group of people cannot go on changing their citizenship after every break-up. India broke-up, and they went to East Pakistan. Then Pakistan broke-up, and they now want to migrate to what was West Pakistan.

As to the religious dimension, there is little to be said. The Biharis are Muslims, they are in Bangladesh, which is a Muslim country. Pakistan is no better than Bangladesh as a Muslim country. In fact, it has been made worse by fundamentalism, sectarianism, and terrorism. If they are invoking Islam, then there are fifty-six Muslim countries, some of them better Muslims than others, and some extremely rich. So, they have a wide choice provided they are accepted. If Pakistan had accepted them, the problem would not have lingered for thirty years.

The issue has also been agitated at the humanitarian level. If that is the case, then no one should talk of their right to come to Pakistan. Humanitarian concern makes it a universal concern. Rich and under-populated countries can offer to accept them on humanitarian grounds. But, the problem is that the 'stranded Pakistanis' will not accept such a situation, as they consider themselves Pakistanis.

The real issue underlying the agitation is the ethnic affinity between the Muhajirs of Sindh and the Biharis in Bangladesh. These 2.5 lakh Biharis can no longer go to India. They could have easily done so in 1971, when three lakhs did crossover to India. They do not want to stay in Bangladesh as ethnically they refuse to integrate with the locals. They would pay any price to join their ethnic counterparts in Sindh. This demand is made as a matter of right which is based on the assertion that they made sacrifices for their dreamland. Bangladesh, as far as they are concerned, was a dreamland when it bore the label of Pakistan. Their dream was shattered when it seceded.

They accepted coming to the Punjab where Prime Minister Nawaz Sharif settled the first group of sixty-three families during his first term of office (1990-93) as a part of the coalition agreement with the MQM.

This action of the IJI-MQM coalition was condemned by Sindhis of all political shades. Strong objections were raised against the issue of Pakistani national identity cards to the Biharis by the Pakistani high commission in Dhaka. Here is the summary of the press coverage by some Sindhi daily newspapers, which reflect the unanimous Sindhi verdict: The PML (N) chief minister of Punjab, Ghulam Haider Wyne's statement to the effect that Biharis were Pakistanis, and that they were free to go anywhere in Pakistan, was vehemently condemned.[4] Wyne had built 1000 houses for them. But, after sixty-three houses were occupied, further repatriation was stopped. Then, in 1999, the PML (N) foreign minister, Sartaj Aziz, declared that they were not Pakistanis. Thus, the PML (N) used Biharis as political pawns for bargaining with the MQM. The Biharis repatriated to Mian Channu had shifted to Sindh, and that was aggravating the ethnic conflict in Sindh.[5] It was alleged that Prime Minister Nawaz Sharif and Chief Minister Ghulam Haider Wyne were allowing repatriation not out of sympathy for the Biharis but to punish the Sindhis for casting their vote for the PPP.[6] A warning was issued to express deep concern against converting Sindhis into a minority in their own province.[7] Some papers gave sane counsel that such a controversial issue should be resolved with mutual consent through a dialogue between the Sindhis and the Muhajirs, the two concerned parties.[8] Sindhis were bitter that they were not even consulted by the PML (N) before making a commitment which hurt their vital interests and threatened their existence in their home province.

It is the ethnic basis of the issue that is at the root of the problem. It makes Pakistanis synonymous with the Muhajirs, and makes a mockery of the federation and the nation-state. It is in this perspective that the resentment of the Sindhis against the repatriation of 'stranded Pakistanis' can be properly understood. The resentment is not confined to a particular group or a party of Sindhis. All Sindhis, irrespective of their political creed, oppose repatriation. Their opposition is not based on hatred or rancour against the Biharis. In fact, Sindh had welcomed the Bihari refugees even before the creation of Pakistan.

Today (7 January 1947), the first meeting of the Bihar relief committee was held under the chairmanship of M.A. Khuhro, Chief Minister. Among those present was Maulana Abdul Quddus Bihari. The meeting considered ways and means of rehabilitating the Muhajirs arriving in Sindh as a result of the tyranny and bloodshed caused by the riots in Bihar (India). It was decided to take necessary steps to rehabilitate the Biharis in Sindh by providing employment, housing, etc. District-wise quotas of rehabilitation were assigned. Each minister was assigned a district. They were to complete the job within two weeks after consulting local *zamindars* and Muslim League office bearers, and submit a compliance report to the provincial Muslim League.[9]

The above quoted passage has many messages to convey. The rehabilitation plan included housing and employment. The refugees were distributed in groups in various districts to enable them to integrate with the locals, in keeping with the centuries-old tradition of Sindh to absorb diverse people within its loving embrace and display unity in diversity. Besides, it was an eloquent testimony to Sindh's commitment to Pakistan, its ideology, and its total involvement in the problems confronting the new state. Finally, it showed that although the subject of refugee rehabilitation was outside the purview of the provincial government, Sindh went out of its way to help its Bihari brothers in distress.

Seen in this perspective and in the backdrop of the history of the attitude and the conduct of the MQM towards the Sindhis, it should not be difficult to understand why the Sindhis have *en masse* opposed the repatriation of 'stranded Pakistanis'. Sindhis see in the MQM demand an opportunity to set off one community against the other, having nothing to do with the ideology of Pakistan, or Islam, or the humanitarian aspect. The MQM strategy has been to inflate and strengthen its own constituency in Sindh, by fair means or foul. If illegal immigration of the Muslims from India and the Biharis from

Bangladesh have contributed towards that goal, why not make a bid for opening a legal channel of immigration of the Biharis from Bangladesh? The number of 'stranded Pakistanis' remaining in these camps have already shrunk to 250,000. So, the burden on Karachi, which is already bursting at the seams due to illegal immigration, will be negligible, it is argued.

All these justifications, whether ideological, or Islamic, or humanitarian, are a smoke screen to hide the real agenda of the MQM. What were the ideological, Islamic, or humanitarian compulsions leading to terrorism, violence, collapse of the economy, and ethnic polarization? What were Altaf Hussain's compulsions for burning the national flag and repudiating the ideology of Pakistan? And, why did Nawaz Sharif discontinue the repatriation of the 'stranded' people after building 1000 houses for them in Mian Channu and settling the first batch of sixty-three families? And, why did Nawaz Sharif's foreign minister, Sartaj Aziz, refuse to call them Pakistanis in 1999 after having committed in the coalition agreements of 1989 and 1997 that they would be repatriated to Pakistan? Benazir, being a Sindhi, could be 'accused' of entertaining 'Sindhi prejudice'. But, what about Nawaz Sharif and Sartaj Aziz, whose commitment to repatriation was clear, unambiguous, and free of prejudice? Why did they go back on their commitment? The answer to all these question is that the 'stranded Pakistanis' have been made political pawns by the concerned parties in their power game.

Since the issue of 'stranded Pakistanis' has been raised by a powerful, well-knit, and financially rich urban political party, it has shaken the foundations of Pakistan and raised an enormous dust cloud. Almost every politician has given vent to his feelings. Makhdoom Khaliq-uz-Zamman says that if the Bangladeshi Biharis wish to be repatriated, they should go back to Bihar (India).[10] Benazir Bhutto called them Bangladeshi Biharis in her statement in Kuala Lumpur.[11] Later, Azim Tariq said, 'Anybody who is a Muslim has the right to Pakistani nationality'.[12]

Muhammad Shukruddin, secretary-general of the Stranded
Pakistanis General Repatriation Committee (SPGRC), claimed
that (a) they are neither Biharis nor Muhajirs but 'stranded
Pakistanis', (b) at least 600,000 were killed in fighting with the
Mukti Bahini, and (c) had they not voted for Pakistan, there
would have been no Pakistan.[13]

Kazi Zafar Ahmad, the prime minister of Bangladesh, said
that 'stranded Pakistanis', numbering two and a half lakhs
(in 1990), are Pakistanis as they opted for Pakistan and were
keen to go there. There was no question of their absorption in
Bangladesh. Economically, they were better off than many
Bangladeshis.[14] Veteran Sindhi politician Rasool Bux Palijo, in
a well-argued article, gave an enlightening picture of what would
happen to Pakistan if its doors were opened to immigration on
the basis of ideology and Islamic brotherhood. He warned that
this would open a Pandora's box and millions of Muslims of
South Asia would flood and drown Pakistan.[15]

There is little doubt that a minor issue has been exaggerated
because of the bargaining power of the MQM, exercised mainly
on the non-Sindhi political elite of Pakistan, who agreed to the
repatriation more as a political bribe than a justifiable claim.[16]
It was a question of two and a half lakh Biharis. Almost all of
them are under thirty years of age, and were born after the
emergence of Bangladesh. They are allowed to move out and
go anywhere without a permit or visa by virtue of their birth.
Some of them have openly come up with the suggestion to
request for Bangladeshi citizenship.[17] The millions of dollars
collected for them by the Rabita Alam Al Islami can be utilized
for settling them in Bangladesh, provided the MQM stops
making political guinea pigs out of them. If the Biharis had
been able to see that they were being used as pawns, they might
have acted differently, and they could have earned a place of
honour for themselves in the state of Bangladesh. 'Their
travails would have been over, had they merged their identity
with that of the Bangladeshis. Little did they realize that those
who made the policies in Pakistan, would for all practical
purposes disown them and the Pakistani foreign minister

(Sartaj Aziz), after his latest visit to Dhaka, would make the blunt statement that they were not Pakistanis at all.'[18] If the PML (N) did not consider them Pakistanis in 1999, how did it consider them Pakistanis in 1990 or 1997? Was it a political bribe to the MQM? As long as the bribe worked, they were called Pakistanis, but when it broke down in 1998, these 'stranded Pakistanis' were reverted to being just Biharis.

Many reasons have been advanced on their behalf for their refusal to merge with the locals. Lieutenant-Colonel (retd.) Safdar A. Siddiqui thinks that their integration was impossible. The Biharis spoke Urdu, and admired the poets Iqbal and Ghalib, while the Bengalis spoke Bengali and admired Rabindranath Tagore and Nazar-ul-Islam. The cultural gulf kept them apart. The Hindu population of Bangladesh fuelled the fire of hatred.[19] Similar reasons have kept the Muhajirs apart from the Sindhis and brought Sindh to the brink of collapse. But, the foundations of Sindh have been shaken by two factors. Firstly, the political clout gained by the MQM on the basis of the size of the Muhajir population. Secondly, the Muslim League's acceptance of the MQM conditions, as dictated by the latter in the coalition agreements, which undermined the interests of Sindh.

NOTES

1. Some of these 'stranded Pakistanis' were settled in Mian Channu in the Punjab by Prime Minister Nawaz Sharif in compliance with the MQM-IJI agreement of 1989. Later, all of them disappeared from Mian Channu. Their destination is officially unknown, but otherwise obvious.
2. *Dawn*, 23 March 1999.
3. Ibid.
4. Daily *Al-Waheed*, Karachi, 24 September 1992.
5. Daily *Ibrat*, Hyderabad, 23 September 1992.
6. Daily *Awami Awaz*, 25 September 1992.
7. Daily *Sindh Sujag*, 23 September 1992.
8. Daily *Hilal Pakistan*, Hyderabad, 24 September 1992.
9. *Al-Wahid* (Sindhi) 8 January 1947. Translated into English by the author.
10. *Herald*, January 1990, p. 56.
11. Ibid.

12. Ibid., p. 54.
13. Ibid., pp. 52-3.
14. *Herald*, January 1990, p. 48.
15. Rasool Bux Palijo, 'The Other Side of the Picture', *Dawn*, 11 October 1992.
16. Repatriation of 'stranded Pakistanis' was a part of the PML (N)-MQM agreements in 1989 and 1997.
17. Letter by Javed Hilali from Austin, USA in *Dawn*, 14 October 1998.
18. M.H Askari, Extracts from his article 'Stranded or Abandoned', *Dawn*, 17 March 1999.
19. Letter by Lieutenant-Colonel (retd.) Safdar A. Siddiqui in *Dawn*, 23 March 1999.

8

JINNAHPUR—THE ULTIMATE GOAL

Sindh is our province—we don't want its division.
— *Altaf Hussain (September 2000).*

Every political party has a goal, and the MQM is no exception. The goal is usually set forth and defined in the party manifesto, which is issued, revised, and updated to suit the political agenda of a party in a given situation. The goal may be short-term or long-term depending upon the objective conditions, guided by the party's philosophy, motivation, strength, structure, resources, and strategy.

The party may declare the goal openly or keep it secret, either wholly or partly, as dictated by the circumstances, which may determine its actions and responses at a given time. Premature declaration of a goal may lead to frustration of the goal by forces more powerful than the party. For example, the secession of East Pakistan was neither declared nor negotiated as a goal, and yet it happened soon after the negotiations on autonomy broke down, due to circumstances that were beyond control. Once the secession became a reality, the founder of Bangladesh declared that total independence was precisely the goal he had been working for all along.

Some parties declare the goal openly, but modify it as it is put to public debate, discussed, analysed, considered, and reconsidered during negotiations. Quebec separatists have not yet succeeded in mobilizing majority opinion in favour of secession. Moro liberation has been deferred following the grant of autonomy by the central government in Manila. The Irish Republican Army has suspended its militant activities and joined the Protestant unionists to work for a united Northern Ireland, following the prolonged negotiations guided by British Prime Minister Tony Blair.

Whether a party opts for peaceful methods or resorts to violence, or adopts both, either simultaneously, or as and when necessary, are decisions which are guided by a review and an assessment of the progress that the party has made towards achieving its goal. These decisions then determine the party's strategy and tactics. Take the case of the Tamil Tigers of Sri Lanka. Their strategy and tactics have remained constant, namely, violence, for a long time, on the basis of the strong backing and motivation from their kin in neighbouring India. Against this backdrop of separatist movements around the world, whether violent or non-violent, whether seeking freedom or autonomy, where does the MQM fit in? An attempt is made to examine, analyse, sift evidence, listen to the MQM leadership, adversaries, neutral observers, and come to some conclusions:

> Kamran Rizvi, member central executive committee of the MQM (H) has stated that without defining the goal, the movement degenerates into arrests, abscondence, and exile. The MQM's goal is the creation of a southern Sindh province. The struggle for its attainment is non-violent. The leader of this movement, Chairman Afaq Ahmad, is among us on the scene of the struggle. Those who wrote slogans in 1997 drenched Karachi in blood, and transferred blood money to London. The tyrant (Altaf Hussain) is again pretending to appear as a victim.[1]

From its very inception in 1992, the MQM (H) has been frank, forthright, and blunt in demanding the division of Sindh and the creation of a Muhajir province. Since it has no representation in any elected forum, its survival and growth depends upon its pressure tactics to expose and run down the MQM (A). One of the tactics it successfully adopted was to move its militants to physically occupy and control some of the constituencies won by the MQM (A) during the 1997 elections.

This surreptitious occupation was so menacing that even those MQM (A) parliamentarians who had won elections from these constituencies could not enter their own areas. These areas became notorious, and came to be known as 'no-go areas' whose restoration to the MQM (A) formed a part of the PML (N)-MQM (A) coalition agreement, one which the PML (N) government did not fulfil in order to keep up the pressure on the MQM (A). Following Prime Minister Nawaz Sharif's ultimatum to the MQM (A) in October 1998 to surrender the alleged killers of Hakim Said or be prepared for the consequences, Altaf Hussain accused Sharif of masterminding the murder of Hakim Said, and ordered the MQM activists to go underground. In retaliation, Afaq Ahmad issued a rejoinder:

> Muhajir youth must reject the call to go underground. Our goal is to divide Sindh to create a Muhajir province in southern Sindh. To fight false prosecutions against Muhajir activists, I am forming a legal aid committee comprising senior lawyers... Today, my Muhajir nation has forgotten the repatriation of stranded Pakistanis, elimination of the quota system, unemployment of Muhajirs, opening of the Khokhrapar border with India, and a metropolitan police set-up. Those who captured votes on the basis of these demands have been the greatest obstacle to these demands... My 400 activists have been murdered... I shall avenge their blood... Parents must ensure that their young activists do not go underground.[2]

The concept of the division of Sindh is as old as the demand for declaring the Muhajirs a separate nationality. This demand was made in the party manifesto of the MQM. It formed a part of the election manifesto of the MQM in 1988. It was proposed by the MQM as one of its conditions for the PPP-MQM coalition in 1988, but was rejected by the PPP. However, rejection by the PPP did not banish the concept from the political agenda of the MQM and other groups of young Muhajirs.

In 1991, an angry Muhajir doctor, named Salim Haider, shot into prominence as chairman of the Muhajir Ittehad Tehreek.[3] In 1991, he published a booklet in Urdu, *Ab Sindh Taqseem Hona*

Chahye (Sindh should now be divided), and launched it in Karachi.[4] He tried to present his case for the division of Sindh. The book claimed that Sindh had never been independent, and that Sindh's separation from Bombay was achieved with the help of the UP and Bihari leaders. According to the plan, the Muhajir province would include the Karachi division, Hyderabad, Kotri, Tando Adam, Tando Muhammad Khan, Tando Allahyar, Mirpur Khas, Shahdadpur, Nawabshah, and Sukkur.[5]

The foundation of the movement for the division of Sindh seemed to have been laid. The MQM (A) had occupied ministerial positions and moved into the driving seat under a coalition agreement with the IJI, headed by Nawaz Sharif at the centre, and an over-ambitious Jam Sadiq Ali in Sindh.[6] Under government patronage, it was easier and safer to plan and make a successful bid to break up Sindh. In 1992, Karachi was ripe for a terrorist shock. The streets of Karachi were drenched in blood. The magnitude of killings was beyond the control of the police or rangers. The prime minister could not order the army to move in and restore order. The army chief, General Asif Nawaz, took the initiative and struck at the terrorists in May 1992.

In mid-July 1992, Brigadier Haroon took a group of newsmen to Karachi and revealed that 'there were confirmed intelligence reports that some of the MQM leaders were trying to create a separate state.'[7] The matter had taken a serious turn when terrorism reached a high pitch. More evidence of the plan for the division of Sindh was unearthed, including a map. But, it seemed that the army was severely handicapped in dealing with MQM terrorism, as admitted to by the Karachi corps commander, General Naseer Malik, in an interview to the BBC.[8] Since the security of Pakistan had come under threat, the matter moved from the streets of Karachi to the floor of the National Assembly. Responding to desperate questions from the members, the parliamentary secretary, Berjees Tahir (IJI), revealed a list of twenty-one torture cells unearthed by the army.[9] These torture cells were discovered during the army operation which began on 28 May 1992. The National Assembly was also given a list of 121 persons accused of setting up these torture cells. The list included Altaf Hussain, Dr Imran Farooq, Salim Shahzad, Kunwar Khalid Younus, and others. Altaf escaped to London. Imran Farooq, Salim Shahzad, and Azim Tariq went underground. MNA Kunwar Khalid Younus, Councillor Zahid Qureshi, and Councillor Abdul Majid Bajwa were arrested.[10]

For the senior partner at the federal level in the IJI ruling coalition, the revelation by the intelligence agencies and the disclosures made on the floor of the National Assembly to the effect that its junior coalition partner at the federal level and the senior coalition partner at the provincial level, was involved in a clandestine plot to break up Sindh (and Pakistan) and resorted to terrorism as a *modus operandi*, came as a rude shock. The opposition took the government to task for encouraging the diabolical designs of the MQM. Benazir Bhutto said:

> MQM promoted a sub-conscious sense of separation amongst the ethnic group it tried to isolate from mainstream Pakistan. Fifty per cent leaders (of the MQM) were illegal immigrants from India who created a state within a state in the urban areas of Sindh where they were only short of printing their own currency. But the real objective of creating such a state within the state was to go for a state outside the state.[11]

This was a devastating attack made by the leader of the opposition on the floor of the highest parliamentary forum in the country, on the basis of the allegation made by the government itself. Opposition members, including Farooq Leghari,[12] accused the government of joining the MQM in the conspiracy to break up the country and, in support, quoted the visit of Nawaz Sharif to London to meet Altaf Hussain. An adjournment motion on the issue, introduced by the opposition, was voted out amidst slogan shouting and pandemonium.[13]

The army action in Karachi effectively restored normal conditions on the surface. On a long-term basis, the results were not conclusive. To begin with, General Asif Nawaz wanted powers under article 245 of the constitution, to be able to deal conclusively with the culprits involved in terrorism, and to foil the MQM plan to create an independent Jinnahpur in urban Sindh. But, these powers were denied to him and, therefore, his officers were reduced to the status of SHOs, who found it difficult to prove such sensitive cases in an ordinary court of law.[14] Intelligence reports on MQM terrorism as well as the details that were revealed in the National Assembly were ignored by the ruling party to escape embarrassment, and these were, therefore, relegated to the dustbin of unsubstantiated history. Altaf Hussain remained in exile, and with the passage of time, was allowed to control the damage and heal the wounds.

In this process, certain actions of the army also came to the rescue of the MQM (A). There was a split in the ranks of the MQM, and it was alleged that the split was engineered by the army. The dissidents called themselves the MQM (H). Who encouraged the split in the MQM is not important. Splits do take place within parties, and almost all parties in Pakistan have gone through this phase. A 'democratic' political party represents a voluntary association of like-minded persons, and people keep joining or leaving it. There is nothing wrong in this. The MQM has to learn to live with dissidents, and not consider those deserting it or disagreeing with it as traitors who have to be punished.[15] Take the case of Azim Tariq, who resurfaced on 28 November 1992:

Had I not come out today, I might have been forced to join MQM (H). I do not want to do any thing against my conscience. I don't know if I am right or wrong. People know, God knows, and history will judge. I am just a human being... I see a pool of blood in this city... I do not want anyone to come with me. It is their own wish. If they want to come, good. If not, it is their wish.

I had four options: (1) to remain underground, (2) resign from the party, (3) join MQM (H), (4) come out and save the party. God knows better (about terrorism and torture cells). How long would Karachi bleed and innocent lives of young people lost... I strictly believe in politics of peace and accommodation, forget and forgive and no confrontation. Those who have committed excesses will never be safe from the wrath of God.[16]

Azim Tariq's disclosure was a devastating indictment, and the final verdict on MQM's terrorism. He decided to resurface and make a determined bid to reform the MQM (A), but he knew the consequences—death stared him in the face. He sought protection from the corps commander, and the latter assured him that he and his family would be provided protection. A few days later, he was assassinated. His death shook the conscience of the thinking, sane, and senior Muhajir intellectuals, who began to raise their voice through newspaper articles and letters to the editors. Retired Ambassador Birgis Hasan Khan wrote:

When we have leaders who will lead and not put themselves at the head of the mob, the problem of Sindh will be solved. The first agreement would be to control the extremists on both sides. The Muhajirs must be made to realize that Sindh can not be partitioned. The old Sindhis must be made to understand that Muhajirs cannot be pushed into the Arabian Sea, dispossessed or reduced to serfdom.[17]

A good piece of advice was given to the Muhajirs by Iqbal Jaffar, a retired bureaucrat and an intellectual of high calibre. He said:

The Muhajir community has reason to feel deprived and defenseless in the face of many challenges, but in the storm raised in the militant rhetoric, it overlooked the fact that most of the causes of deprivation were not peculiar to it as a community. It shared most of the ills with others living in Sindh... However, the Muhajirs were persuaded to believe that a separate battle had to be fought by them and for them... There is nothing that Muhajirs can take from others.... There is too little to share. Also, there is nothing that others can take away from the Muhajirs, for their assets, education, talent, and enterprise—are not capable of being stolen, usurped, or distributed. But there is much that they can create and there is much that they can give—they can be a catalyst for change and progress.[18]

There were some speculations that Jinnahpur as a homeland for the Muhajirs could not have been the brainchild of any Muhajir. S.H. Zaidi has taken the view that this term must have been invented by some agency to beat back the movement of Sindhu Desh:

> The Muhajirs in general, even those in MQM, have never been known to support anti-Pakistan movements. An urban community, with no clout with the military and no choice but to be loyal to Pakistan, has no use for such adventurism. In fact, whoever coined the term Jinnahpur (with a separatist connotation) forgot that no real Urdu speaker would coin this word, containing the Hindu suffix of 'pur' (used for the name of cities rather than region or states) and on top of it, associate the name of the founder, which is held in veneration by them, with it... It is quite conceivable and highly probable that the Jinnahpur bogey was invented to divert attention from Sindhu Desh and remove what was perceived as the main obstacle in its path by its protagonists.[19]

Irrespective of the validity of the argument that the term Jinnahpur must have been coined to thwart the movement for Sindhu Desh, the fact remains that any attempt to divide Sindh would serve the same purpose. By the same token, it can be argued that the Sindhu Desh concept demolishes Jinnahpur. Mirza Jawad Baig, chief of the Pakistan Awami Tehrik, made a formal demand for a Karachi *Suba*, which was sought to be achieved by the same method as for Jinnahpur.[20]

The issue of the division of Sindh has never been allowed to die down; it has simmered all along, with occasional flare-ups, either in Karachi or in London, or both. On 20 February 1994, Altaf Hussain dropped a bombshell through a fax message to *Dawn* Karachi, saying:

> Scores of people suggested to me through fax and telephone that Muhajirs should now have a separate province. The concerned authorities should not take it as a joke. They should try to improve the situation and take practical steps towards it.[21]

The publication of this message threw the entire country into a quandary. The people of Pakistan were shaken at all levels—the Parliament, the print media, the political parties, and ordinary citizens. On 28 February 1994, the Sindhi-Muhajir strife was the subject matter of an adjournment motion in the Senate, moved by Ijaz Ali Jatoi:

> If Sindh is divided then Pakistan will also be divided. Sindh will only be divided on the bodies of hundreds of thousands of Sindhis. Had Pakistan not been created, those who have been demanding division of Sindh would have been begging in the streets of UP and CP. Creation of Pakistan would not have been possible had Punjabis, Pathans, Balochis, Sindhis and Bengalis not provided their land for the country. We had provided our lands for Pakistan without liquidating and foregoing our cultural, historical, linguistic and social rights...
> Sindhis divided their homes to provide shelter to them at the time of partition when no other province was ready to accept them. We know how the special trains of Muhajirs were shot at in Mardan and how they were treated in Punjab and Balochistan. These Muhajirs never supported Sindhis in any struggle since the creation of Pakistan. They always supported military dictators and all those who flouted the constitution.[22]

Having thrown the trial balloon of Jinnahpur, and gauging the reactions, the MQM thought that was the right moment to put pressure on the PPP government for the withdrawal of all cases against their leaders and activists in connection with terrorism which had paralysed Karachi since 1992. This pressure, exerted through ' secret and open channels', was rejected by the PPP federal law minister, Iqbal Haider, who declared on 5 May 1994 that the law would take its own course, and who then went on to advise Altaf Hussain to 'give up the politics of hatred and violence.'[23]

Commenting editorially, *Dawn* of Karachi warned that:

> Mr Altaf Hussain's choosing to raise it (the issue of division of Sindh) now adds a fresh complication to an already complicated situation. Sindh faces multifarious problems all of which deserve to

be tackled together: the army operation, the near breakdown of civic services, the law and order problem, violence, crime and strife and the lack of employment opportunities which breed frustration. The MQM's grievances, while important, cover just a part of this larger spectrum of problems. How does the demand for a separate province fit into this perception?[24]

The daily *Jang* conducted an opinion survey and recorded the views in its issue of 25 September 1994:

Pir Pagara said that the creation of a Karachi Suba would weaken the federation and, therefore, the entire Sindh would oppose it. He supported federal control over Karachi. He asked if the proposed province would be confined upto Port Qassim, or would it also include Hyderabad and Sukkur? Mumtaz Bhutto said that Karachi Suba would be harmful for the Muhajirs who lived in the interior Sindh. Sherbaz Khan Mazari said that the MQM has a mandate from urban Sindh which was not being accepted, and that had caused a sense of deprivation. Mairaj Muhammad Khan warned that this was no time for demanding a separate province, and that Altaf Hussain must abandon the demand, otherwise it would trigger a wave of transfer of population and lead to bloodshed. He added that the matter would not be confined to Sindh alone. Iqbal Yusuf (PPP) opposed the proposal based on ethnic grounds and said that it would cause mass migration. Ghulam Sarwar Awan (PPI) said that the proposal would open a Pandora's box and the country would face one division after another. Rasool Bux Palijo (Awami Tehrik) held the establishment responsible for spreading these ideas. Abdul Hameed Jatoi said that if the Muhajirs could not integrate, they should go back to India. Nisar Ahmed Halepoto (PPP) said that a new province in Sindh cannot be created by a notification. It would be a replay of the tragedy of 1947. Pasha Kazi (PPP) thought the division would break the country. Shamshad Memon (PPP) thought the demand would create ethnic hatred. Vishnu Mal (Sindh Hari Tehrik) thought that this slogan was anti-Pakistan. Dr Qadir Magsi (JSTP) called it a dream which would never come true. Ismail Rahu (Awami Tehrik) claimed that no power could divide Sindh.
Azad bin Haider said that the demand was premature before the census. Mirza Jawad Baig said that the provinces were created for administrative convenience and not for creating a nationality. Mushir

Pesh Imam was in favour of a division, but agreed that it was not easy and called for cool-headed thinking. Prof Hasnain Kazmi said that the MQM mandate should be accepted and provinces should be reconstituted. Dr Manzoor Ahmed said that naming Muhajiristan would make no difference, the real issue was the problems of the people. All the provinces should sit together and reconstitute the provinces. Ijaz Mahmood (Muhajir Rabita Council) argued in favour of the division of Sindh. Shoaib Bukhari (convenor of the MQM coordination council) said that the MQM would take the final decision on the issue after ascertaining the wishes of the people. Hafiz Taqi and Dr Salim Haider (MIT), the author of the book, *Sindh Should Now be Divided*, claimed that this demand was an integral part of his party agenda.[25]

Muhajir intellectuals, scholars, and columnists, who saw in the threatened division of Sindh a replay of the tragic events of 1947 and 1971, issued repeated appeals and warnings to the MQM leadership not to lead the Muhajir youth into adopting an extremist position. M.B. Naqvi, a senior columnist, called the new development, a 'brewing storm over Sindh', and said:

MQM Chief Altaf Hussain's statements from London are becoming threatening and even more paranoid. He not only envisages agitation against the PPP government in cities but has begun hinting at being forced to demand a division of Sindh. The Muhajir Rabia Council (MRC) has already demanded bifurcation of Sindh... Some of the basic considerations need to be reiterated for keeping the perspective. First, keeping Sindh united, democratic and culturally plural is in the long term interest of the Urdu-speaking Sindhis; it is also vital if we want Pakistan to remain a united and democratic, albeit federal, country. The processes of division in any part of Pakistan, and far more so in Sindh, will unleash totally uncontrollable forces that may badly hurt Pakistan's unity and integrity. The point is so obvious that one hates to argue the point at any length. That makes it obligatory on the Urdu-speaking intelligentsia to convince the leadership of MQM, irrespective of its factions, to stop acting and talking in a manner that smacks of a divisive or exclusionist attitude; even as a talking point, by way of merely threatening the PPP government. This kind of thing is tantamount to playing with fire (because it familiarizes the concept that can lead to suicidal results). No grievance, no matter how genuine or resulting from the PPP government's stupidity or cussedness, can justify cutting the branch on which the so called Muhajirs have to survive.[26]

What could have been the motivation behind the threat of division issued from distant London? Could it have been the tough negotiations between the PPP and the MQM failing to result in another coalition agreement whereby the MQM could have shared power once again? But, the MQM had shared power twice before, once with the PPP, then with the IJI, and both times the agreement had gone up in flames amid allegations and counter-allegations of breach of trust, followed by terrorism of all kinds. Any party, the PPP included, would have been over-cautious in dealing with the MQM after the events of 1992 and 1993. Any political bargain would have been a hard one to strike. Was the threat from London to serve as an ultimatum? If it was, then it was ill-advised and immature. The PPP was a mainstream party, with following in all the provinces and a functioning government at the centre and three provinces (PPP government in Sindh, and coalitions in the Punjab and NWFP). Whereas, the MQM, though a well-knit party, had a narrow urban base in Sindh only. It was in no position to issue ultimatums over an issue which had repercussions in all the provinces as well as at the federal level. M.H. Askari, a senior columnist, gave sane and practical advice to the MQM.

...The time to create linguistic or ethnic provinces in Pakistan was shortly after partition, which is when it was done in India. Too much emotion has been generated since then to make any change in the present boundaries of the provinces anything but an extremely painful process. In Sindh, particularly, the present ethnic polarization would only become more acute. It is difficult to redraw a map of Sindh in a way in which the entire population in any of its parts would be ethnically or linguistically homogeneous.[27]

The ghost of Jinnahpur, since it was created, has haunted the political landscape of Sindh. Its maximum impact was visible during the PPP rule in 1993-96. The motive was obvious—to blackmail the PPP into offering the same terms as the PML (N), against the interests of Sindh. Every thinking Pakistani was jolted by this new phenomenon which became a hot topic of discussions at all levels and a source of serious public debate in the print media. The MQM had succeeded in creating an environment charged with anxiety and indignation, reminiscent of the dismemberment of Pakistan in 1971. Here is the assessment of columnist Rifaat Hamid Ghani:

...What then could Jinnahpur imply? The name came into circulation through a kind of retrospective, revealing news item. One of the bits of evidence unearthed against the MQM early in operation clean-up was a fragment of what was purported to be a map of a place called Jinnahpur. Was it trumped up? The military could have spoken out unequivocally, but to this day, public understanding remains an informed guess. Jinnahpur in itself is a strange hybrid: the annexation of territory by a defeated occupying force. The demographic 'triumph'of the Muhajir over Sindh, and by extension, Pakistan, for the province is part of the federation... What then is Jinnahpur? A Karachi falsely severed from its hinterland, leaving the Muhajirs in the rest of urban Sindh the option only of migration to a Karachi that is already bursting at the seams in which the non-Sindhi settlers, other than Muhajirs, also account for a significant portion of the population. That kind of Jinnahpur, however, still seems far-fetched... Yet popular lore on the background of differences and division within the MQM, prior to the commencement of operation cleanup, includes disagreement as to the visualization of a separate Muhajir territorial space.[28]

While Jinnahpur was a ghost to some, it was a reality to others. To the Sindhis of every political shade, it was a challenge, as it was to the Punjab, Frontier and Balochistan, and indeed to the federation of Pakistan. After suffering for half a century from factors which destabilized the country, even a simple issue of renaming a province had become sensitive.[29] Division of a province, therefore, was certain to cause a chain reaction, and Pakistan was ill-prepared to face the possible consequences. The attempted division of Sindh had international implications due to its international links, and the MQM's ultimatum of a unilateral declaration of independence was based on reliance of external support. These were the fears expressed by Benazir Bhutto when she said, 'Brigadier Haroon had disclosed the map of Jinnahpur in 1992 and yet those who had plotted and conspired against Pakistan were released unconditionally and paid relief compensation through state funds for kidnapping Major Kalimullah, killing DSPs, rangers and thousands of Karachiites.'[30]

In 1928, the Nehru Report recommended Sindh's separation from the Bombay Presidency, subject to the creation of a Hindu province in the south of Sindh.[31] Two decades later, Sindhi Hindus migrated to India following the creation of Pakistan. But, six decades later, the Muhajir immigrants, who had occupied the places vacated by the Hindus, and maintained a separate political status, as the Hindus did before independence, are demanding the creation of a Muhajir province roughly in the same geographical location as was indicated in the Nehru Report. History creates its own ironies, anomalies, and strange parallels. Political divergence between Sindhi Muslims and the pre-independence Sindhi Hindus has been reincarnated in the shape of the ghost of the MQM separation. Both separatists— the outgoing Hindus and the incoming Muslims—have the same rationale, and the same motivation for the parting of ways with the Sindhi Muslims, whose endeavours to maintain the unity, integrity, and solidarity of Sindh, its culture and history, have been under threat, first by fellow Sindhis, and now by fellow Muslims.

What is common between the two parties trying to divide Sindh? One wanted to create Hinduland or Nehrupur in and around Karachi, the other wants to create Muhajirland or Jinnahpur. One was to create a separate homeland on the basis of religion while the other is to create a separate homeland on the basis of ethnic diversity. While the motivation in both cases is political, Hinduland would have repudiated secularism, a pillar of the Hindu political weapon, the other would repudiate the two-nation theory, the pillar of the Muslim demand for Pakistan. Paradoxically, the Muhajir province is being demanded in the name of Jinnahpur, which is an insult to the memory of Jinnah, a born Sindhi, a son of the soil, who chose Karachi as the capital of Pakistan and who, in his 14-points (1929), had demanded Sindh's separation from Bombay to create a Muslim majority province.

How did the two compatriots treat Sindhi Muslims while co-existing in the same province? Hindus felt that their economic dominance came under threat by the separation of Sindh from Bombay. When the Government of India Act of 1935 became effective in 1937, and elections were held, the Hindus tried to regroup and consolidate political gains. They took advantage of the backwardness of the Muslims, opposed legislation to uplift the rural community, tossed around one cabinet after another, and converted ministerial chairs into musical chairs. Essentially, the MQM is doing the same.

Public debate on Jinnahpur is an on-going exercise. Most of this debate is carried out through letters to newspaper editors, feature articles by prominent columnists, and occasional statements by political leaders. Some of these opinions are well-argued, others offer practical and pragmatic advice. However, there is one line of argument for the division of Sindh which ignores the realities specific to Sindh and Pakistan, and which must be addressed seriously. One correspondent argues that Sindh should be divided because:

India created 32 states out of 8 in 1947. Lord Curzon divided Bengal in 1905. Sindh was separated from Bombay in 1935. Multan was forcibly annexed to the Punjab by the Sikhs. Bahawalpur was never a part of the Punjab. Potohar has a distinct cultural identity. NWFP should be divided into Pakhtunkhwa, Hazara and DIK, Balochistan should be divided into 3 provinces, Canada has 12 provinces.[32]

The correspondent may be living in Sindh, but he needs to know more about this province. He has the right to express his opinion, but his opinion will carry more weight if it is based on the realities of Sindh. None of his examples apply to Sindh. Administrative problems can be solved through greater autonomy upto the grass roots level and not through a division. Dividing Sindh means dividing the same people—the Sindhis and the Muhajirs. Is he dividing the land or the people? If it is the land, then ask the owners. If it is the people, then why not ask the people? Since the controversy has gone on for far too long, it has now degenerated into loose talk, which has lowered the level of the debate. The latest example is the ultimatum given by Altaf Hussain, saying that if the killings of the Muhajirs was not stopped, he would have no other option but to launch an armed struggle and seek support from a neighbouring country. He accused the Punjabi establishment of refusing to accept the Muhajirs and the mandate given to the MQM by the people. He denied the charge that he was planning to create Jinnahpur and that he was an agent of RAW (Research and Analysis Wing—India's intelligence agency). He prayed to God to help him in making a unilateral declaration of independence. He accused the Punjab of running Sindh as its colony, and of engineering linguistic riots in Sindh in 1972. He appealed for Sindhi-Muhajir unity.[33]

Altaf Hussain did not specify whether he meant unilateral declaration of independence of Sindh or Karachi. However, since he has said it in the context of Sindhi-Muhajir unity, it is assumed that he was seeking the secession of Sindh from Pakistan. Firstly, Sindh does not want to secede. The only group favouring secession is the Jiye-Sindh whose founder was not sure if he wanted an independent Sindh or a confederation.[34] Secondly, he does not have any mandate from Sindh to speak for the Sindhis. Thirdly, he has appealed for Sindhi-Muhajir unity, which means that the unity does not exist. That being the case, how can he give a premature call for independence? Even if unity is achieved, it may not lead to a consensus on the issue of secession. On the contrary, a great majority of Sindhis and

Muhajirs would oppose any such move. Altaf Hussain has denied his links with RAW and yet he relies on India's help in his war of independence from Pakistan. Finally, it is the killing of the Muhajirs that prompted him to issue the ultimatum, and this is a serious matter which needs to be discussed in detail.

That the MQM has been engaged in terrorism is beyond question. A terrorist party kills its opponents and its own members get killed in return. It has to accept casualities as a part of the killing game. It has killed the Pathans, the Punjabis, the Sindhis, policemen, rangers, and army men. In return, they have killed the MQM activists. It has been a mini civil war, and casualities must include innocent people on both sides. So, what is the complaint about? Does it mean that all these people, namely, the Pathans, the Punjabis, the Sindhis, the police, the rangers, and the army, are determined to eliminate the Muhajirs from Sindh? The very formulation of such a theory is absurd and, therefore, the allegation that the Muhajirs are being killed cannot be taken at face value. They have a right to live as peaceful citizens and no one can eliminate them. The MQM's new found urge to close ranks with the Sindhis is a welcome development. G.M. Syed tried it, but failed because Altaf Hussain set up a separate agenda for the Muhajirs that created a wide gulf between the Sindhis and the Muhajirs. Altaf now speaks the same language that Syed spoke in 1986. Syed was on the same grid till he died in 1995, with his dream of Sindhi-Muhajir unity unfulfilled, mainly due to Altaf Hussain's ill-conceived isolationism and his obsession with Muhajir rights, as distinct from the rights of the people of Sindh. Altaf has begun to mend fences with the Sindhis since late 1998 when he was rebuffed by Prime Minister Nawaz Sharif, who exposed the terrorist face of the MQM.

Should the Sindhis interpret this new development as a signal that the MQM has abandoned its goal of Jinnahpur? There is no easy answer to this question. They must judge for themselves on the basis of the MQM's past performance. Sindhis are divided in three broad groups. The majority belong to the mainstream Pakistan parties. A minority supports Sindhu Desh. Another minority supports a confederation. All the three schools have been consistent in their political choice. By contrast, the Muhajirs have been shifting their political loyalties. They have been in the Muslim League, the JUP, the Jamat-i-Islami, the Muhajir-Punjabi-Pathan (anti-Sindh) Mahaz, the PPP, the PML, and in the MQM. They have been fundamentalists, secularists, rightists, centrists, and left of centre, to suit their changing loyalties. Altaf himself has been shifting his loyalties to suit his changing moods. He pleased G.M. Syed in 1986, pleased Ziaul Haq by staying out of the MRD, burnt the Pakistan flag, signed an agreement with the PPP in 1988, signed an agreement with the PML (N) in 1997, broke it in 1998, and finally signed an agreement with the JSQM in 1998, which cannot be broken because it has no substance. The MQM's latest demand is the autonomy of Sindh, but it has taken no concrete action to achieve this goal. Altaf's ultimatum to give a call for independence does not inspire confidence even among the Sindhi nationalists, mainly because he lacks consistency. The mainstream Sindhis and Muhajirs dismiss his threat as one of his political gimmicks. Could he be seeking a UDI of Sindh as a bargaining chip, with his eyes fixed on Jinnahpur—his ultimate goal?

The MQM still carries the stigma of an ethnic party. Despite the change in its name from Muhajir to Mutahida, there has been no significant move or any visible progress to make it appear as a mainstream party representing various ethnic groups within or outside Sindh. Nor have its activities since 1992, when the name was changed, substantiated its claim to become a broad-based mainstream party. An agreement with the JSQM and a few statements do not reflect any change in policy. The focus of the MQM, therefore, remains confined to the Muhajirs, and its goal limited to Jinnahpur. The terrorist style of the MQM politics and its divisive goal have encouraged the Sindhis to support the mainstream parties as a means to counter the MQM. This sudden pro-Sindh rhetoric of the MQM leadership is unlikely to impress the Sindhi leadership. How can the MQM live down its history of terrorism and bloody encounters with all the non-Muhajir communities in Sindh by issuing a sugar-coated statement from London? The MQM has to do a lot of homework and frame a consistent policy before its new posture is taken seriously.

When Altaf Hussain alluded to a neighbouring foreign power that would help him in his unilateral declaration of independence against the Pakistani establishment, he had India in mind. But, in inviting India he would be playing the role of Sheikh Mujibur Rahman, rather than that of his stranded Bihari brothers who had actively supported the pro-Pakistan establishment in their bid to keep the country united. Now, in the changed scenario, with the role of the MQM reversed, what will be the fate of the stranded Biharis? Will the demand for their repatriation to Pakistan be withdrawn?

Since the goal of Jinnahpur became a hot subject, its meaning and interpretations have undergone many changes. Dr Salim Haider demanded the division of Sindh roughly into two equal halves, the lower half, including Karachi, Hyderabad, Mirpurkhas, etc. was to be an exclusive Muhajir domain.[36] Other Muhajir intellectuals wanted the creation of a Karachi Suba, with an unspecified area as its hinterland, where the Muhajirs could set up their own government. The MQM (H) has been uncompromisingly consistent on the issue of Muhajirland. The main representative political party of the Muhajirs, the MQM (A), has been vague on the issue. But, because of its political clout and its street power, its vagueness has caused ripples throughout Pakistan, in general, and in the parliament, in particular.[35] Quite often, rumours were floated that the Muhajirs, aided by a foreign power, planned to create an independent state in Karachi, and make it a free port like Singapore. In this accumulated confusion has been added the latest call by the MQM (A) for the unilateral declaration of independence of Sindh. Since any thoughts of the Muhajirs and the Sindhis joining for the independence of Sindh makes no political sense, the discussion must be confined to the issue of the division of Sindh. The Muhajirs claim that they are a nation. To make a group of people a nation, there has to be a three way relationship between language, consciousness, and territory. They have Urdu as the language. Their consciousness has been sufficiently created and aroused by the MQM. But, the third element, namely, the territory, is missing. There are Muhajir concentrations in the urban areas of Sindh but these concentrations, neutralized as they are by the non-Muhajir population in the same urban centres, hardly constitute a Muhajir territory. Muhajir pockets and neighbourhoods, irrespective of how surreptitiously they were created, do not add up to a Muhajir territory. The reality is that there is no such thing as a Muhajir territory. There is only one territory, namely Sindh, and both Sindhis and Muhajirs share the same territory, as their common wealth. The earlier they learn to live together, the better for them and for Sindh.

In this connection, the MQM must heed the timely warning:

What a tragic phenomenon in Pakistan's history the MQM has been? In the right hands it could have laid the foundation of a new middle class-oriented politics. In the hands of its present leadership it has become a blind instrument of terror, pursuing messianic goals which are based upon thoroughly unrealistic considerations. The Awami League, helped above all by geography, could carve out an independent state. The MQM, try it might, cannot sever Karachi from the rest of Pakistan. What is more, even revolutionary parties avoid pitting themselves against the armed might of a state, especially when that might is cohesive. The Bolshevik resolution succeeded when the Tsarist military disintegrated. Khomeini's revolution in Iran succeeded when the Shah's military broke up. Altaf Hussain, blazing the trail of a new revolutionary doctrine, is trying to pit his movement against the armed might of the Pakistan state. Not only is this venture inherently foolish, it also puts the MQM's constituency in a suicidal course of action... It is difficult to negotiate with a movement which draws sustenance from a very narrow chauvinism and whose actions proclaim that it is committed to the use of violence for furthering of its aims.[36]

There is one aspect of Jinnahpur which needs to be brought out as an essential part of the discussion. If the Sindhu Desh demand represents a challenge to the integrity of Pakistan, Jinnahpur represents a challenge to the integrity of Sindh as well as to

Pakistan. If Sindhu Desh has been on the cards for three decades, Jinnahpur demand is only a decade old. Is it possible to explore and establish a relationship between the two projects? In his letter to *Dawn*, S.H. Zaidi had hinted that Jinnahpur was a bogey invented (by the establishment) to divert attention from Sindhu Desh.[37]

Altaf Hussain, being a political strategist, employing the services of experts sitting in London, must have foreseen the likely repercussions before formulating his call for the division of Sindh. First, he timed his call to coincide with the scandal regarding the acceptance of a bribe (from the PML-N) by his team consisting of Senator Ishtiaq Azhar and others during the negotiations with the PPP for a coalition in 1993. The scandal was floated by the PML (N) to thwart the MQM-PPP negotiations. Unnerved, the MQM disengaged its team members instantly, named a brand new team, and announced severance of any contacts with the PML (N). This move could have been aimed at damage control which was essential at a crucial time when:

1. The army was busy surrounding various MQM concentrations in Karachi to unearth thousands of unauthorized lethal weapons concealed in their houses and hideouts. When a locality was surrounded, the inmates would quietly place the weapons out in the street in darkness, so that the real culprits could never be apprehended.

2. The MQM had earlier been accused in a whispering campaign during the 1993 NA elections of having accepted bribes for not contesting the elections. But, seeing that the bribe-givers were not benefiting from the MQM boycott (which they claimed was on account of the alleged army victimization), they re-entered the electoral battle for the provincial assembly two days later, and bagged all the seats from the MQM constituencies in Karachi, Hyderabad, and elsewhere. That strategy of damage control, which had worked well, served as a guide for future use.

3. While the new MQM approach was more an act of showmanship than a serious negotiating attempt, substantial dialogue never really began.

4. Rather than enter into a dialogue with the PPP, and having
   declined the PML (N)'s request to participate in anti-
   government strikes and rallies, the MQM decided to release a
   bombshell, to coincide with anti-PPP government strikes and
   rallies. That bombshell was to reinject the topic of the division
   of Sindh and create confusion so as to blur the political
   environment of Sindh.
5. The call for the division of Sindh was worded cleverly. The
   demand was not made in clear cut-terms. It was thrown as a
   straw in the wind, to invite public debate, to throw anti-
   division Muhajir elements off balance, and to convince the
   borderline Muhajir elements that their salvation lay only in
   the division of Sindh. The message was also clear to the
   Pathan community, whose leaders had been in regular contact
   with the MQM leadership prior to this call, to work out a
   modus vivendi between the Muhajirs and the Pathans in the
   Muhajir part of divided Sindh.

If Sindhi reaction is analysed, it becomes clear that Altaf's
call threw them off balance. They failed to condemn it at a
national level by organizing an all parties conference in
Islamabad, Lahore, Peshawar, Quetta, and Karachi.
Condemnation by the PML (N) was tame and lifeless. Religious
parties like the JUP, the JI, the JUI, and others, which hold such
strong views on religious issues, remained non-committal. Sindhi
nationalists used strong language, including demands that the
dividers go back to India. By doing so, they fell into the trap
laid for them. Threats cannot be nullified by counter-threats.
The threat of the division of Sindh must be countered by a firm,
decisive, well-orchestrated initiative at the right places,
conducted on a sustained basis. The call was given by a united,
disciplined, politically conscious party, well equipped with all
imaginable resources, including men, material, finance,
international support, and an up-to-date worldwide communication network. By contrast, Sindhis are divided, poor in
resources, undisciplined, and faction-ridden. Besides, they are
feudal-dominated, and the feudals have a history of joining even

the devil for personal gains at the cost of Sindh. The Punjab, Frontier, and Balochistan must be brought into the forefront to oppose the division of Sindh. And, if some elements among them are directly or indirectly encouraging the issue, they should be exposed at all levels.

Sindhi nationalists, apart from being a divided house, are also suspected by the Punjabis to be unpatriotic. This suspicion must be removed through dialogue at an appropriate level, even if it means agreeing to a quid pro quo. Besides, they have a negligible representation in elected forums which enfeebles their voice in comparison to that of the MQM which has a solid mandate. This factor alone reduces the nationalist Sindhi reaction to empty rhetoric. If the MQM threat is based on genuine grievances, the Sindhis should openly voice their support for the redressal of such grievances in order to remove the sting from the threat. In the battle of ideas, there should be no room for threats or bullets. Sindhis must fight back with better and superior ideas, and project them in a non-violent, convincing, wise, mature, and calculated manner to silence the supporters of the division. Threats and counter-threats will only advance the case for division.

Sindhis should determine if the idea of Jinnahpur is home-grown or foreign-inspired. The Sindhi response should be formulated accordingly. Could Altaf Hussain be testing the wisdom and political maturity of the Sindhis? The Muhajirs are aware that this commodity is in short supply among the Sindhi politicians. But, what about Sindhi thinkers, writers, and intellectuals? The MQM may also be testing the reaction of the Punjab and the army. Both have the power, but do they possess enough wisdom to counter Altaf on a political plane? They failed to effectively split the MQM in 1992, and to defeat it in the elections in 1993. They can fail yet again. Could the MQM be fishing for a *modus vivendi* with the Punjabi lobby which controls the economy? Could the idea of Jinnahpur have been planted by the army to provoke the MQM into yet another foolish action which the army could then move to crush.

All parties, whether directly or indirectly involved in Jinnahpur, are aware that this dream cannot be made into a reality, if at all, in a peaceful manner. There is bound to be a clash between the Sindhis and the Muhajirs in all the cities and towns of Sindh, and the MQM is aware that such clashes would only hasten the achievement of their goal just as the communal riots hastened the partition of India. Will the federal authorities (and the army) permit the situation to deteriorate to the point of a civil war? The army intervened every time it suspected this outcome, irrespective of whether the MQM itself was one of the ruling parties. Besides, a civil war would escalate from a limited Sindhi-Muhajir conflict into a much wider Muhajir-non-Muhajir clash. For example:

• The Punjab has high stakes in trade and industry, and it cannot remain a silent spectator to the destruction of its economic interests. It is aware that if Sindh is split, it will trigger a chain reaction.

• The Pathans have high stakes in a peaceful Sindh because they wish to protect their transport monopoly, job opportunities, and their invisible trade, which accounts for billions of rupees.

• The Baloch element in Karachi is considerable. They are a peaceful lot, engaged in middle and lower level trades. Any socio-political upheaval will destabilize their economic life.

• Among the Muhajirs, the intellectual, professional, executive, and affluent classes will dissociate themselves from any bloody conflict, irrespective of their political leanings. Even those who support the idea do not support an armed conflict over the issue. But the groups of Muhajirs who call the shots, and who tend to decide the issues on the streets of Karachi, are the ones who really matter. They have proved their strength through the bullet as well as through the ballot.

• It is widely believed that the Jinnahpur demand is motivated by greed rather than grievance.

The Jinnahpur enthusiasts seem to be counting on one possible scenario. If they escalate the crisis into a bloody conflict, Sindh would become insecure for the Sindhi Hindus, who, for fear of being included in Jinnahpur, would flee to

India and cause a refugee problem. It will be worthwhile to foresee the possible consequences of such a development in the light of recent history, and take steps to avert such a catastrophe.

The MQM should also consider the fact that the world around them is fully aware of the possible short-term and long-term goals of Jinnahpur, and would have made contingency plans to meet the consequences. One such observation may suffice:

> ...The logical outcome of the ideology, demography, and localized concentration of popular support for the MQM is the demand for a separate Karachi or a Muhajir province; and such a province, if it comes into being, will only be a stepping stone to a demand for a separate state, because having a Muhajir province will satisfy Muhajir grievance no more than the existence of Sindh and Balochistan has satisfied Sindhi and Balochi aspirations... Even if such a province comes into being, its Muhajir character can be assured only by an ethnic cleansing that will dwarf the horrors of Bosnia, for, despite Muhajir nationalists' absurd demographic claims, Muhajirs will have, if at all, no more than a razor thin majority in such a province.[38]

In Karachi, the most frequently asked questions are: Why is Altaf Hussain living in exile in London since 1992? Why can't he return to Pakistan and sink and swim with his people? His stay in London has more to it than meets the eye. Talk to an MQM leader and he will say that Altaf is staying away because the government has implicated him in false and fabricated cases, involving him in murder, conspiracy, etc.; that he would be arrested on his return and would never be released; that he does not expect justice, given the limitation of Pakistan's judicial system, etc. Others feel that he will be physically eliminated by the establishment as soon as he sets foot on Pakistani soil, or by the MQM dissidents or his political rivals. Being a symbol of Muhajir aspirations, he must stay abroad and live, guide, and inspire his followers.

How do the people look at his self-imposed exile? He fled during the army crackdown in 1992. The cases against him must pertain to 1992, filed by his coalition partner. In 1993, the coalition partners were dismissed and their opponents, the PPP, came to power. That was an opportunity for him to return and plead against the 'false and fabricated' cases. But, he chose to stay on in London. In 1996, the PPP government was dismissed and the PML (N) returned to power. They made a fresh start, visited London, reconciled with Altaf, healed the old wounds, and cut a new deal, under which the MQM rejoined the government as a reconciled coalition partner, and was promised the governorship and the chief ministership of Sindh, being the senior partner. Thousands of MQM activists were released from detention. Leaders were released on parole to enable them to occupy ministerial positions. That was the most appropriate time for Altaf to return and lead his party. But, he chose to stay on in London.

Could there have been a persuasive reason for him to stay on in London? Here is one theory:

1. A separatist movement can best he conducted from abroad. He remains immune from harassment by the local authorities. He has access to all the gadgets, techniques, and contrivances to cloak the real goal of the MQM, and play up the issue of human rights which wins easy and popular support in Europe and America.

2. He has abundant expertise available outside Pakistan. Sympathetic Muhajir minds in Europe, the USA, and the Gulf are there to draw upon. Then, there is a vast pool of talent available in India to which he has free access, but only from London.

3. Separatist movements thrive on donations by individuals and sympathetic foreign sources. Donations from Pakistanis have been generous.[39] For a prolonged campaign, extra help on a generous scale from sympathetic foreign powers becomes necessary. If the movement has the potential to split Pakistan, Indian help would be readily available.[40]

4. Most of the revolutionary movements are guided from abroad. The Iranian revolution was directed from Baghdad and Paris. Tamil Tigers have their base in India. Living in London facilitates contacts with fellow revolutionaries around the world.

5. The battle for Jinnahpur now extends from the killing fields of Karachi to the Human Rights Commission in Geneva, Amnesty International, the European Parliament, the United Nations, and the corridors of power in London and Washington. London provides easy access.

6. The ideology which brought the Muhajirs from India to Sindh is worn out, as demonstrated by Altaf's flag burning at the Quaid's Mazar in 1979. They did not integrate with the locals. They made frantic efforts to get the Khokhrapar border post opened, but Pakistan did not oblige. They moved mountains for the repatriation of stranded Pakistanis, but Pakistan ignored them. Pakistan took steps to stop illegal immigration from India. That explains the MQM's alienation from Pakistan. They have to have links with their kin in India. The hostility between India and Pakistan has prevented the re-establishment of these links. There is a good chance that Jinnahpur will provide the missing link. The role of the Indian Muslims in the international network of the MQM has been well known.

Many educated Sindhis have failed to grasp the true significance of the repeated and frequent eruptions of MQM terrorism. On the face of it, it may appear as a reaction of a deprived and persecuted community. But, this is only a pretext which masks the real aim which is obvious to those who can understand. MQM terrorism is provoking the Sindhis to retaliate in kind and resort to counter-terrorism which could then escalate into a civil war and force a division of Sindh as a solution. Mature Sindhi politicians have seen through this game and have counselled a cool-headed approach. But, there are hot-headed Sindhis, who, in their blind love for Sindh, have done immense harm to their cause. One such 'devoted' Sindhi of Shikarpur once boastfully told the author that the MQM people (he meant the Muhajirs) had been driven out of their city which had been 'cleansed' of the trouble makers. The author lamented that Shikarpuri Sindhis, by their act of 'ethnic cleansing', had pushed Sindh one step closer to a division. Was this example of Sindhi chauvinism a manifestation of anti-Muhajirism, or a knee-jerk reaction of a misguided group? Fortunately, the incident was localized, but its message carried a warning for the Sindhis.

The quotation at the beginning of this chapter is what the Mutahida chief, Altaf Hussain, said in London on 18 September 2000, in a public gathering, in the presence of nationalist leaders, including Attaullah Mengal, Mahmood Khan Achakzai, Syed Imdad Muhammad Shah, and others. This declaration represents a change of strategy. The MQM (A) has to revise its manifesto, follow it up with concrete action to distance itself from its own past, and make a new beginning. But, a new beginning appears a distant dream when in the same breath Altaf condemns the partition of India, which calls into question his faith in Pakistan.[41]

NOTES

1. *Jang*, 8 November 1998. The MQM (H) is the breakaway faction of the MQM (A). It openly preaches the division of Sindh while the MQM (A) uses it as the ultimate weapon. The MQM (H) relies on the use of street power while the MQM (A) uses the combination of elected power and terrorism.

2. *Jang*, 8 November 1998.

3. The Muhajir Ittehad Tehrik (MIT) soon faded out of existence.

4. I attended the launching of the book. The speakers included Naim Siddiqui, Yusuf Advocate, Dr Khwaja Sharful Islam, Azad Bin Haider, Zuhair Akram Nadeem (subsequently murdered by MQM [A] activists), and others. They made hard-hitting speeches.

5. See page 90 of the booklet '*Ab Sindh Taqseen Hona Chahye*' by Salim Hyder. The areas earmarked for the Muhajirland excluded small pockets of rural areas for Sindhis to set up their 'reservations' on the pattern of the Red Indian reservations in the U.S.A.

6. The MQM was the senior coalition partner in Sindh in 1990, and yet it agreed to join the cabinet as a junior partner for motives which were revealed in 1992 during the army action.

7. See report of Nusrat Javed in The *News International* of 10 October 1992.

8. Gen. Naseer Malik told BBC '...If the hands of the army were more open, it could arrest suspected persons involved in the crimes.' See Ayaz Amir's column in *Dawn*, 31 August 1992.

136   A TESTAMENT OF SINDH

9. Location of twenty-one torture cells: (1) Pilli Kothi Qasimabad, Liaqatabad (2) F. No. E-1/1, Bl-1, 3rd Al-Karam Square (3) Commercial College, Azizabad (4) Sector Office, Block-14, F.B. Area (5) Doctor's Flat, Abbasi Shaheed Hospital (6) House Opposite 5-1/27, Nazimabad, Sikandarabad (7) Pk Sikandarabad, Liaqatabad (8) House in Kachhi Abadi, New Karachi (9) House No. 47, Gali No. 4, Jacob Lines (10) Barrack No. 55, Jut Lines (11) House No. 447, Jacob Lines (12) St. No. 36-37, Area D1, Kachhi Abadi, Malir (13) Muhajir Khel, 36B Landhi, (14) Councillor's Office (Haji Jalal), Landhi (15) House of Asghari Begum, Landhi (16) Ibrahim Alibhoy School, S.F. Colony (17) Mullah Shor Garden, Block No. 5, Shah Faisal Colony (18) Civil Defence, S.F. Colony (19) Sector Office, Halqa 86, Landhi (20) C-1 Area, Halqa 86, Landhi (21) St. No. 9, Sector Z.E., Orangi Town, See *Dawn*, 11 September 1992.

10. See *Dawn*, 11 September 1992.

11. National Assembly debate reported by Nusrat Javed in the *News International* of 10 October 1992. Significantly, Nusrat Javed called the Jinnahpur goal as 'The last refuge of a scoundrel'. Also, see *News*, Karachi of 28 October 1992, *Nation*, Islamabad of 28 October 1992, and *Jang*, Karachi of 28 October 1992 and 30 October 1992, regarding arrest of M. Naim for issuing thousands of NID cards to Indian nationals at Rs 2000 per card. Under this conspiracy, many Indian nationals became Pakistan's enlarged MQM vote bank, and a source of political support for Jinnahpur.

12. Farooq Leghari became the president in 1993, and resigned in 1997.

13. *Dawn* report of 13 October 1992.

14. *Dawn*, 21 November 1998. Analysis by Faraz Hashim.

15. Fazal Qureshi's opinion in *Dawn*, 4 December 1993.

16. Ghulam Hasnain reports in *Dawn*, 29 November 1992.

17. See *Dawn*, 7 May 1992.

18. Iqbal Jaffar's article, 'Isolation of Muhajirs', see *Dawn*, 3 October, 1992.

19. Letter by S.H. Zaidi in *Dawn*, 29 January 1993. 'Pur' may be a Hindu suffix, but Muslims seem to have fallen in love with it. Examples: Muhammadpur, Alipur, Ahmadpur, Noorpur, Khairpur, Islampur, Mirpur, Shahdadpur, Budhapur, Mahrabpur, Saidpur, Shahpur, Salihpur, Risalpur, Khanpur, Shikarpur, Bahawalpur, Deenpur, Tajpur, Nasarpur, etc. If the Hindu suffix can go with Muhammad and Ali, why not with Jinnah?

20. See *Dawn*, 14 December 1993.

21. *Dawn*, 21 February 1994.

22. Senate debate. See *Dawn*, 1 March 1994.

23. *Dawn*, 6 May 1994.

24. *Dawn*, editorial 28 September 1994.

25. Daily *Jang*, Karachi 25 September 1994 published details of the opinion survey on the issue which had shaken the conscience of the people of Pakistan.

26. See *Dawn*, Karachi, 21 February 1994.

27. *Dawn*, 23 November 1994.

28. 'The goals of Jinnahpur', Karachi diary by Riffat Hamid Ghani, *Dawn*, 27 Otober 1994.

29. The Awami National Party of the NWFP wanted to rename NWFP as Pakhtunkhwa, but it was not allowed to do so by its senior coalition partner, the PML (N), even at the risk of breaking-up the coalition in 1997. The PML (N) felt that there were seeds of disintegration in the proposed change of name.

30. *Dawn*, 21 November 1998.

31. Anthony Read and David Fisher, *The Proudest Day—India's Long Road to Independence*, W.W. Norton and Company, New York and London, 1998, p. 215, Extracts: 'The only significant concession to Muslim interests was a proposal to create two new Muslim majority provinces by giving NWFP full provincial status and separating Sindh from Bombay. But this was matched by the creation of a Hindu Province in the South.'

32. Letter by Feroze Shah Gilani, published in *Dawn* of 8 December 1999.

33. *Dawn*, 27 October 2000. It is a revelation that the linguistic riots of 1972 in Sindh were engineered by the Punjabis.

34. G.M. Syed's Sindhu Desh has been analysed in great detail in M.S. Korejo's book, *G.M. Syed—An Analysis of his Political Perspectives*, Oxford University Press, Karachi, 1999.

35. In 1994, the Senate was shaken by threats of the division of Sindh issued by the MQM (A).

36. Ayaz Amir, Islamabad Diary—Karachi, 'Has the Tide Turned?' *Dawn*, 26 February 1996.

37. Letter by S.H. Zaidi in *Dawn* 29 January 1993.

38. Dr Feroz Ahmad, 'Ethnic Politics is a Dead-End Street—How to Bridge the Divide', series of articles, *Dawn*, 23 November 1995.

39. Over Rs 700 million were collected annually. Rs 600 million were transferred, as disclosed by the late Ishtiaq Azhar, ex-convenor of the MQM Co-ordination Committee, (see chapter 3 pps. 50 and 62).

40. In a declaration issued by Altaf, quoted elsewhere, he hinted at such a possibility.

41. *Dawn*, 19 September 2000 reports Altaf Hussain's speech made in London on 18 September 2000, in which he declared his opposition to the division of Sindh and his condemnation of the partition of India in 1947.

9

DIALOGUE OF THE DEAF

THE MQM-JIYE-SINDH: -FIRST HONEYMOON

By an accident of history, the Sindhis and the Muhajirs have come to share the same piece of territory. They share a common religion. They also shared a common historical experience while under the British rule. In certain points of history, like the Khilafat Movement, the trial of the Ali brothers in Karachi, during the struggle for Pakistan, and the communal riots in India, they developed a close emotional bond. This accumulated store of mutual understanding was expected to serve as a bedrock for forging a mutually beneficial relationship between the two communities.

For reasons explained in detail elsewhere, the two communities began to drift away from each other soon after the creation of Pakistan. This drift has continued unabated through the decades, and after over half a century of sharing the territory of Sindh, the gulf has become so wide that the best political brains of Pakistan find it difficult to bridge. The spirit with which they joined to create Pakistan, and the foundation on which the two stood shoulder to shoulder in 1947, crumbled. The binding force between them melted away, and the two began to be inspired by philosophies which were not only different in origin, but had very little in common.

Among the Sindhis, a school of thought came into being in the early 1970s, under the leadership of G.M. Syed, the founder of the Jiye-Sindh Movement (JSM), which preached the dismemberment of Pakistan. At around the same time, the Muhajir leadership started to articulate Muhajir grievances which ultimately led to the emergence of the Muhajir Quomi Movement (MQM). The newly formed MQM denounced its faith in Pakistan, demanded the recognition of a separate Muhajir nationality at par with the other four nationalities (Punjabi, Sindhi, Pakhtun and Baloch), and burnt the national flag as a gesture of open rebellion against Pakistan.[1]

Thus, in 1980, when General Ziaul Haq and his associates, both civil and military, were at the peak of their power and glory[2] after having executed Z. A. Bhutto (1979), these two forces made their debut on the political stage of Sindh. Both forces were nourished on a diet of frustration, deprivation, and bitterness that had accumulated over a period of three decades. Since the PPP, the only mainstream party functioning at that time, stood smothered, and its leadership either in exile or in prison, the deck was cleared in Sindh to facilitate the rise of two separate streams—the Sindhis and the Muhajirs.

An impression was sought to be created that Sindhi politics was dominated by the two newly emerging forces, namely, the MQM in urban Sindh and the JSM in rural Sindh. The compliant press and the controlled electronic media also contributed to the creation of this impression. The two parties, having achieved a measure of success, were guided by an invisible hand to engage in a Sindhi-Muhajir dialogue.[3]

The stage-managed Sindhi-Muhajir dialogue took place during Syed-Altaf meetings. As a result, the JSM and the MQM reached an understanding over most of the issues, as may be seen from the following proclamations of Altaf Hussain:

- Pakistan ideology should be opposed.
- Federalism was a tool for the exploitation of the smaller nationalities by the Punjab.
- Sindh was being crushed by the centre under the pretext of crushing the dacoits.
- Kalabagh Dam was planned to crush Sindh.
- Pano Akil cantonment was planned to crush Sindh.
- Shooting of Sindhis at Thori Phatak was condemnable.[4]
- The Pakistan Army was dominated by the Punjab.[5]

– Movement of the Punjabis and the Pathans into Sindh was converting the Sindhis and the Muhajirs into a minority within their own province.[6]

To all appearances, the formative years of the MQM were the golden years of the Sindhi-Muhajir dialogue. Altaf Hussain became the favourite spokesman of the downtrodden Sindhis and Muhajirs. Slogans of 'Sindhi-Muhajir *Bhai-Bhai*' and 'Syed-Altaf *Bhai-Bhai*' were raised at political rallies, Syed-Altaf meetings, and at Syed's birthday parties, which had come to acquire the status of a great annual political event.

Then came the 1983 MRD movement. Both the JSM and the MQM played their assigned roles—that of abstention. Any movement for the restoration of democracy was not their concern because to them democracy meant rule by the Punjab and enslavement of Sindh. Also, the MRD was PPP-sponsored, and since the PPP stood for the federation, which had been denounced by the JSM and the MQM, the two joined forces to eliminate the PPP. Thus, while the MQM and the JSM watched as spectators, Zia proceeded to ruthlessly crush the MRD in rural Sindh.

The Sindhi-Muhajir dialogue of the early 1980s was a disappointment. Firstly, the parties had overestimated their representative status. In the 1985 elections, which were contested on a non-party basis, the MQM had failed to have their sympathizers elected even though the PPP had boycotted the elections. Both parties made a poor showing. The understanding between Syed and Altaf had not taken a formal shape or status and had been confined to public utterances and political rhetoric. Even if it had acquired a formal status, it would have been washed away by the election results. As it turned out, the entire drama of the so-called Sindhi-Muhajir or Syed-Altaf honeymoon, which had no substance, direction, or grass-root support, was stage-managed by Ziaul Haq to show that he had effectively driven out the PPP and the ghost of Bhuttoism from the soil of Sindh. In the process, the lack of political acumen of the JSM and the MQM stood exposed.

THE MQM-PPP AGREEMENT

The 1988 elections led to the emergence of three distinct political forces which had a direct bearing on the urban-rural relationship in Sindh, and their fallout on the formation of the federal government. The PPP emerged as the largest single party in the National Assembly, short of an absolute majority. In rural Sindh, it won almost 100 per cent of the seats in the National and Provincial Assemblies. In urban Sindh, the MQM emerged as the dominant force; in the Punjab, the PPP trailed behind the Islami-Jamhoori Ittehad (IJI)[7], a coalition between the Pakistan Muslim League (Nawaz Group)[8] and the Jamaat-i-Islami, in the National and Provincial Assemblies. At the federal level, the PPP was called upon to form the government, subject to obtaining a vote of confidence. In Sindh, the PPP could form the government on its own, but in the interest of ethnic peace and harmony in urban Sindh, the need for involving the MQM in the affairs of entire Sindh, and also because the PPP needed MQM support to form the federal government, a PPP-MQM dialogue was initiated for the formation of a coalition.

The MQM announced its 25-point demand as the basis for the dialogue. These were:

1. Sindh domicile to be granted after twenty-five years residence in the province, and all existing domicile certificates to be cancelled. Identity cards to be issued on the basis of domicile certificates. The Muhajirs arriving from Bangladesh should be exempted from the application of this condition.
2. Jobs in the police and intelligence services be given to the locals only.
3. Issue of arms licences to the Sindhis and the Muhajirs be made as easy as obtaining a TV or a radio licence.
4. Afghan refugees to be shifted to the Pak-Afghan border, and their acquisition of property and business be prohibited.
5. People of other provinces be given jobs in their own provinces.

6. *Katchi abadis* settled upto 1978 be regularized; others made illegal; land grabbing (by settlers from other provinces) be stopped by the police; land allotment to non-locals as political favours be stopped.

7. Urban transport to be modernized, and government transport services be transferred to the municipalities; drivers should be matriculates, and professional driving licences be issued only to the locals.

8. Priority be accorded to the locals in government and semi-government jobs; non-locals in such jobs be sent back to their provinces; priority be accorded to the locals in trade, industry, licences, quotas.

9. Right of vote to the locals only.

10. Reduce voting age to eighteen.

11. Separately ascertain the population of the Sindhis and the Muhajirs, and give them jobs, authority, and admissions to educational institutions in proportion to their numbers.[9]

12. The Muhajirs be declared a separate nationality.[10]

13. In private and government jobs, the locals be given priority.

14. In the federal and provincial government and semi-government departments and corporations, anti-Muhajir policies be withdrawn and the doors opened for the employment of the Muhajirs.

15. 'Stranded Pakistanis' in Bangladesh be repatriated.

16. Khokhrapar route to India be opened.

17. Postal rates for India to be the same as with other neighbours.

18. Locals to get priority in admissions to educational institutions in Sindh.

19. Sindh Medical College be given a new hospital.

20. All homeless people in Sindh be given plots at concessional rates, and loans for house building.

21. Separate the Karachi Electric Supply Corporation (KESC) from the Water and Power Development Authority (WAPDA), and transfer the non-locals from the KESC to WAPDA.

22. Vehicle tax be collected by the municipal committees.

23. Fuel adjustment charges be uniform throughout the country.

24. The Sindh government should collect the sales tax.
25. Public holidays on the birth/death anniversaries of Shah Latif
    and Liaquat Ali Khan.

Some of the conditions laid down were tough for any party to
agree to, and it became apparent that in the name of getting
civil amenities and economic opportunities for the Muhajir
community, the MQM wanted to exploit its balancing position
in the vote of confidence at the federal level, and as a price for
ethnic peace in Sindh. Certain issues raised in the list of demands
had defence and foreign policy implications, which were not
debated in the election campaign. Also, the parties did not have
the requisite data and information to make an informed decision.
Over some issues, non-MQM members were elected on the basis
of conflicting and contradictory manifestos. Other issues could
only be raised on the floor of the National Assembly in order to
arrive at a national consensus. Certain issues could create inter-
provincial bitterness at the very start of the process of
democracy, which had just been restored after eleven years of
dictatorship.

With this highly controversial list of demands as the basis,
the PPP and the MQM began a dialogue at the end of November
1988. The next day's headlines carried the news that the MQM
had increased their conditions from twenty-five to forty. On the
third day, the conditions were increased to fifty-seven.
Apparently, the MQM sensed that the PPP desperately needed
their support at the federal level and would pay any price, hence
the temptation to blackmail the PPP and inflate the demands.
A serious political dialogue was thus reduced to a futile and
ridiculous exercise. A more irrational bargain in the quest for
power could not be imagined. The PPP might as well have
prolonged the dialogue till the MQM had scored a century. But,
they got unduly unnerved and called a halt at fifty-seven. Both
sides congratulated each other, and themselves, for laying the
foundation for a new era of peace and prosperity in Sindh.

It is noteworthy that the PPP negotiators were all Sindhis in
their capacity of provincial representatives. They negotiated on

issues which varied from the municipal level, through provincial and national, to the international level. The MQM did not consider it fit to split the issues for discussion at appropriate levels, and they put the onus on the PPP which, as the party in power at the federal level, would be bound to honour the commitments in respect of the national and international affairs. In doing so, the MQM ignored the fact that the electorate in the Punjab, Frontier, and Balochistan (the last two did not give any mandate to the PPP), let alone the electorate in Sindh, was not aware of what was cooking between the MQM and Sindh PPP negotiating teams.

Such half-baked agreements are not unusual in a Third World country where political parties lack maturity and experience. At any rate, the PPP-MQM agreement was signed in good faith, at a time when democracy was about to dawn. It was held as a step forward, and it received full support from the print media and the general public. A study of the fifty-seven clauses of the agreement shows that the PPP made an attempt to pacify the passions of the MQM, which was entering the corridors of power for the first time since its creation. The spirit behind the accord was to remove the doubts and misunderstandings, and provide an opportunity to the MQM to think on a national plane and see things in a national perspective. The PPP was aware that elementary civic facilities were denied not only to the squatters of the *katchi abadis* of Karachi, but to hundreds of thousands of rural folk in Sindh who demanded no less attention. But, since the MQM was more concerned about the civic problems of the urban population, the PPP had to agree to their demands.

On contentious issues, the PPP negotiators tried to remove the sting of bitterness from the MQM demands, without dismissing them outright. For example, it tried to rationalize the *katchi abadis* as being the outcome of socio-economic pressures, a situation exploited by land grabbers. The MQM demand for being declared a distinct ethnic nationality was rejected, and the MQM was made to agree to work with the PPP to create a society based on social, ethnic, and economic justice, not only within Sindh but also between Sindh and other provinces. The PPP also made the MQM agree to encourage mobility of students within the province as a step towards national integration, though it did agree that Karachi girls would not go to the Nawabshah Medical College. Opening of the Khokhrapar border, which was demanded outright without delay, was linked by the PPP with the normalization of relations with India, imperatives of national defence, and other related issues—matters which the MQM had ignored due to their agitational mode of politicizing sensitive defence and foreign policy issues to gain popularity, catch votes, and inflame passions of the urban crowds.

On the burning issue of immediate repatriation of 'stranded Pakistanis' (Biharis) in Bangladesh, the agreed clause read: 'Such Pakistanis who are living abroad on their own or under compulsion will have equal rights of Pakistani citizens.'

This amended clause was a trap in which the MQM landed unwittingly. Stranded Biharis were called Pakistanis by no one except by the MQM. The term used for them should have been non-controversial and in keeping with a mutually agreed interpretation. Even the PML(N) changed the interpretation to suit political expediency. The agreed version of the clause could not bind the PPP to repatriate the Biharis. On the issue of domicile certificates and ID cards, the MQM demand was heavily weighted against the Punjabis, the Balochis, and the Pathans, and in favour of the Muslims of Indian origin. The PPP left it to the Sindh Assembly to examine it. On the issue of census, the Muhajirs insisted on being counted separately, but the PPP, being aware that the never-ending influx of Muhajirs from India would not only drown Sindh but also tip the scale between Sindh and other province, finally agreed, perhaps reluctantly, that there should be a column in the census form to indicate the birthplace of the father. Sindh PPP negotiators had no authority to agree to this provision, which had far-reaching implications. If the father's birthplace sets one Sindhi apart from another Sindhi, then this calls into question the very concept of Pakistan, as held by the Muhajirs, whose nationalism is not land-based or birthplace based, but based on ideology. Yet, the population of Sindh was sought to be split on that absurd formulation, for working out the quota in jobs until 1993.

The demand for the cancellation of domicile certificates and ID cards issued after 1978, even though justified prima facie, was not accepted outright but referred to a committee.

Immediately after signing the PPP-MQM agreement, in December 1988, the following events took place:

- The MQM began accusing the PPP of non-implementation of the agreement.
- Secret contacts were established with the MQM by some IJI leaders from the Punjab.
- The MQM began to boycott cabinet meetings and the Provincial Assembly sessions.
- A secret agreement was negotiated between the MQM and the IJI from March 1989 onwards, was formalized in August 1989, and signed in September 1989.
- A no-confidence motion was moved against the PPP government, with the support of the MQM, in October 1989.

Coalition agreements are intended to be made in good faith between responsible political partners, and are meant to be implemented. Non-implementation of any such agreement leads only to one consequence, namely, a break-up of the coalition, and possible collapse of the government. But, implementation of such agreements always takes time. Also, since the agreement was made after the election, the PPP had to prepare the ground, not only within Sindh, but also in other provinces, and at the national level, to ensure acceptance, harmony, and understanding. Besides, the process of democracy had just started and the top most priority was to be given to the setting up of institutions. Just before the elections, tempers had run high, and so sufficient time was needed to cool down, for reflection, and for a meeting of the minds. The agreement was made by the leaders, but the people on whose behalf the agreement was signed had not even been consulted. Wide gaps in the perceptions of the Sindhis and the Muhajirs had existed, and these had to be narrowed down to facilitate implementation.

Committees were appointed to carry out an in-depth analysis of the conditions agreed upon, the problems involved, and possible options and solutions that would promote inter-ethnic harmony. Finally, solutions were to be provided in the shape of bills to be moved in the National and/or Provincial Assemblies, because they were the competent institutions to frame policies that would accommodate the MQM demands.

The impatience with which the MQM pursued its agenda, the manner in which its elected members mounted the propaganda war inside and outside the Assemblies, and entering into secret negotiations with the Opposition within a few months of signing the agreement, displayed a degree of bad faith on the part of the MQM. It was, and still is, the third largest party of Pakistan, and was expected to show patience, restraint, and political maturity in dealing with local, provincial, national, and international issues.

It is noteworthy that none of its demands pertained to rural Sindh. It had moved away from the position taken during the Altaf-Syed meetings, in general, and in respect of the rights of Sindh, in particular. Almost the entire thrust of the MQM was concentrated on the problems of the Muhajirs, assuming that either similar or even more serious problems did not exist in rural Sindh, or even if they did, then that was not part of the MQM agenda.

The MQM tried to isolate the Muhajir issues from the provincial or national issues. They refused to see these in the context of larger issues, and insisted on being treated separately, a special case, irrespective of what happens to the Sindhis or the rest of the population of Pakistan. While the MQM accused the PPP of non-implementation of the agreement, the latter took the plea that action had been initiated on many issues and, in any case, even if action had been taken, it would have been frustrated owing to the secret negotiations carried out by the MQM with the Opposition, which amounted to a breach of trust and an act of political sabotage.

MQM-IJI AGREEMENT 1989

This agreement was secretly negotiated during the currency of the MQM-PPP agreement of December 1988, and finalized in October 1989. The immediate aim was to bring down the PPP government at the centre through a no-confidence motion in October 1989. The MQM-IJI agreement aimed to achieve the goals of national integration, inter-provincial understanding, and inter-ethnic harmony. These goals were sought to be achieved through the implementation of sixteen operational conditions. The parties agreed to cooperate at the provincial and federal levels. The MQM signed on behalf of itself (and the province of Sindh) while four Punjab-based MNAs signed on behalf of the federation. The IJI team was unable to find a negotiator or a signatory from Sindh, Balochistan or the NWFP. Nor could the MQM find a Sindhi, belonging to any party, to put a stamp of approval. In other words, the fate of Sindh was decided without involving a Sindhi. The immediate goal of the secret agreement was to topple the PPP government at the centre through a no-confidence motion. Following brisk horse-trading and floor-crossing activity, the no-confidence motion was lost. Thereafter, under a coordinated strategy, the MQM defied the Sindh government while the IJI government of the Punjab defied the federal government. Failure of the no-confidence motion against the PPP government in Islamabad led to an escalation of confrontation. Finally, President Ghulam Ishaq Khan intervened, dismissed the PPP government in 1990, and ordered fresh elections within three months. The ensuing elections were rigged.[11]

Whereas the ill-fated MQM-PPP agreement contained fifty-seven conditions in December 1988, that with the IJI concluded six months later contained only sixteen conditions. The inference could be that the remaining forty-one conditions were either implemented by the PPP, or were too frivolous to be included in the MQM-IJI agreement. The MQM dropped its demand for cancelling the domicile certificates and ID cards issued through fraud or otherwise to the Punjabis and the Pathans. Emphasis was shifted from providing jobs for the locals (the Sindhis and the Muhajirs) to the combined opportunities, jobs, and common interests of the Muhajirs, the Punjabis, and the Pathans living in Sindh. The MQM was to be consulted for all appointments in Sindh. Both parties felt that the Muhajirs were in a majority in Sindh, and, therefore, in the next census (1991) they should be separately counted, not only on the basis of their fathers' birth place, but also on the basis of their distinct mother tongue. On that basis alone was the voters list to be prepared and job quotas distributed. The agreement fixed Karachi's population as ten million, and called for allocation of resources on this basis. The 'stranded Pakistanis' (Biharis) in Bangladesh were to be issued Pakistani passports, and the MQM would sit on the board to supervise the repatriation.

The agreement was to complete its third anniversary in August 1992, but it fizzled out in June 1992, when the MQM quit the coalition, following the army crackdown against MQM terrorism.

The MQM had surrendered forty-one conditions as a trade-off for dubious promises which were never fulfilled. It surrendered more ground for immigration into Sindh from the Punjab and the Frontier. The IJI was aware that the census on the basis of ethnic groups would eventually divide and disintegrate the country. It had to discontinue the census in the preliminary phase in 1991 amid charges of rigging made by the Muhajirs against the Sindhis, and vice versa. The stage was set for a bloody showdown. To prevent this from happening, the army had to be called in May 1992.

In the agreement, the MQM represented Sindh but its contact with rural Sindh was non-existent. Its focus was urban Sindh and the Muhajir community. Following the crackdown, a split within the MQM ranks began to show. Altaf Hussain fled into exile to escape arrest. The MQM president, Azim Tariq, its secretary-general, Salim Shahzad, MNA Dr Imran Farooq, and scores of other leaders went underground.[12]

While sharing power in 1990-92, the MQM was the senior partner in the coalition in Sindh and yet it was deprived of its claim to the slot of the chief minister because it had opted to stay as a separate ethnic party in preference to joining a mainstream party at the provincial or federal level. Its self-imposed isolation compelled it to accept Jam Sadiq Ali as the chief minister, even though the latter had no party and his only qualification was his ability to put together a patchwork coalition by using all fair and foul means, including intimidation and horse-trading. That the MQM, as a party of educated people, urban elites, and a politically conscious community should have served under him was a sad reflection on its political vision. Thus, the MQM-IJI agreement of 1990 ended in disgrace, without any condition having been implemented, except the repatriation of sixty-three families of 'stranded Pakistanis' to Mian Channu in the Punjab. The repatriation came to an abrupt halt. In 1999, they were declared non-Pakistanis by the same ruling party (PML-N).

THE ABORTIVE MQM-PPP DIALOGUE 1993-96

The Sindhi-Muhajir dialogue had already experienced three abortive phases. The first phase, in 1986, was a trial phase between the MQM and the Jiye-Sindh, marked by a fanfare of 'Sindhi-Muhajir *bhai bhai*' and 'Altaf-Syed *bhai-bhai*' slogans, and by expressions of goodwill between the two communities occupying the same piece of land and sharing common interests in the political future and economic well-being of Sindh. Unfortunately, these pious hopes and great expectations remained unfulfilled following the phenomenal success of the MQM in the elections of local bodies in 1987, and of the Provincial and National Assemblies in 1988.

The second phase, beginning with the MQM-PPP coalition agreement in 1988, ended inauspiciously in 1989, leaving a trail of bitterness and rancour among the parties. The PPP may have had a power base in the Punjab, but its leadership was Sindh-based and so was its overwhelming support. Besides, the coalition agreement was negotiated entirely by the Sindhi component of the PPP, mainly with the idea of providing a bipartisan and fully representative administration to the troubled province of Sindh. The impatience of the MQM with regard to the non-implementation of the fifty-seven conditions of the agreement brought an end to the coalition in less than a year. The MQM also played a significant part in the dismissal of the PPP government in 1990. The ensuing elections (1990) were rigged by the establishment to keep the PPP out of power, both at the centre and in Sindh. The MQM may not have participated in the rigging, but it reaped the harvest by entering into a coalition with the rivals. This was enough to indicate an anti-PPP prejudice within the MQM. Since the PPP was the most popular party in Sindh, this prejudice was seen and interpreted as an anti-Sindhi posture adopted by the MQM. Such a posture by a party that existed and thrived in Sindh contributed to the hardening of positions taken by the Sindhis in future negotiations.

When the MQM occupied a position of authority, it made its presence felt through political terrorism against its opponents, who might have belonged to any community, including the Muhajirs themselves. In 1992, MQM terrorism invited army action, which dealt a severe blow to the terrorists, exposed their torture cells, and brought a premature end to the MQM-IJI agreement in June 1992. In 1993, the IJI government was also dismissed.

In 1993, the establishment, having been disillusioned with the performance of the IJI, did not interfere in the elections. Predictably, the PPP won the round, and it formed the federal government in coalition with the PML (Chatha group), and the Sindh government on its own strength. It did not need the MQM in any coalition partnership, but since the MQM had an overwhelming mandate from urban Sindh, it had to be accommodated in the power structure in the interest of peace, stability, harmony, and smooth functioning of the administration. So, negotiations between the MQM and the PPP were restarted, and in order to make the dialogue meaningful, each side was to keep in view the past history of the other party, and also to ensure that the accord had a reasonable chance of success.

In conducting the dialogue, the MQM did not rush into making demands. Instead, it took time to do its homework to prepare a solid base for its demands. On 4 June 1994, it issued a 32-page memorandum, delivered to newspaper offices, setting forth its position on the issues pertaining to the Muhajirs in Sindh.[13] A summary of the preamble is as follows:

Over 15 million Muhajirs constitute 50 per cent of Sindh's population[14]; more than 75 per cent provincial revenues are derived from cities like Karachi, Hyderabad, and Sukkur, but only about 10 per cent is spent on the development of these urban centres. During 1988, Rs 702 million were recovered from Sindh as excise duty and taxes, out of which Karachi alone contributed Rs 543 million. During 1987-88, Karachi's contribution towards federal revenue was more than 60 per cent but hardly 5 per cent was spent on the city. In the same year, Karachi contributed Rs 37,509 million as custom duties which constituted 41 per cent of the total federal revenue. During the same period, Karachi contributed 3,592 million or 52 per cent of the total central excise duty of Rs 6,849 million. On the political front, the share of the Muhajirs in the National and Provincial Assemblies has been reduced to 50 per cent of their actual strength.

The demands made to mitigate the wrongs and to compensate for the deprivation suffered by the Muhajirs were listed as under:
1. Operation clean-up directed (by the army) against the Muhajirs (in 1992) be discontinued.
2. Representation of the Muhajirs in the Provincial and National Assemblies and the Senate should be increased in proportion to their population. Census should be conducted by an impartial authority.[15]
3. Enhance urban quota in federal and provincial services from 7.6 to 9.5 per cent and from 40 to 50 per cent respectively.
4. Positions of the governor and the chief minister should be shared equally, in rotation, by the Sindhis and the Muhajirs.
5. Urban areas of Sindh should receive a proportionate share of the federal and provincial funds for development.

6. Undo the bifurcation of the Hyderabad Municipal Corporation, and the creation of the Malir district and the Lyari Development Authority.
7. Immediate repatriation of 'stranded Pakistanis' in Bangladesh.
8. Grant of autonomy to municipal bodies.
9. Reinstate all employees arbitrarily sacked from federal, provincial, and semi-government services.
10. Compensation be given to thousands of MQM activists who were killed, kidnapped, arrested, tortured, and maimed, and their properties looted and burned, during the previous two years (mostly during the IJI-MQM coalition rule).
11. An independent commission to conduct an enquiry into the looting by investigation teams of household goods, jewellery, and other valuables worth billions of rupees, and the victims be compensated for their losses.
12. Hold a judicial enquiry into custodial murders by the army, law-enforcing agencies, and Haqiqis, and punish the guilty.
13. All cases against MQM activists be withdrawn unconditionally.
14. Muhajir recruitment in police according to the population.
15. Admission of the Muhajir students in professional institutions in the rural and urban areas.
16. Hold a judicial enquiry into massacres of the Muhajirs, and the looting and burning of their houses.
17. Assignment of B-Class jails to the MQM prisoners.
18. Cease raids on the MQM headquarters, and looting of the MQM properties; stop political victimization, restore telephone lines, and pay full compensation.
19. Army action was to be used in rural Sindh against criminals. But, it was used in urban Sindh against the MQM to break the party. Stop operation clean-up. A judicial commission be set up to determine the excesses of the army.

These demands were not made face to face, as was done in 1988, but were issued as a memorandum in the press for public consumption. Apparently, the two parties were not on talking terms with each other. The MQM was still basking in the sunshine of its alliance with the PML(N). It had not yet been able to live down the various disclosures that had been made regarding the way it was 'delivered' to the PML(N) in 1989 by General Aslam Beg.[16]

Mercifully, the list of the MQM demands on the PPP in 1994 was very modest as compared to the one prepared in 1988. It had omitted the demand of its recognition as a separate nationality, knowing that it had been rejected by the PPP in 1988. Regarding the repatriation of 'stranded Pakistanis' in Bangladesh, the PPP had diluted it in 1988 to the point where it had become meaningless. But, since the PML(N) had accepted the demand in 1990, albeit in a tongue-in-cheek manner, the matter was revived again. Most of the demands made in 1994 pertained to the consequence and grievances arising out of the army action carried out under the PML(N) while the MQM itself was a part of the ruling coalition.

The PPP government in 1994 could not possibly redress the grievances arising out of the army action in 1992. However, the army did continue its presence in Karachi because the city was still in turmoil. This prompted General Naseer Babar to crack down on the MQM once again in 1995. Incidentally, 1994 was the year in which the MQM had mounted the demand for Jinnahpur which had created an uproar in the National Assembly and the Senate. These developments in combination had undermined the value of the memorandum issued by the MQM containing its charter of demand. In fact, tempers in Sindh had reached a boiling point and, in that scenario, no party was in a frame of mind to take the MQM charter of demands seriously. If the MQM had been serious about its own demands, it would have refrained from terrorism, restrained itself from issuing the threats of Jinnahpur, and created a climate conducive to a political dialogue. A charged atmosphere was hardly propitious for any dialogue. In spite of these negative inputs, the PPP authorized Chief Minister Abdullah Shah to explore a meeting

ground with the MQM in the interests of peace and harmony in
Sindh. On 23 December 1994, *Dawn* noted:

> It was agreed during the Wednesday (21 December 1994) meeting
> that all efforts would be made jointly to defuse tension and restore
> peace and tranquility. The onus of this must necessarily be with the
> MQM, which will be expected to restrain its militants, just as the
> government side must also avoid any provocative actions. For the
> PPP, it has been a major effort to enter into talks with a party
> which was once regarded as harbouring terrorists. It should be
> remembered that the PPP has to be mindful of Sindhi nationalist
> sentiment, and that has its own pressures and limitations. The party
> has always had to contend with the lobby which has been against
> any deal with the MQM. If violence continues now even after
> negotiations have been started with the MQM, the PPP's hawks in
> Sindh would be strengthened. The MQM's active support will,
> therefore, be needed to isolate trouble makers and bring the situation
> in Karachi to something approaching normality.[17]

Expectations rose as the dialogue proceeded. *Dawn* noted
some headway:

> ...some tangible progress as was the case on Monday. Not only has
> the government accepted two of the MQM's demands, the non-
> acceptance of which was proving to be a sticking point in the talks,
> reportedly it has also agreed to implement the MQM's 10-point
> charter of demand before 4 February 1995 when the next round of
> talks is scheduled to take place... The two demands accepted, relate,
> firstly, to the announcement earlier this month of 'head money' for
> the arrest of those MQM leaders who are said to be in hiding, and,
> secondly, to the trials within jail premises of arrested MQM leaders
> charged with specific offences. The head money notification is to
> be withdrawn and the trials are now to take place in open court...
> while the Sindh government is called upon to show some
> generosity... the MQM has refused to put on the robes of
> moderation...[18]

Unfortunately, the dialogue made little progress, as commented
by Ayaz Amir in his Islamabad diary:

Admittedly, it is difficult to negotiate with a movement which draws sustenance from a very narrow chauvinism and whose actions proclaim that it is committed to the use of violence for furtherance of its aim. In Karachi, however, what is generally understood by a political solution does not necessarily have to result from negotiation...[19]

On February 26, *Dawn* lamented that 'The dialogue which had been started last year has more or less fizzled out'.[20] *Dawn* analysed the issue further, and said:

...when the army began its 'operation cleanup' in June 1992, the MQM, or at least its top leadership, gave every sign of being psychologically devastated. That was the time to make political overtures to the MQM but the moment passed and soon the MQM lost its fear of the army and there was a resurgence of violence in Karachi.[21]

Whether this hypothesis would have worked or not, the opportunity was missed by the PML(N) which remained a passive spectator of the scene till it was dismissed in 1993. By the time the PPP came into power, the MQM had already regained its breath, lost its fear of the army, regrouped, and resumed its terrorism. The MQM-PPP negotiations were foredoomed to fail because the MQM was simultaneously conducting a dialogue with the PML(N). The initiative for such talks had been taken in September 1994. Nawaz Sharif and his negotiating team visited London in March 1995 to re-establish the thread broken by the army action of 1992, and strike a political bargain with Altaf Hussain.[22]

It seems that the MQM was sailing in two boats at one and the same time, each pulling in the opposite direction. Apparently, the PML(N) offered a better deal which led to the breakdown of the PPP-MQM dialogue. The deal would reveal itself after the dismissal of the PPP government in 1996, which brought Nawaz Sharif back into power in 1997. Looking back, it appears that sitting in London, Altaf Hussain had learnt the fine art of political bargaining. Little did he realize that a party which is not in power (as the PML-N was in 1995-96) would be extra generous in offering lucrative terms. Besides, since Nawaz Sharif did not represent Sindh, he could afford to make tall promises and offer attractive incentives to Altaf about Sindh, knowing full well that when it came to the implementation, he could easily put the blame on the Sindhis for not co-operating, and get away with it. In short, this kind of bargaining betrayed the political naivete and inexperience of the top MQM leaders, who, in their greed for power, were blinded by the deceitful offers made by the leaders of the PML(N). To make such offers appear genuine, the PML(N) cleverly put a cloak of secrecy on them on the plea of preventing a possible Sindhi backlash.

MQM-PML(N) AGREEMENT 1997

Late in 1996, the PPP government was dismissed by President Farooq Leghari, and fresh elections were scheduled to be held within ninety days. As expected, the PML(N) captured the National Assembly with a heavy mandate,[23] while in Sindh, the PPP was returned as the largest party, but without an absolute majority. Once again, the MQM moved closer to the centre of power, namely, the PML(N), and signed a brand new coalition agreement in order to keep the PPP out of power in Sindh. This agreement was signed in February 1997, but its terms were not announced. The reasons for keeping it secret could have been to avoid a Sindhi backlash in case some of the conditions were considered to be against Sindhi interests and, secondly, to evade a public debate on contentious issues. Keeping public issues shrouded in secrecy was an exercise in bad faith. Since some of the issues were highly contentious and controversial, as it turned out later, both the PML(N) and the MQM were sacrificing the interests of Sindh at the altar of party interests.

As events unfolded, the ill-advised agreement proved to be devastating for the MQM. Allegations of non-implementation were made against the PML(N) not long after it was signed.

MQM Senator Aftab Shaikh complained on 14 October 1998 that in February of the same year, 272 MQM activists were murdered, and yet no one had been arrested. He also cited examples of non-implementation of the following commitments.[24]

1. Opening up of the 'no-go' areas.[25]
2. Rehabilitation of displaced persons of the 'no-go' areas.
3. Establishment of a judicial commission to probe into the extra-judicial killings of MQM activists.
4. Equal development of both the rural and urban areas of Sindh.[26]
5. Equal representation in the provincial cabinet.[27]
6. Parity with the Sindhis in representation in the administration.
7. Participation in the Law and Order Committee.
8. Compensation to the victims killed during the PPP regime (in 1995-6) when General Naseer Babar was the federal interior minister.
9. Repatriation of 'stranded Pakistanis' (Biharis).
10. Release of persons illegally detained for alleged crimes.
11. Opening of the Khokhrapar border with India.

Assuming that all these allegations made by the MQM(A) against the PML(N) were correct, and there is no reason to doubt the credibility of ex-Senator Aftab Shaikh, the above list of non-implementation of the agreement by the PML(N) reveals a complete and total disregard of the commitments made by the senior partner. That being the case, it seems that the MQM(A) was taken for a ride for a good two years (1997 and 1998). This would have continued for another three years, or even more, at the expense of the vital interests of Sindh, had the MQM not been subjected to humiliating accusations made by the PML(N) members, individually and collectively, both in the National Assembly and outside it.[28] Pushed to the wall, the MQM walked out of the coalition on 21 August 1998, and denounced the agreement. Senator Aftab Ahmad called a press conference and listed the grievances of the MQM, accusing the government of bad faith with regard to the terms of the agreement. That was followed by an unending series of talks, including the visits of Prime Minister Nawaz Sharif and Chief Minister Liaquat Ali Jatoi to London to pacify Altaf Hussain. However, nothing tangible came out of these talks. The coalition agreement was kept suspended in order to keep the door open for the re-entry of the outgoing MQM ministers.

Then occurred the tragedy which turned the tables. On 17 October 1998, Hakim M. Said was murdered. During investigation, it was revealed that the arrested suspects belonged to the MQM(A). One of the arrested MQM(A) activist, named Fasih, died in custody during the investigation. Involvement of the MQM(A) in the murder was becoming obvious to the people at large. There were theories and counter-theories advanced in relation to the cause of Fasih's death. The MQM attributed it to police torture. The police theory was that he poisoned himself to avoid making a confession. An award of half a million rupees was announced for any clue leading to the arrest of the culprits. A list of terrorists was prepared for arrests in connection with the murder.

On 23 October, following a snap decision, the MQM(A) abruptly and unceremoniously rejoined the coalition with the PML(N) government. Political analysts linked this panic decision to the emerging scenario following the murder of Hakim Said, to forestall any intended action to implicate the MQM. This return to the coalition took place unconditionally, as none of the demands made at the time of exit from the coalition had been met. Some well-meaning observers, while welcoming the re-entry of the MQM, were still at a loss to understand as to how this sudden about turn would contribute to the clearing of the mess that had been created in Karachi by the very people who had been at the helm of affairs for quite some time.[29]

On 29 October 1998, Prime Minister Nawaz Sharif bewildered the MQM by issuing a firm and forthright ultimatum to them, in a news conference, to hand over the accused persons within three days. These were named as: Aamirullah, ex-ASI Naushad, Arif Khan, Masroor, Asif Chitta, Wahab Bandhani, Ajmal Pahari, Rehan, and MPA Zulfiqar Haider. The prime minister claimed to possess 'credible and incontrovertible' evidence of the MQM's involvement in the murder, and warned that if the accused persons were not handed over within three days, there would be a 'parting of ways'.[30]

The MQM ignored the ultimatum and stood expelled from the coalition. In retaliation, they accused Prime Minister Nawaz Sharif of killing Hakim Said and MQM activist Fasih. Besides, Altaf Hussain asked MQM activists to go underground.[31] This was a response typical of a wounded lion instinctively seeking to strike back. Pakistani politics at the highest level had degenerated into a tribal warfare.

Many questions arise out of the diabolical and ill-fated secret partnership between the MQM and the PML(N):

1. If the agreement was secret, whom were they hiding it from? From the Sindhis? Did it hurt the Sindhis? If it did, it was doomed to failure, which is what came about.

2. If non-implementation of the agreement was a pre- planned strategy, as seems to be the case, then it was a political gimmick, a fraud, and a trick to misguide the people of urban and rural Sindh.

3. Both partners knew beforehand that many clauses in the agreemet could not be implemented. Yet, if they signed it, they did so to occupy ministerial positions, to enter the corridors of power, to keep their rivals out of power, to collect the price to the tune of millions, and to legitimize fascist methods and recovery of *bhatta*.[32]

4. The agreement was anti-Sindh in tone, tenor, content, and intention, calculated to keep the majority party in Sindh out of power. This real goal of the agreement was exposed in October 1998, when, on the collapse of the PML(N)-MQM(A) coalition, the opposition was denied the opportunity to form the government, and Sindh began to be ruled from Islamabad, up until the army takeover on 12 October 1999.

5. The agreement was one-sided because it did not stipulate that the MQM would abandon terrorism, of which the PML(N) was aware. It gave the MQM the licence to kill.

If the history of coalition partnership is any judge, it casts a shadow of gloom and hopelessness. Any dialogue to be meaningful and worthwhile must begin with a clear conscience and a sense of commitment to Sindh. The dialogue between G.M. Syed and Altaf Hussain in 1986 was within the framework of Sindh, but it took place between two alien parties, having separate agendas and divergent goals. The election results of 1988 weaned away the MQM from the Jiye-Sindh, which had lost the elections to the PPP. The goal was changed to share power with the PPP as its coalition partner. In the process, the Jiye-Sindh-MQM dialogue was allowed to wither away. This power game, with its ups and downs, continued upto 1998 when the MQM quit, or was expelled from the coalition with the PML(N).

What is the balance sheet of coalition agreements and partnerships? The MQM got entangled in the power game, acted rashly, antagonized the Sindhis, delivered no benefits to the Muhajirs, antagonized the army, and received repeated poundings and psychological shocks. Were any lessons learnt from these experiences? Altaf Hussain has said that (a) Sindh has become a colony of the Punjab, (b) the Punjab was creating hatred between the Sindhis and the Muhajirs, (c) the Punjab engineered the language riots in 1972 to create a Sindhi-Muhajir rift, and (d) if the establishment did not stop killing the Muhajirs, he would have no option but to launch an armed struggle and seek support from a neighbouring country, as the MQM was close to making a unilateral declaration of independence (UDI).[33]

Altaf Hussain claims to be the spokesman of the Muhajirs.[34] He neither speaks nor claims to speak for the Sindhis who constitute the majority in Sindh.[35] Sitting in London, and without consulting the Sindhis, how can he issue a UDI? The majority of the Sindhis supported the PPP since 1970, and the PPP stands for the federation of Pakistan. Minority Sindhi groups follow different political programmes, varying from the federal, to the confederal, to seeking outright independence.[36] Thus, Sindhis neither share the political line contained in Altaf's threat, nor have they been consulted by him. If Altaf was convinced about the Punjabi domination of Sindh, he should not have shared power with them, and if he did, he should have done that openly and exposed their domination, rather than signing secret agreements with them. If he wants independence for the Muhajirs only, he should have been more specific about it. By threatening to wage war against Pakistan, and inviting a neighbouring country to support him, Altaf has insulted his forefathers who rendered sacrifices for Pakistan. Finally, his ultimatum is a challenge to the Muhajir community of Sindh whose loyalty and commitment to the ideology of Pakistan have been put to a severe test. They must pinpoint the provocation which led to Altaf's ultimatum. The provocation is said to be the killing of the Muhajirs. But, the MQM has constantly made this complaint ever since its creation. Only the killers have changed—namely, the Sindhis, the Pathans, the Punjabis, the PPP, the IJI, again the PPP, the PML(N), the police, the rangers, and finally the army. Does it mean that everyone in Pakistan is out to eliminate the Muhajirs, if Altaf is to be believed? There seems to be something wrong with the Muhajir label. Why not get rid of the label and join the mainstream? If that can happen, it will be the end of the dialogue on an ethnic basis—the dialogue which has created so much suspicion, so much bitterness, and so much intolerance.

MQM–Jiye-Sindh: Second Honeymoon

This agreement was signed in Karachi in July 1998 between the MQM and the Jiye-Sindh leaders. The MQM was represented by Anis Qaimkhani, Anis Advocate, Dr Farooq Sattar, and Shoaib Bukhari. The Jiye-Sindh was represented by Imdad Muhammad Shah, Bashir Khan Qureshi, Abdul Waheed Aresar, Jalal Mahmood Shah, and Shafiq Muhammad. Under the agreement, a joint committee was formed to formulate a common strategy for joint action on major issues, namely, the Kalabagh dam, the share of Sindh in the National Finance Commission award, and the 1998 census. Upto now, no joint action strategy has been formulated, nor is one expected. Both sides entertain strong reservations about their respective population ratio.

To make the accord meaningful, the two sides had to sort out contentious issues that had widened the gulf between them for long. For example, the MQM demands a separate nationality. It has often threatened to divide Sindh, and this threat is directed at the Sindhis. Besides, the MQM insists on repatriation of 'stranded Pakistanis' (Biharis) and the Jiye-Sindh (the entire Sindh) opposes this demand. The MQM has to disown terrorism and expel militants from its ranks. It has to discontinue secret deals which hurt the interests of Sindh. On the other hand, the Jiye-Sindh's goal is the creation of Sindhu Desh and the MQM, since signing the agreement with the JS, has been condemning the Punjab for treating Sindh as a colony. It has to define its position whether it wants autonomy within the federation, or seeks a confederation, or outright independence. In that context, it has to clarify what does the unilateral declaration of independence (UDI) imply, and which foreign power is Altaf Hussain going to invite to help him in his struggle for independence from Pakistan. All other Sindh-based parties have taken concrete action in seeking autonomy, while the MQM's contribution is limited to issuing statements and threats which can be easily dismissed. Being the most organized and well-knit Sindh-based party, it was also expected to take some concrete action, failing which no one would take it seriously on this issue.

To sum up, the MQM has been in confrontation since its inception with every government, both in Sindh and at the centre. It fell out with the PPP government in Karachi and Islamabad in 1989. It issued a warning to the military government of General Pervez Musharraf in January 2000 of waging a war with the help of a foreign power, and of making a unilateral declaration of independence. The history of this party is there for everyone to observe and judge. The performance has to be judged on merit, which includes its patriotism, terrorism,[37] secretive and underhand deals, threats of division of Sindh, and threats of waging a war and issuing a UDI. Its founder and chief, Altaf Hussain, and his senior advisors, Dr Imran Farooq and Saleem Shehzad, are sitting in London, in exile, 6000 miles away from home, issuing statements and policy directives to the party by telephone and e-mail. All the governments of Pakistan, since 1992, consider them proclaimed offenders. Their resilience, power of endurance, and capacity to absorb shocks are remarkable and unmatched. They have bounced back every time they have faced adversity. They have changed the name from Muhajir to Mutahida to join the mainstream, but this change is more tactical and cosmetic than serious and meaningful. No non-Muhajir has joined the party[38] because only its name has changed, but the image remains the same, which is ethnic, terrorist, secretive, chauvinistic, separatist, undependable in partnerships, extortionist,[39] etc. These labels are too old, too firm, too damaging, and too devastating to be erased by mere cosmetic changes.

NOTES

1. In 1979-80, Altaf Hussain launched himself in Muhajir politics by burning the Pakistani flag at the *mazar* of the Quaid-i-Azam. He was arrested, put on trial, then released. He went into exile in the USA. The Muhajirs forgot the flag burning incident. (p. 84, Shahid Kamrani: *Sindh Ka Manzarnama*).
2. The Jamaat-i-Islami joined Ziaul Haq to provide religious underpinning to the military regime.
3. General Zia had developed an understanding with G.M. Syed by paying some special attention to him. For details, please see General Jahan Dad's revelation in his book, *Pakistan-Leadership Challenges*, OUP, Karachi, p. 255. Rahim Bux Soomro, an ex-minister of Sindh, revealed to me on 8 August 2000 that he arranged two meetings between Zia and Syed, and that he encouraged Syed to approach Zia to get two jobs for Syed's family members, and that Zia obliged.
4. Shahid Kamrani, *Sindh ka Manzarnama*, p. 86.
5. Ibid., p. 96.
6. Ibid., p. 102.
7. The IJI was midwifed by the ISI by combining the PML (N), the JI, and other groups to defeat the PPP.
8. The PML (N) fared poorly in the Punjab in the National Assembly elections. So, it used the slogan '*Jaag Punjabi Jaag*' for the Provincial

Assembly elections, which took place two days later. The slogan worked wonders, and the PML(N) won a majority.

9. At that point, the MQM had claimed that there were twenty-two million Muhajirs in Sindh which meant that they would be in a majority in the province and consequently, would be entitled to a major share in the jobs, admissions, and political representation in Sindh.

10. This was a prelude to the demand for the division of Sindh.

11. Election rigging was admitted to by the caretaker Prime Minister G.M. Jatoi and General Mirza Aslam Beg. Rs. 140 million were distributed among the Muslim League candidates, including Nawaz Sharif and Pir Pagaro. Involvement of the ISI in the rigging was also disclosed by General Beg.

12. Azim Tariq surfaced later in 1992, and since he took a soft line, he was murdered. Dr Imran Farooq and Salim Shahzad surfaced in London in 1999, and as hardliners, they man the top executive posts in the MQM.

13. The *News International* of 5 June 1994 published a summary of the 32-pages memorandum of the MQM.

14. From twenty-two million claimed earlier, they reduced their population voluntarily to fifteen million. The 1998 census indicated that their population was about 7.5 million. The MQM has rejected that figure.

15. Census was conducted by the army in 1998, according to which the Muhajirs were estimated to be about 25 per cent of the population of Sindh. This was rejected by the MQM which claimed a majority in Sindh.

16. See M.B. Naqvi's article in *Dawn* of 23 April 1994.

17. *Dawn*, editorial (extract), 23 December 1994.

18. *Dawn*, 25 January 1995 (editorial comment).

19. Ayaz Amir, 'Islamabad Diary', *Dawn*, 26 February 1996.

20. *Dawn*, 26 February 1996 (editorial extract).

21. *Dawn*, 29 February 1996 (extracts from editorial).

22. *Dawn*, 20 March 1995, report by Athar Ali.

23. PML(N) got 12 per cent of the listed votes.

24. The agreement was kept secret until the MQM leaders began to allege non-implementation of the conditions, which began to be revealed one by one.

25. The MQM(H) had allegedly taken control of some areas in Landhi, Malir, etc. where the MQM(A) leaders, including their elected members, could not enter. The agreement provided that the PML(N) government would evict the MQM(H) from these areas and restore them to the MQM(A).

26. This meant that rural Sindh was being developed while urban Sindh was not. On the face of it, this was an inaccurate statement.

27. This was meant to claim parity with the Sindhis, if the MQM claim of being in majorily was not accepted.

28. Revelations were made by MNAs Khwaja Asif and Ejaz Shafi alleging Altaf Hussain was both bribed and compensated monetarily by the PML(N). On 29 October 1997, Prime Minister Nawaz Sharif appointed a

judicial commission, headed by a Supreme Court Judge, to probe into the alleged extra-judicial killings so that compensation may be paid to the affected people. The commission did not meet, and the probe was not carried out, but the federal government released Rs 100 million as compensation. By April 1998, 492 families, out of 706 claimants, were compensated at the rate of Rs 100,000 per family. No one was held responsible for the murders. (*Dawn*, 3 October 2000).

29. See *Dawn*, editorial of 25 October 1998.

30. See *Dawn*, 29 October 1998.

31. See *Dawn*, 30 October 1998. The accused persons were arrested, tried, and awarded the death sentence on 25 May 1999. Accused MPA Zulfiqar Haider was absconding. The High Court set aside the sentence, and acquitted the accused on 31 May 2001.

32. Revelations were made in the National Assembly by MNA Ejaz Shafi alleging that payments were made to the MQM(A). These allegations were denied. Also, ex-MQM Senator Ishtiaq Azhar revealed that Rs 600 million were sent to London by the MQM, as confided to him by Hakim Muhammed Said just before the latter's assassination.

33. Published in *Dawn* of 28 January 2000.

34. Javed Jabbar, while reviewing this author's book, *G.M. Syed-Analysis of his Political Perspectives*, on 23 December 1999, at PACC, Karachi, stated that the MQM was supported by only 20 per cent of the Muhajir community.

35. Census of 1998.

36. The Jiye-Sindh groups stand for Sindhu Desh which has been analysed in detail by the author in *G.M. Syed*, OUP, Karachi, 1999.

37. Some MQM activists have been convicted for murders and extortions. For details, see the chapter on Political Terrorism-Judicial Verdicts.

38. Mr Ali Ahmad Brohi, a Sindhi intellectual, joined the MQM on 1 September 2001.

39. Apart from *bhatta*, they recovered millions from the government, as revealed by ex-Senator Ishtiaq Azhar and ex-MNA Ejaz Shafi.

10

RELIGION AND THE STATE – I

Sindh has the unique distinction of being the birth place of Muhammad Ali Jinnah, who has been rated by some scholars as the greatest Muslim since Salahuddin Ayubi.[1] He was the founder of the largest Muslim state in the world, established against heavy odds in 1947, in keeping with the traditions of the Holy Prophet of Islam (PBUH). Both Salahuddin and Jinnah were brave soldiers of Islam. Salahuddin had a vision, and so had Jinnah, of the ultimate triumph of his faith. Salahuddin used the prevailing weapons, reinforced with his determination, to regain the glory of Islam. Jinnah used his superior intellectual faculties and negotiating skills, reinforced by the overwhelming support of the Indian Muslims, to win the battle. His formidable adversaries included the British, who ruled one-fourth of the world on the strength of their achievements in the fields of science, technology, industry shipping, and commerce. They were unmatched in their advancement in modern warfare, political evolution, economic growth, public administration, communication network, and the art of diplomacy. They had perfected the techniques of ruling peoples in Asia and Africa through centuries of trials and experimentation.

The other adversary of Jinnah was the Indian National Congress, led and guided by political stalwarts like Mohandas Gandhi, Jawahar Lal Nehru, Raja Gopal Achari, Rajendra Prasad, Maulana Abul Kalam Azad, Sardar Patel, and others. These leaders had the benefit of wisdom, statecraft, and diplomacy practiced in India for thousands of years by legendary thinkers and pioneers like Lord Krishna[2], Gautama Buddha,[3] Mahavira, Asoka, Chandergupta, Akbar the Great, and many others, tempered and updated by new developments in the contemporary world, and acquired through modern education.[4]

To wrest Pakistan from the jaws of these powerful adversaries was a feat performed almost single-handedly by Jinnah, who relied mainly on his powers of persuasion, iron will, single-minded devotion, intellectual honesty, and political astuteness. He knew better than any other Indian Muslim why a Muslim state should be established on the soil of India, and what constitutional and socio-economic shape the newly created Pakistan would take. During the crucial years of hard bargaining, he fought his battles as a sick man, and within a year of the achievement of his goal, he died. But, during this short period of one year before his death, he gave clear indications and unmistakable guidelines to the effect that Pakistan was going to be neither a *mullah*-dominated state nor a fundamentalist country. Instead, he clearly enunciated that he wanted Pakistan to be a modern, democratic state, guided by the universal principles of social justice and equality, as enshrined in Islam, and one which would keep pace with contemporary developments.

Jinnah's well considered thoughts on the future shape of Pakistan were forcefully and fearlessly projected in his memorable speech delivered to the Constituent Assembly on 11 August 1947. He said:

...if you work together in a spirit that every one of you, no matter to what community he belongs, no matter what relations he had with you in the past, no matter what his colour, caste or creed, is first, second and last, a citizen of the state with equal rights, privileges and obligations, there will be no end to the progress you will make.

...you are free to go to your temples, you are free to go to your mosques, or to any other places of worship in this state of Pakistan. You may belong to any religion or caste or creed – that has nothing to do with the business of the state... We are starting with the fundamental principle that we are all citizens and equal citizens of one state.

Now I think we should keep that in front of us as our ideal and you will find that in the course of time Hindus would cease to be Hindus, and Muslims would cease to be Muslims, not in the religious sense, because that is the personal faith of each individual, but in the political sense as citizens of the state.[5]

Compare Jinnah's words with that of Kemal Ataturk, the founder of modern Turkey:

All our troubles come from the misuse of religion... it is a weak man who needs religion to bolster his rule... Religion is a personal matter. Each citizen of the republic may decide his religion for himself.[6]

While Ataturk was lucky to have lived and translated his ideas into concrete shape in the Turkish constitution, Jinnah's thoughts were mutilated during his lifetime and his dream was frustrated after his death. The following portion of his 11 August speech was blacked out.

Now I think we should keep that in front of us as our ideal and you will find that in the course of time, Hindus would cease to be Hindus, would and Muslims cease to be Muslims, not in the religious sense, because that is the personal faith of each individual, but in the political sense as citizens of the state.

This portion, like the rest of the speech, was in conformity with the ideals of Islam. Jinnah followed the example of ideal Muslim rulers in the history of Islam. Who ordered the omission of these crucial words from the official speech made by Jinnah in the constitutional forum? Coming as it did from the founder of Pakistan, the speech had the sanctity of a proclamation, a guarantee, and a blueprint. Each and every word that Jinnah said, particularly in the Constituent Assembly, was well-considered and calculated, to lay the basis of the future constitution. Those who tampered with Jinnah's thoughts on the constitution must be held accountable for the constitutional crisis that has afflicted Pakistan, including the crisis leading to the separation of East Pakistan. The crisis still continues.

Although Jinnah's speech is quite candid, and does not admit of more than one meaning, it must have raised many eyebrows, not only in the fundamentalist camp, but also in the inner circles of the Muslim League. After all, thoughts of an Islamic ideological state must have been present in the very concept of Muslim separation. If a state was being created on the basis of Muslim nationhood, did it not imply that such a state should seek its inspiration from the pristine principles of Islam? But, these remarkable words of Jinnah are said to have come straight from his heart as he was not reading from a prepared text but making an extemporaneous speech.[7]

Similar questions arose in the mind of Jinnah's biographer, Stanley Wolpert:

What was he (Jinnah) talking about? Had he simply forgotten where he was? Had the cyclone of events so disoriented him that he was arguing the opposition brief? Was he pleading for a united India – on the eve of Pakistan—before those hundreds of thousands of terrified innocents who were slaughtered, fleeing their homes, their fields, their ancestral villages and running to an eternity of oblivion or a refugee camp in a strange land?[8]

These and similar other comments on Jinnah's speech tend to confuse the thrust of the Indian Muslim struggle for the partition of India to create a Muslim state with that of a nation-state, created on a territorial base, consisting of Muslims and non-Muslims, the former being in a majority. Jinnah's speech tried to separate religion from the Pakistan movement, which had turned emotional, and had given rise to unintended and unforeseen massacres and mass evacuation. The emotion and the tragedy had to be put behind—that had become history. The task of nation building called for a new approach, a fresh start, a reconciliation, a building up of mutual confidence, a pledge of equality and justice to the non-Muslims, a word of consolation to the Indian Muslims who had supported Pakistan, and finally,

a message of peace and harmony to neighbouring India. To
Jinnah, partition did not mean a confrontation between the two
emerging South Asian states—one Hindu and the other
Muslim—but that the two civilized, modern, liberal states, who
failed to reach an understanding to live in a united India due to
an accumulated mistrust, had decided to live as friendly but
independent neighbours. If the two states were to become liberal
democracies, as Jinnah would have wished them to be, there
was ample room for liberalism in both Hinduism and Islam, and
Jinnah knew it better than his followers who let him down.[9]

Those who questioned the constitutional implications of
Jinnah's speech had overlooked the fact that he was in fact
basing his ideas on the spirit of the charter of Medina which
Prophet Muhammad (PBUH), the great law-giver of mankind,
promulgated while setting up the state of Medina:

> To the believers whether of the Koraish or of Yathrib and all
> individuals of whatever origin who have made common cause with
> them, all these shall constitute one nation. The Jews...shall have an
> equal right with our own people...and all others domiciled in
> Yathrib shall form with Muslims one composite nation; they shall
> practise their religion as freely as the Muslims...the Jews shall join
> the Muslims in defending Yathrib against all enemies...[10]

Thus, under this first-ever written constitution of the world,
the people of multi-religious and multi-racial Medina were
bestowed equal rights, equal privileges, and equal respons-
ibilities, as citizens of the first Muslim state in history.

During his short life of one year as head of the state, a sick
Jinnah took time off from his heavy pre-occupations to visit a
Christian ceremony in a church in Karachi on 7 August 1947, as
a gesture of his assurance to that community that they were
equal citizens of Pakistan. Had he lived longer, he would have
also attended similar ceremonies of the Hindus, the Parsis, the
Sikhs, and others. However, he did meet a Hindu delegation in
Dhaka and a Parsi delegation in Quetta. His successors did not
bother to follow in his footsteps. The culture of religious

tolerance and accommodation, initiated by Jinnah, was reduced to mere lip service by his successors. Thus, Jinnah's commitment to religious pluralism and ethnic diversity was eroded by clever manipulation by orthodox Islamic elements who preached Islam's universalism but practiced narrow sectarianism. Some of them even questioned Jinnah's knowledge of Islam.[11] Jinnah did not claim to be a scholar of Islam. But, he had the clearest vision of what a Muslim state should be like in the modern world. By contrast, not a single Islamic scholar has so far produced a model by synthesizing the Islamic concept of a state with that of modern liberal democracy. Pakistani rulers and scholars have used the name of Jinnah to project their personal image and pigeon-holed him as an Islamic reformer.[12] It is true that there is nothing inherently contradictory between Islam and democracy. But, to make the two fully compatible and harmonious in the present context, certain rules and practices in traditional Islam must be subjected to *ijtihad*, which has to be a continuous exercise. This has not been possible due to the rise of fundamentalism in Muslim society.

Was Jinnah's perception of nation-building on the basis of liberalism guided by the universal principles of Islam, as elucidated in his 11 August 1947 speech in the Assembly, a part of his conviction, or was it an afterthought, or a sudden change in his outlook? To find an answer, one has to go back in history, to the evolution of the concept of a nation-state during the first half of the twentieth century. When pan-Islamist Iqbal went to Europe, he found a proliferation of nation-states in Europe which were bound by their ethnic and linguistic identities. This concept had also been adopted by the Muslims of Turkey, Iran, Egypt, and the Arab world. He found his dream of one *millat* and a united *ummah* as a political force overtaken by the rise of Turkish, Egyptian, Iranian, and Arab nationalism. Racial and linguistic unity had replaced religion as a binding element for nation-building.

How much was Iqbal influenced by these changes could be seen in his address to the Allahabad Muslim League session in 1930, where he declared that these facts, however unpleasant, could not be ignored by the Indian Muslims. People around the world were seeking nationalist solutions to their problems. Nationalism was a fact of life in all the Muslim countries, with territorial frontiers constituting an integral part of the basis of nationhood, and each one going its own separate way under the banner of its own nationalism.[13]

> True statesmanship cannot ignore facts, however unpleasant they may be. The only practical course is not to assume the existence of a state of things which does not exist, but to recognize the facts as they are, and to exploit them to our great advantage.[14]

Iqbal presented his solution by shifting his focus from pan-Islamism to Indo-Muslim nationalism in the light of contemporary developments around the world, to enable the Indian Muslims to keep pace with the changing political scenarios. His address laid the basis for the grouping of the Muslim majority provinces in western India to constitute a nation-state. The Lahore Resolution of 1940 was a re-affirmation of the same thesis, and goes beyond, by conceding autonomy and sovereignty to the federating units, precisely based on the European and Muslim world's contemporary models, in recognition of the racial and linguistic realities of the federating units.

The above discussion provides a historical perspective to Jinnah's speech of 11 August 1947, which, as can be seen, was neither a casual utterance, nor an emotional outburst, nor based on his so-called 'incomplete knowledge of Islam and an Islamic state'. Seen in restrospect, it was a well-considered and deliberate declaration, and a specific guideline for the essential pre-requisites of the newly established nation-state of Pakistan. If Jinnah had a vision of Pakistan, he surely had the vision of its constitution as well, which he revealed in the appropriate forum, the Constituent Assembly. Uprooting of Jinnah's concept has plunged Pakistan into an identity crisis and thrown nation-building into disarray.

The creation of Pakistan did not *ipso facto* build a nation. The nation had to be built by cementing the federating units, framing a constitution, and establishing institutions to strengthen democracy. Two schools of thought emerged, both contradictory and mutually exclusive, to prescribe the cementing link for the federation. The Islamists claimed that we were Muslims first and Pakistanis afterwards. The secularists claimed that we were Pakistanis first and Muslims (or Hindus, Christians, and others) afterwards. Besides, they saw no contradiction between being a Sindhi, a Balochi, a Pathan, a Punjabi, and a Bengali on the one hand, and Pakistanis on the other. The Islamists prevailed, and in consequence, the task of nation-building has not been accomplished and Pakistan became a split nation from its very inception.

Historically, Pakistan was not a civilizational entity like India, Iran, China, Egypt, etc. For establishing its identity and ensuring its integrity and growth, it had to build itself brick by brick, using tools which would work, and not those based on abstract theories which would create chaos and disharmony. Half a century after its creation, Pakistan is a picture of chaos and disharmony, which indicates that the tools used for nation building were outdated and obsolete.

As a democrat, Jinnah would not have dictated his terms to the Constituent Assembly on the type of constitution that it ought to adopt. But, with his vision, insight, and grasp of the subject, which none else possessed, he would have surely guided the course of the debate. His death deprived the Assembly of his wisdom, guidance, powerful influence, and persuasive ability. His followers in general, and Prime Minister Liaquat Ali Khan in particular, all honest men, good Muslims, and well-intentioned, did not possess the vision of Jinnah. They were a group of idealists, who were still nourishing the dream of an Islamic renaissance which, in their perception, had taken a concrete shape in Pakistan—the land of the pure—where an Islamic state would be established to serve as a model to the entire world. In this environment, charged with Islamic emotions, they created an opening for the fundamentalists, who had opposed the creation of Pakistan, to enter the constitutional debate in the print media and through public speeches in streets, but outside the elected assemblies since they had no representation in any elected forum.[15]

As long as Jinnah was alive, the fundamentalist lobby was held in check. His broadcast talk to the people of the United States, made in February 1948, was still fresh in their minds:

> The Constitution of Pakistan is yet to be framed by the Pakistan Constituent Assembly. I do not know what the ultimate shape of the constitution is going to be, but I am sure that it will be of a democratic type, embodying the essential principles of Islam. Today, they are as applicable in actual life as they were 1,300 years ago. Islam and its idealism has taught us democracy. It has taught equality of man, justice and fair play to everybody. We are the inheritors of these glorious traditions and are fully alive to our responsibilities and obligations as framers of the future constitution of Pakistan. In any case, Pakistan is not going to be a theocratic state—to be ruled by the priests with a divine mission. We have many non-Muslims, Hindus, Christians, and Parsis, but they are all Pakistanis. They will enjoy the same rights and privileges as any other citizen and will play their rightful part in the affairs of Pakistan.[16]

Had Jinnah visualized that within three decades General Ziaul Haq would run Pakistan as a theocratic state, with a 'divine mission', obtained through a fraudulent referendum, he would probably have given a time limit of a few months to the Constituent Assembly to adopt a constitution in order to prevent any future tampering with it by military adventurers and their proteges. Did he put too much trust in the ability of his successors?

On 7 March 1949, Liaquat Ali Khan moved the Objectives Resolution, which was adopted by the Constituent Assembly on 12 March after:

> ...a stimulating debate that brought out the implications of the constitution. It envisaged a state in which the principles of democracy, freedom or equality, tolerance and social justice, as enunciated by Islam, would be observed; where Muslims would be able to order

their lives in accord with Islam, and minorities could practice their religion and develop their culture; a state which would guarantee fundamental rights, including freedom of expression and association, which would secure the independence of the judiciary, and safeguard the integrity of the federation, so that the people of Pakistan may prosper and attain their rightful and honoured place among the nations of the world and make their full contribution towards international peace and progress and happiness of humanity.[17]

The debate preceding the passage of the resolution raised many issues. The rights given by Jinnah, such as equal citizenship to Muslims and non-Muslims, were washed away by the classical concept of treating non-Muslims in an Islamic state as *zimmis*, who are accorded full protection and allowed religious freedom, but are not given equal rights at par with the Muslims. Although the validity of the concept of *zimmis* is now open to debate, there has been no rational dialogue on the subject, in the light of contemporary realities and in keeping with the universal declaration of human rights, to accord equal treatment to religious minorities.

Ms Fatima Jinnah was not a professional politician, nor was she involved in the framing of the policies or laying down the guidelines for constitution-making. But, being so close to Jinnah, she knew his mind, and was in a position to probe his thoughts. She once said:

We are a Muslim state. That doesn't mean a religious state. It means a state for the Muslims... We are not a state run by priests or a hierarchy.[18]

Non-Muslim members of the Constituent Assembly, Sris Chandra Chattopadhyaya, Birat Chandra Mandal, and Bhupendra Kumar had taken Jinnah at his word and had visualized Pakistan as he did, as a modern democratic state, with sovereignty vested in the people, and non-Muslims having equal rights of citizenship regardless of their religion, caste, or creed. They protested that the Objectives Resolution ran counter to Jinnah's concept of Pakistan, proclaimed by him to be a secular state.

They claimed that had the Resolution been presented in his lifetime, its shape would have been different.

The Resolution was defended by the Muslim members, led by Liaquat Ali Khan, Sardar Abdur Rab Nishtar, Dr Isthtiaq Hussain Qureshi,[19] Mian Iftikharuddin, and others. Sardar Nishtar said that if Jinnah gave pledges to the minorities, he also gave a pledge to the majority.[20] The ulema declared that Jinnah's conception of a modern nation-state became obsolete with the passage of the Objectives Resolution.[21] Ironically, the Resolution was strongly supported by Foreign Minister Chaudhry Zafarullah Khan in a speech lasting fifty minutes. Within four years of the passage of the Resolution, Zafarullah Khan's own sect, the Ahmadis, became the target of widespread riots, politically motivated, but crushed by military action.[22] The riots erupted again during Z.A. Bhutto's rule (1972-7) as a consequence of which the Ahmadis were declared non-Muslims.

It has been argued by some Islamic scholars that Jinnah was not conversant with the Islamic legal system, its political theory, and the historical realities in their evolution, even though he was familiar with the broad principles of Islam.[23] Jinnah's ideas about the shape of Pakistan's constitution have been examined by Justice Muhammad Munir in the context of the Objectives Resolution:

1. Jinnah wanted state sovereignty to rest with the people. In the Resolution, the sovereignty rests with Allah.
2. The Resolution refers to the protection of the right of the minorities to worship and the practice of their religion, whereas Jinnah had stated that there would be no minorities on the basis of religion.
3. The distinction between religious majorities and minorities takes away from the minority the right of equality, which again is a basic idea of modern democracy.
4. The provision relating to the Muslims being enabled to lead their life according to Islam is opposed to the conception of a secular state.
5. The Objectives Resolution differs from the Lahore Resolution (1940) in which two sovereign states were demanded.[24]

All the fears expressed against the Objectives Resolution have come true. Ahmadis were declared a religious minority under the Islamic state. General Ziaul Haq used his martial law powers to shift the Objectives Resolution from the preamble to the main body of the Constitution. For eleven years, Zia ruled Pakistan as a unitary theocratic state. He enacted laws prescribing penalties and enforcing an economic system without updating it to suit the existing realities. When he found that his system was unworkable, he blamed it on his prime minister who had exposed his Islamic pretension.[25] His legacy was kept alive by Prime Minister Nawaz Sharif (1990-3 and 1997-9), who tried to further amend the constitution of 1973, already Islamized by Ziaul Haq, to make Pakistan a 'truly Islamic' state, by introducing the fifteenth amendment. However, before the amendment could be passed, he was dismissed in October 1999.[26]

In his memorable lectures, Allama Muhammad Iqbal strongly advocated *ijtihad*, but his voice has fallen on deaf ears in Pakistan, the land of his dream:

> ...the day is not far off when religion and science may discover hitherto unsuspected mutual harmonies...there is no such thing as finality in philosophical thinking. As knowledge advances and fresh avenues of thought are opened, other views, and probably sounder views than those set forth in these lectures, are possible. Our duty is to carefully watch the progress of human thought, and to maintain an independent critical attitude towards it.[27]

To Iqbal, Islam is dynamic and its claim to universalism can be sustained only through maintaining an independent and critical attitude towards its system, and update it to fit into the modern scientific mould and contemporary thought. His son, and spiritual heir, Justice Javed Iqbal, claims that his illustrious father considered an Islamic state a truly secular state.[28] He says:

Islam does not recognize the distinction between the 'spiritual' and the 'profane'. The spiritual and temporal obligations are not only connected with each other but it is incumbent on every Muslim to constantly endeavour to realize the spiritual values while performing the temporal obligations. Hence secularism is an integral part of Islam and it is for this reason the the Islamic state assimilates the qualities of an ideal secular state.[29]

Elaborating further, Javed Iqbal goes on:

Iqbal was the first thinker to give the right of *ijtihad* to an elected parliament instead of an individual. Iqbal endorsed the Turkish Parliament's abolition of polygamy in Islam as he thought that even Quranic injunctions could be held in abeyance to meet the requirements of the Muslim community. He believed that *ijtihad* should not be confined to the ulema but to experts in their respective fields like science, technology, and other similar subjects. Ulema could declare that *riba* was prohibited but they failed to offer a substitute on which modern banking should be based.[30]

Jinnah's thoughts and utterances were in perfect harmony with Iqbal's interpretations. If any one imagined that Jinnah, not himself an Islamic scholar, but a Muslim leader with a high level of education, a perfect understanding of political currents and cross-currents, a deep insight into the communal problem of India, and a vision for the future state of Pakistan, would formulate a constitutional strategy based on the orthodox interpretation of political Islam by fundamentalists like Maulana Maudoodi, or the ulema of the Deoband or the Barelvi schools in India, he was gravely mistaken. Jinnah needed no lessons in political Islam, and if he did, the thoughts of Iqbal were there to confirm his own beliefs.

While addressing the Karachi Bar Association on the birthday of the Holy Prophet (PBUH), on 25 January 1948, just months before he died, Jinnah declared that people were making mischief when they rejected the idea of an Islamic state. Some were misled by propaganda. Islamic principles today were as applicable to life as they were 1300 years ago. He insisted that the Constitution of Pakistan would be formulated on the basis of *sharia*. A few weeks later (at Sibi Darbar on 14 February 1948), Jinnah once again repeated the same theme, using almost the same ideas and words, 'It is my belief that our salvation lies in following the golden rules of conduct set for us by our great law giver, the Prophet of Islam (PBUH). Let us lay the foundations of democracy on the basis of truly Islamic ideals and principles.'[31]

The reader must note that Jinnah's concept of an Islamic state was the same as that of Iqbal. His emphasis was on democracy, underlining the sovereignty of the people who would be guided by the 'ideals and principles' of Islam. In concrete terms, this is what he believed should have been the shape of Pakistan's constitution:

1. He was opposed to a theocratic government.
2. He wanted a secular, democratic government.
3. There was to be one nation, the Pakistani nation, regardless of the individual's creed, religion, or sect; that religion would be an affair of the individual and would have nothing to do with the administration of the state.
4. Such government was to be based on Islamic principles and tradition.
5. For him Islamic principles signified a society based on social justice, equality, and brotherhood of man, tolerance, equity, justice, and fair play. He used the words Islamic socialism in a pragmatic sense.[32]

The fundamentalists twisted the logic to say that if it is what Jinnah wanted, then why was the Islamic card played up and why was Pakistan demanded for the glory of Islam? That was a propaganda ploy used by the fundamentalists. In reality, they knew the justification for the partition of India as much as Jinnah knew, and that was:

The aim of obtaining a Muslim majority area and establishing therein a government of the majority was no more than freedom from Hindu domination and running their own government in that area. That the object was to establish a religious state in the region was neither in Quaid-i-Azam's mind nor in that of Allama Iqbal. But, of course, implicit in the Constituent Assembly's power was to frame any kind of constitution it liked... But so far as the Quaid-i-Azam is concerned, he was strongly in favour of a modern secular constitution and if during Quaid-i-Azam's life, Liaquat Ali Khan had even attempted to introduce the Objectives Resolution of the kind he got through the Assembly on 25 March 1949, the Quaid-i-Azam would never have given his assent to it. The real object of Quaid-i-Azam was to save the Muslim majority areas from the political domination of the Hindus as well as to save them from economic exploitation of the kind that emerged from the facts and figures given by the Congress and the Sikhs in claiming the inclusion of Lahore in India before the Boundary Commission. Another object, perhaps a more important one, was to preserve the identity of Musalmans but, what was this identity? Had it to be defined or taken as it was at the time of the partition? Underlying the speech of the Quaid-i-Azam is the economic objective – raising the standard of living of the mass man who was grinding under poverty because partly for lack of self-help and partly his exploitation by the Hindu, he was a pitiable human being, and his lot could be improved if the Muslims of the majority areas had their own government. Thus, the primary object of establishment of Pakistan was the self-government of territory in which the Muslims would have a majority and could show to the minorities how just and equitable that government was. But, theocracy in any form he had expressly ruled out.[33]

Pakistan was created for the glory of Islam. What kind of Pakistan would bring glory to Islam? A theocratic Pakistan? A liberal, tolerant, and compassionate Pakistan? Once again, let Jinnah provide the answer:

...to ask whether Jinnah was a secularist or a fundamentalist is conceptually fuzzy and sociologically meaningless because we are taking current categories and forcing them on the people who lived over half a century ago in a different political and cultural context. Besides, to lift these terms from Western discourse, where they originated, and apply them to non-Western societies is misleading...

the more interesting question, perhaps, is what kind of Islam Jinnah would have wanted to be practiced in his state. Did he advocate what could be described a more compassionate and tolerant form of Islam, one in accordance with the most scholarly thinking within the religion yet embracing all humanity, or a more literalist, rigid Islam in confrontation with other religions?[34]

In retrospect, Pakistan was close to secularism in its formative years because of the lingering influence of its founder on some of the civilian and military rulers.[35] But, these rulers failed to carry forward the ideals of Jinnah at the popular level due to their lust for power and their failure to strengthen democratic institutions. The common man has been completely marginalized, and his basic problems have been ignored in the confusion created by an unending debate on an Islamic state versus a secular state, and the terrorism unleashed in the name of religion. There has been a flood of letters to the newspapers demanding secularism as a solution. A sample letter is reproduced:

Secularism in a Muslim country does not necessarily mean an atheistic or a materialistic political system. This assumption is quite wrong and unacceptable. Secularism is a system in which justice is guaranteed regardless of anyone's creed, race, ethnic background, religion, sect, social or political status. Pakistan is divided into different ethnic, religious and linguistic ranks. We are Arains, Rajputs, Jats in the Punjab. There are also the Punjabi-Pathans and the Hazarvi-Pathans... some smaller groups such as the Brauhis in Sindh and Seraikis in the Punjab, are also ethnically different. Then there are the Pathans in the NWFP and the Sindhis in Sindh. The Muhajirs constitute 10 per cent of the total population. In Balochistan, the Balochi and the Brauhi people have distinct identities. Similarly, the Kashmiris consider themselves separate. This ethnic composition is further differentiated due to different languages like Punjabi, Sindhi, Pushto, Urdu, Balochi, Brauhvi and Seraiki... We are Sunnites, Shiites, Christians, Hindus, and Sikhs. The Sunnites and Shiites are further sub-divided into sub-sects... different Islamic parties are striving to achieve goals of their respective sects in the name of Islam.[36]

Is it possible now to amend the constitution and secularize it within the framework of an Islamic state? The answer is yes. Islam is a universal faith, valid for all times; it has room for *ijtihad* to be able to move with the times and to deal with new situations. To begin with, a few amendments would be needed:

1. Make all citizens equal in all respects irrespective of their faith, gender, and race.
2. Replace the separate electorate with a joint electorate.
3. Strict observance of the Charter of Universal Human Rights.
4. Men and women be given equal rights in all respects— inheritance, divorce, court testimony, etc.
5. Sovereignty should rest with the parliament which should be unfettered by any *sharia* court. The parliament may seek advice from scholars, jurists, economists, scientists, etc.

NOTES

1. Akbar S. Ahmed in his book: *Jinnah, Pakistan and Islamic Identity – The Search for Saladin*; Routledge, London 1997, has this to say on p. xviii:

   Saladin and Jinnah are both known in history for their victory – Saladin recapturing Jerusalem and Jinnah winning Pakistan... Both were outsiders in mainstream Muslim society. Saladin was not an Arab in a world dominated by the Arabs and their language; indeed he was a Kurd, a tribal people with their own culture and language. Jinnah did not belong to the culture of UP and Punjab, which dominated the Muslims of India. He was from Sindh, originally Gujarat, and was a member of a minor sect in Islam. He did not speak Urdu... Both Saladin and Jinnah took on the most renowned opponents of their age... Saladin fought Richard the Lionheart and Jinnah challenged Mountbatten, Gandhi and Nehru... Saladin and Jinnah both tried to echo the ultimate leadership model for Muslims, that of the Holy Prophet (PBUH).

2. Lord Krishna (1500 BC, ninth incarnation of Hindu god Vishnu) was considered the greatest political theorist and expert in statecraft. He advised the warrior prince Arjuna (of *Mahabharat* fame), who was reluctant to wage war with his cousins fearing tragic consequences, to proceed to war as it was incumbent upon a kshatrya to go to war irrespective of consequences.

184

A TESTAMENT OF SINDH

3. Gautama Buddha, eighth incarnation of the Hindu god Vishnu, pioneer of the philosophy of ahimsa, which was used by Gandhi as a very potent weapon.

4. Mahavira, the last Tirthankar of Jainism, and contemporary of Buddha, made ahimsa an article of faith of Jainism, which inspired Gandhi. Akbar is rated as the most successful Mughal Emperor on the basis of his pragmatism, secularism, and statecraft. In his attempt to liberalize religion, he created a new religion and antagonized the ulema.

5. These are extracts from the Quaid-i-Azam's speech. Portions of his speech which guaranteed equality to non-Muslims were blacked out from publication in the newspapers.

6. Quoted from Shamee A. Khalid's letter in *Dawn*, 30 October 1999.

7. Such questions were raised by intellectuals and columnists from time to time. See Ayaz Amir's column in *Dawn*, 31 January 1988.

8. Stanley Wolpert, *Jinnah of Pakistan*, Oxford 1984, Pakistan Edition 1989, p. 340.

9. Iqbal considered an Islamic state as a truly secular state, as interpreted by his son, Javed Iqbal, in his book, *Ideology of Pakistan*, Ferozesons Ltd. pp. 2-4. Jinnah's vision of Pakistan was the same as Iqbal's. Iqbal conceived it, Jinnah achieved it.

10. Ameer Ali, *The Spirit of Islam,* Pakistan Publishing House, Reprint 1969, pp. 58-9.

11. Shariful Mujahid in his monumental work, *Jinnah—Studies in Interpretation*, Quaid-i-Azam Academy, Karachi 1981, pp. 255-6, says: 'But to expect him to synthesize the Islamic concept of state with that of the modern Western concept was to ask for the impossible. Jinnah was not cut out for that.'

12. Among the rulers, General Ziaul Haq and his sponsored politician, Nawaz Sharif, justified their fundamentalist twist to Pakistan's polity by using the name of Jinnah in their speeches and slogans broadcast on the electronic media.

13. Shariful Mujahid's article, 'Iqbal – a man of vision', *Dawn*, 9 January 1999.

14. Extract from Iqbal's speech at the Allahabad Muslim League Session (1930), quoted from 13 above.

15. Among the fundamentalist parties which had opposed the creation of Pakistan were the Jamaat-i-Islami, the Jamiat-ul-Ulama-i-Hind, the Jamiat-ul-Ahrar, the Khaksars, and other orthodox groups of Islamic scholars. Pakistan was achieved in spite of opposition from this quarter. But, the fundamentalist groups have now successfully obfuscated Jinnah's vision of Pakistan.

16. Shariful Mujahid, *Quaid-i-Azam Jinnah—Studies in Interpretation*, Quaid-i-Azam Academy, Karachi, 1981, pp. 650-1. Zia ruled Pakistan as a priest in a military uniform with a 'divine mission'.

17. Extract from the Objectives Resolution. The laws and practices, later enacted under the Constitution, using the Resolution as a guide, discriminated between the Muslims and the non-Muslims, and men and women, much against the spirit of the Resolution.

18. James A. Michener, *The Voice of Asia*, New York, 1952, p. 298, quoted by Shariful Mujahid in *Jinnah—Studies in Interpretation*, Quaid-i-Azam Academy, Karachi, 1981, p. 265.

19. Dr Ishtiaq Hussain Qureshi, a top Muslim Leaguer, had written a pamphlet 'The Future Development of Islamic Polity' in the Pakistan Literature Series in which he said, 'We have to create in our people a grim determination to live honourably like men with some purpose greater than the purpose of daily bread, higher than mere physical existence. There are incidents in earlier Islamic history of state capitalism on a very limited scale. Will it not be better to go back to these antecedents and adopt a modern and more developed form of state capitalism to develop our resources? The Russian experiment has a great deal to teach us in the methods of increasing our industrial and material power in spite of lack of capital. I am a believer, as were our jurists, in the doctrine of human labour being the real producer of wealth. All our population will have to be regimented for the purpose of reconstruction which will have to be carefully planned.' Quoted by Khalid Bin Sayed in *Dawn,* 28 November 1999. Later, Dr Qureshi became an orthodox Muslim, as is evident from the tenor of his speeches in the Parliament and his writings. It seems he surrendered his socialism under the pressures built by the fundamentalist lobby which became active after the creation of Pakistan. Even the leftist, Mian Iftikharuddin, was carried away by the strong current of the same lobby.

20. Going by Nishtar's logic, it is the duty of the majority to redeem the pledge made to the minority, and not the other way round.

21. Shariful Mujahid, op.cit., p. 55, quoting 'The Munir Report' on anti-Ahmadi riots in Lahore, p. 203.

22. Kunwar Idrees's comment in *Dawn,* 6 October 1999.

23. Shariful Mujahid in *Jinnah—Studies in Interpretation*, has made this claim on p. 255, which is debatable. Jinnah did not claim to be a scholar of Islam. All such scholars had opposed the creation of Pakistan and they were rejected by Indian Muslims who reposed full confidence in Jinnah who created a state for them. He knew better what kind of state was to be established for them.

24. Chief Justice Muhammad Munir, *From Jinnah to Zia*, Vanguard Books Ltd., Lahore. 1979, pp. 36-7.

25. Zia dismissed Prime Minister Junejo in 1988, and one of the charges was that the latter did not enforce the Islamic system.

26. Nawaz Sharif's tenure as prime minister is known for its harsh application of the blasphemy laws, condoning honour killing by suppressing the

resolution in the Senate to condemn these crimes, discrimination against women, rise of sectarian terrorism, an attack on the Supreme Court, and a campaign against the appointment of non-Muslim judges.

27. Muhammad Iqbal, *Reconstruction of Religious Thought in Islam*, Sheikh Muhammad Ashraf, Lahore, 1977, p. (vi).

28. Javed Iqbal, *Ideology of Pakistan*, Ferozsons, pp. 2-3.

29. Ibid., p. 4.

30. Javed Iqbal's speech on Iqbal's birthday on 9 November 1999, see *Dawn*, 10 November 1999.

31. Akbar S. Ahmad, *Jinnah, Pakistan and Islamic Identity—The Search for Saladin*, Routledge, London and New York, 1997, p. 197. Jinnah spoke of an Islamic state many times. Prof. A. Waheed Siddiqui counted ninety speeches made by Jinnah between 1940 and 1947, in which he spoke of the Islamic state. His concept of an Islamic state was defined and elaborated when he spoke to the Constituent Assembly—the body elected to frame the constitution.

32. Chief Justice (retd.) Muhammad Munir, *From Jinnah to Zia*, Vanguard Books, Lahore, 1979, pp. 32-3.

33. Ibid., pp. 34-5.

34. Akbar S. Ahmad, *Jinnah, Pakistan and Islamic Identity*, Routledge, New York, and London, 1997, p. 194.

35. General Ayub Khan had a secular orientation.

36. Letter by Imran Ahsan Mirza of Mianwali in *Dawn*, 29 October 1999.

11

RELIGION AND THE STATE – II

Prime Minister Z.A. Bhutto was a liberal Muslim with a secular orientation. The constitution which he gave to Pakistan in 1973 has been rated as a great achievement as it was formulated by a consensus. It was the first democratic constitution ever put into effect and one that is still holding the country together despite frequent amendments and military *coups*. But, despite his secular leanings, he had to make compromises with the orthodox lobby in order to achieve a total consensus. The Constitution of 1956, which was abrogated by Ayub Khan, had incorporated the Objectives Resolution as a preamable, declared Pakistan as an Islamic Republic, and specified that the president should be a Muslim. The president was to establish a council to make recommendations for bringing existing laws in conformity with Islam. All the Islamic provisions were washed out under the Martial Law of 1958. Ayub Khan's 1962 Constitution reduced the emphasis on *sharia* in order to discourage sectarian interpretations and the resultant controversies.[1]

Ayub Khan, being a military dictator, was able to get away with liberal laws, like the Muslim family law and the law of inheritance. By the time Bhutto came into power, the Islamic lobbies had regained enough ground to be able to influence legislation. The country had just been split into two, and to hold together the federation of the left-over provinces, the need for a national consensus on the constitution had become paramount. The Constitution of 1973 made the following Islamic provisions:

1. Islam was to be the state religion.[2]
2. The president and the prime minister were to be Muslims.

3. All laws were to be brought in conformity with the Quran and the Sunnah. No law was to be repugnant to the Quran and the Sunnah.

4. A Council of Islamic Ideology was to be formed to include, apart from Islamic scholars, persons with an understanding of the economic, political, legal, and administrative problems of the country, with at least one woman member.[3]

These Islamic provisions were introduced to provide a sense of security to the people who had felt that the separation of East Pakistan had weakened the Islamic foundations of Pakistan. However, Bhutto's urge for 'Islamic Socialism' was satisfied by laying down that:

> The state shall ensure to eliminate all forms of exploitation and the gradual fulfillment of the fundamental principle: from each according to his ability, to each according to his work.[4]

General Ziaul Haq held the 1973 Constitution in abeyance, and ruled Pakistan under the brand of Islam as he and his advisers interpreted it. He legitimized his rule in the name of Islam, by holding a referendum on 19 December 1984, which posed the question:

> Whether the people of Pakistan endorse the process initiated for bringing the laws of Pakistan in conformity with the injunction of Islam as laid down in the Holy Quran and Sunnah... and for the preservation of the ideology of Pakistan, for the continuation of that process and for the smooth and orderly transfer of power to the elected representatives of the people.[5]

A 'yes' vote was deemed to have elected General Ziaul Haq as the president of Pakistan for five years. The people of Pakistan are aware that the 'yes' vote was obtained through rigging. As his legacy, Zia completed and consolidated the Islamic provisions in the 1973 constitution. They read as follows:

Under Article 2, Islam is the state religion. Under Article 2A, the Objectives Resolution was shifted from the preamble where it served as a guideline, to the main body, as a substantive part of the constitution where it becomes mandatory. Article 31(1) makes it obligatory for the Muslims to order their lives in accordance with the fundamental principles and basic concepts of Islam. Article 62A lays down the qualification for the parliamentarians who should possess good character, should not violate Islamic injunctions (non-Muslims exempted), should possess adequate knowledge of Islamic teachings, practices, obligatory duties, should abstain from major sins (non-Muslims exempted), should be sagacious, righteous, honest and *ameen*, have not been convicted of moral turpitude or perjury. Under 203, Federal Shariat Court consisting of not more than four judges and not more than three ulema has been established with powers to decide whether any law is repugnant to the injunctions of Islam, and if so, the government will be given a notice to present its point of view. If the court finds the law repugnant, it will call upon the government to strike the law or amend it to bring it in conformity with Islam. Such law ceases to be effective from the day court decision takes effect. The appeal lies with the Supreme Court Shariat Appellate Bench consisting of three Muslim judges and not more than two ulema. Under Article 227, the laws under Quran and Sunnah become applicable to Muslims, as interpreted by various sects. Non-Muslims' personal law and status as citizens is not affected by Islamic law. Under Article 228, Council of Islamic Ideology is constituted with members not less than eight and not more than twenty, who should be experts in principles and philosophy of Islam and economic, political, legal and administrative problems of Islam. Under Article 230, the Council has to recommend ways and means for ordering Muslim's lives on principles and concepts of Islam, advise whether any law is repugnant to injunctions of Islam, recommend to bring existing laws in conformity with Islam, compile such injunctions of Islam as should be given legislative effect.

Zia's amendments gave definition of non-Muslims, set up a separate directorate for them, subjected them to separate electorates, and what is more, omitted the word 'freely' in connection with minorities professing and practicing their religion and developing their cultures from the Objectives Resolution.[6]

Did Zia really establish an Islamic state during his eleven years' long rule? His failure is implicit in his own action of dismissing Prime Minister Muhammad Khan Junejo, against whom one of the charges was that he had failed to Islamize Pakistan. Soon after Junejo's dismissal (1988), Zia perished in a plane crash. Did he have a model in mind? Knowing his orthodox bent of mind, he may have had the following model in mind:

> A legislature based on adult franchise being alien to Islam, laws would be made by the ulema. *Ijtihad* is individual, not collective. *Ijma* will take place in the assembly of experts, and not elected representatives. Non-Muslims have the status of *zimmis* who have no voice in the making of laws, are not eligible for high office or executive authority. Profit earned on savings is inadmissible. Sculpture, sketching and painting are inadmissible. A woman not observing Islamic *purdah* should be divorced. Engaged couples should not meet before marriage. Ablution is not allowed with lipstick on. Trousers must not reach below the ankles.

Kunwar Idrees collected these and other details from the depositions of scholars of various schools of Islamic thought given before the Punjab Disturbances Court of Inquiry, and from the replies of religious scholars to questions posed by an Urdu daily, and compiled then under the caption 'The Pre-Conditions of an Islamic State'.[7] Some of these provisions may seem frivolous, but these have been gathered from authentic and responsible sources. As to whether Zia would have actually enforced them, the fact is that these ideas are held by the fundamentalists and that Zia was one of them. Even if Zia is no longer alive, there are others who share these ideas. For example, in Kandahar, the Taliban shaved the heads of Pakistani sportsmen wearing shorts, which were considered un-Islamic. (*Dawn*, 16 June 2000). The Taliban have their counterparts in Pakistan. They may not get elected, but they operate in many other ways. In any case they rely on two factors, namely, Zia's provisions in the constitution, and the hope of the rebirth of another Zia. Was not the abortive fifteenth amendment of Nawaz Sharif a fulfilment of Zia's mission?

But, there are people who claim that a truly Islamic state can not be established without preconditions:

Individual and social justice, tranquility of soul and peace of mind, equality of opportunity and a narrowed down gap between the rich and the poor, a state of prosperity in which poverty stands eliminated completely, protection of life, honour and property of the masses, a corruption free administration and a pollution free political environment.[8]

Did these conditions prevail before Zia's rule? If they did not, did he attempt to create such conditions? Facts show that he did the opposite:

He committed treason by subverting the Constitution. He manipulated the judiciary in the Bhutto case. He used Islam to perpetuate his personal power. He and his friends became multi-millionaires by skimming American aid for the Afghan war of liberation.[9] He cheated in the Referendum. He planted the seeds of ethnic politics, sectarianism and nourished fundamentalism. He made non-Muslims second class citizens. He destabilized the process of democracy and destroyed the institutions. He laid the foundation of the gun culture and drug culture through his Afghan policy. He left Pakistan in shambles. All this was a gift from an Islamic reformer who ruled Pakistan under a 'divine mission'. As if that was not enough, his spiritual heirs, Gen. (retd.) Hameed Gul, Lieutenant-General (retd.) Asad Durrani, and Prime Minister Nawaz Sharif, continued his mission, sponsored the IJI and the MQM, rigged elections to wipe out the PPP, and perpetuated the Zia legacy.

Zia's Islamic provisions opened a Pandora's box. The state got itself entangled in a web of sectarian controversies among the Muslims, and the issue of the rights of non-Muslims in an Islamic state. Consequently, various religions and sects were politicized on the basis of their respective faiths, in order to acquire and safeguard their political rights. They organized themselves and trained cadres in their doctrines to be able to agitate for a representative status. That marked the beginning of the proliferation of politicized sects. In a democracy, the lawmakers enact the law and the judiciary interprets it. If the power of the judiciary goes beyond interpretation, into making and enforcing decisions, then the institution of democracy gets weakened and the religious and sectarian elite assume a dominant role. The militant and terrorist role of the religious and sectarian political parties must be seen in this context. The list of such parties, by no means complete, is given below:[10]

1. Tehrik-i-Nifaz-i-Shariat-i-Muhammad (TNSM—movement for the introduction of Muhammad's law).

2. Sipah-i-Sahaba-i-Pakistan (SSP—soldiers of the Prophet's companions – Pakistan).

3. Tehrik-i-Tahaffaz-i-Namoos-i-Risalat (TTNR—movement for the preservation of the Prophet's pre-eminence). This is an alliance of three dozen politico-religious parties.

4. Jamiat-ul-Ulema-i-Pakistan. (JUP Niazi Group—party of religious scholars).

5. Jamiat-ul-Ulema-i-Pakistan. (JUP Noorani Group—party of Islamic scholars).

6. Jamaat-i-Islami (JI—party of Islam).
This party was founded in India before independence by Maulana Abul Ala Maudoodi, a world renowned Islamic scholar. It started as a non-political party, and opposed the creation of Pakistan. For this reason, it converted itself into a political party. After independence, it became most active in denouncing Jinnah's secularism and demanding the establishment of an Islamic state in Pakistan. It joined hands with General Ziaul Haq to establish the rule of *sharia*. The party has considerable street power but its presence in the elected forum is miniscule.

7. Jamiat-ul-Ulema-Islam (JUI—party of Islamic scholars—Fazlur Rehman group). This party has significant representative status in Balochistan and NWFP, and in pockets of the Punjab.

8. Jamiat-ul-Ulemai-Islam (JUI—Samiul Haq Group—party of Islamic scholars).
9. Markazi-Jamiat-i-Ahle Hadith (MJAH—central party of the people of the Prophet's tradition).
10. Jamaat-i-Ahle-Hadith (JAH—party of the Prophet's tradition).
11. Mutahida Jamiat-i-Ahle Hadith (MJAH—united party of people of the Prophets' tradition).
12. Hizb-i-Jihad (party of the holy warriors).
13. Shia Political Party.
14. Khaksar Tehrik (movement of the servants of Allah).
15. Tanzeemul Mashaikh Pakistan (party of the divines).
16. Pakistan Sunni Force.
17. Mutahida Ulema Council (united council of Islamic scholars).
18. Mutahida Ulema Front (united front of Islamic scholars).
19. Markazul Dawat wal Irshad (centre of invitation and guidance).
20. Tehrik-i-Nifaz-i-Fiqh-Jafria (TNFJ—movement for introduction of the Jafria school of jurisprudence).
21. Sipah-i-Muhammad Pakistan (soldiers of Muhammad).
22. Tehrik-i-Jafria – Pakistan (TJP—movement of Jafria school of jurisprudence).
23. Islami-Jamiat-ul-Tulaba (IJT—party of Islamic students— student wing of Jamaati-i-Islami).
24. Islamic Democratic Front.
25. Laskhar-i-Jhangvi (The army of Jhang. Jhangvi is a leader belonging to Jhang. He has raised a private army).
26. Harkat-ul-Ansar (movement of the Ansars. Ansars were the original inhabitants of Medina who welcomed the Muhajirs from Mecca).
27. Jamiat-ul-Mashaikh (JAM—party of the divines).
28. Sunni Tehrik (movement of the Sunnis).
29. Lashkar-i-Taiba (holy warriors). They insist that the Pakistan army must cross the Line of Control to liberate Kashmir, just as India liberated Bangladesh in 1971. (*Dawn*, 9 August 2000).

30. Jamiat-ul-Mujahideen (party of holy warriors).
31. Harkatul Mujahideen (Deobandi Wahabi group).[11]
32. Hizbe Islami.
33. Harkat-ul-Jihad-i-Islami.
34. Tehrik-i-Ittehad.
35. Tanzimul-Akhwan (Brotherhood Party—stands for enforcement of *sharia* by compulsion).
36. Markaz-e-Dawa.
37. Al-Badar.[12]
38. Islami Muttahida Inqlabi Mahaz (IMIM—The united islamic revolutionary front, comprising over twenty religious groups in Peshawar).
39. Shahab-i-Milli—youth front of the Jamat-i-Islami.
40. Jaish-i-Muhammad (army of Muhammad) led by firebrand Maulana Muhammad Azhar.

There may be some more religio-political groups or parties operating underground or beyond the frontiers of Pakistan, either originating from Pakistan or infiltrating into Pakistan. All the parties or groups fall into different categories. Some are peaceful and democratic, others are militant, and yet others are terrorist. Some have been created to confront their opponents. Till recently there was no legal ban on these parties. However, of late the government of General Pervez Musharraf has taken note of the subversive activities of these organizations and has banned a number of these parties, notably Sipah-i-Muhammad Pakistan and Lashkar-i-Jhangvi. During the agitation against Z.A. Bhutto in 1977, the Pakistan National Alliance received massive support from the fundamentalist parties in urban Sindh, demanding the establishment of the *Nizam-i-Mustafa* (the Prophet's [PBUH] system of government). The Nizam-i-Mustafa movement was overtaken by General Ziaul Haq's theocratic regime. In 1988, a political coalition of the PML (N), the Jamaat-i-Islami, and other groups, called the Islami Jamhoori Ittehad (IJI), was midwifed by the ISI to 'save' the Islamic state which was in peril after General Ziaul Haq's demise.[13]

The fact that the student militia (Taliban) who control 90 per cent of Afghanistan (in 1999) were raised, indoctrinated, and trained at least partly in the religious seminaries of Pakistan should be seen in this context. The role of some Pakistani fundamentalist parties, notably the JUI and the JI, has been significant. Some of these holy warrior groups are reportedly recruited from certain Arab countries as well, and are operating in Afghanistan, Kashmir, and in Pakistan. Then there are some fundamentalist groups agitating in certain areas of the NWFP, like Dir, Chitral, and elsewhere, to replace the existing legal system with the Islamic *sharia*. If fundamentalism, sectarianism, and political violence are proliferating under the umbrella of an Islamic state, how can Pakistan blame the world for giving it a negative image and believing every propaganda gimmick employed by India to malign it?

Most of these fundamentalists disagree with one another on issues concerning basic faith, rituals, and other details. Many of them will not pray together.[14] When overtaken by frenzy, they kill each other mercilessly, including in places like mosques, graveyards, and prayer meetings. There have been brutal murders and mass killings in the Punjab, Karachi, Parachinar, Chitral, Gilgit, and elsewhere.

The Shia-Sunni controversy started immediately after the demise of the Prophet (PBUH), but it has not been resolved since and the gulf between the two sects has been widening rather than narrowing. After the Islamization of Pakistan, sectarian intolerance has reached unmanageable proportions. Sectarian terrorism flared up in peaceful areas like Chitral and Gilgit as a result of the social-uplift and health-care programmes being set up in those regions by the Ismaili community.[15]

On 26 September 1999, Maulana Azam Tariq, chief of the militant Sipah-i-Sahaba (SSP), demanded, in Multan, that Pakistan should be declared a Sunni state on the lines of the Taliban system of government.[16] This was followed by the murders of the followers of one sect by the followers of another in the cities of Sindh and the Punjab, and the crisis developed into a mini-sectarian civil war, whose origin could be traced to the fundamentalist policies of the PML (N) government headed by Nawaz Sharif and his political mentor, General Ziaul Haq. Subsequently, the centre of gravity of the Sipah-i-Sahaba shifted to Sindh. On 21 September 2000, the SSP made a massive display of their street power in Karachi to demand that the birth and death anniversaries of all Khulafa-i-Rashidin be declared public holidays. Similar displays of power were made in Hyderabad, Khairpur, Mirpurkhas, and elsewhere. (*Dawn*, 22 September 2000).

The parties and groups most active in sectarian terrorism included the Harkat-ul-Ansar, the Lashkar-i-Jhangvi, the Sipah-i-Muhammad, and the Sipah-i-Sahaba. The Harkat was active in Afghanistan and Kashmir, but later began its operations in Pakistan in concert with the SSP and the Lashkar. Their training in violence and terrorism was conducted in Afghanistan under the Taliban. Pakistan, through its own internal and external policies, encouraged the process of Talibanization of its own society and thereby weakened its own foundation.

Even a moderate newspaper like *Dawn* had to warn against the dangers posed by militant fundamentalists:

> Do we want to keep these militant organizations on our soil? If we do, we should be prepared for the international fallout and for the fact that India will always try to exploit such a situation to its advantage. If, on the other hand, we are concerned about where we stand with the international community, then something will have to be done about the militant organizations which are wedded to waging an armed struggle in occupied Kashmir. What we cannot do is have it both ways: follow our own inclinations and yet expect the international community to see things our way. It does not happen like that in the real world.[17]

Such protests were provoked by attempts made by the militant fundamentalists to dictate the foreign policy of Pakistan. Here is one example:

> Maulana Masood Azhar, one of persons released on 11 December 1999 by the Indian Government on the demand of the hijackers,

claimed that he had 600,000 fighters ready for a war with India...
He appeared before thousands of supporters at Lal Masjid
accompanied by armed guards and police escort... the crowd
chanted, 'Al-Jehad — Al-Jehad'...[18]

The greatest show of sectarian protest was staged in the time
of General Ziaul Haq in 1980 when he enacted laws to suit the
majority Sunni sect to which he himself belonged. Feeling
aggrieved, the followers of the Jafria sect staged a mass rally in
Islamabad by converging on the capital from all over Pakistan.
They spent the night in the open air, and early the next morning,
surrounded all the government secretariat buildings and
physically prevented the entry of any government functionary.
On that day, the government of Pakistan (the Federal Secretariat)
did not function, and rumours went round that the same action
would be repeated daily till the demands of the protesters were
accepted. Ziaul Haq lost his nerve, and in panic, granted some
concessions, like exemption from the compulsory recovery of
zakat, etc. His fundamentalist urges had received their first jolt.[19]

These cosmetic concessions were to prove disastrous,
inasmuch as they aggravated the existing gulf between the sects
and sub-sects, each demanding the enactment of separate laws
to suit its own faith or sub-faith. Under Zia, Pakistan
degenerated from an Islamic state to a sectarian state, and each
sect opened its own teaching centres. With a history of
disagreement going back 1400 years, the training was tuned to
aggravate hatred and mutual bitterness. These teaching centres
or religious seminaries proliferated during the eleven years of
Zia's rule and acquired extraordinary clout on the strength of
state patronage and foreign funding. Their impact and
magnitude were not realized as they operated covertly. By 1997,
such seminaries had numbered 5900 with 500,000 trainees on
their rolls.[20] Their curricula were different from normal schools,
the main emphasis being on classic religious education,
indoctrination, and military tactics.

K.K. Aziz, in his book *The Making of Pakistan—A Study in
Nationalism*, explains the historical background:

Inspiration for the creation and proliferation of these religious seminaries came from 'Dar-ul-Uloom' (house of learning) established in Deoband (India) in 1867, as a counterpoise to Sayyid Ahmed Khan's Western-oriented movement. In matters of faith, this centre was sectarian and propounding the teachings of the Hanafi School of theology. In its sphere of influence it was parochial, its reach confined to the United Provinces and Delhi.[21]

Deobandi theologians together with Jamaat-i-Islami scholars and their fellow supporters were the pioneers, indeed the founders of fundamentalism in Pakistan, after whose creation they infiltrated into urban pockets to create pressure groups, lobbies, political parties, and seminaries.

These seminaries produced mullahs who were skillful in theological hair splitting, competent in expounding the orthodoxies of their particular sect, but completely ignorant of modern movements and developments even in Islam. When these graduates left the schools and began the rounds of the countryside as peripatetic religious teachers, a great many of them in the name of spiritual guidance of the common man have lived on his blood and sweat. They have also fought religious wars against their counterparts of other schools like the Barelvis and Ahli-i-Hadith. Moreover, their purely religious training had kept them aloof and isolated and intellectually estranged from the people educated in secular schools and colleges.[22]

According to official figures, by the year 1997, besides the registered seminaries mentioned above, there were 5000 unregistered training centres, out of which 3393, housing some 3 million youths, were in the Punjab alone. At least a hundred seminaries were known to be imparting combat training in the use of lethal arms. Foreign students numbered about 10,000. Compare these figures with the 1947 figures when only 137 religious *madressahs* functioned and none of them was allowed to impart military training, and then imagine the potential of terrorism now available in the Islamic state.[23]

Each year the ranks of militants of the Laskhar-i-Jhangvi, the Harkat-ul-Ansar, the Sipah-i-Muhammad, the Sunni Tehrik, and other like-minded groups are augmented by brain-washed youths, victims of the Republic's tightening poverty and illiteracy. They are given free lodging and food and free education geared towards sect-oriented indoctrination, memorization of selected texts, emotional appeals, rhetoric, and, for many, weapons training. All this takes place in strictly patriarchal authoritarian environment overseen usually by prejudicial fantasies. Thousands of young citizens are converted into sectarian militants infused with retrogressive tendencies and sent out into the world to fight and to die for their beliefs—here in our Republic, with the Taliban forces, to Kashmir, or to wherever their particular skills can be used.[24]

Well-known and widely-read columnist A.B.S Jafri is shocked that Pakistan has degenerated into a state where sects and sub-sects prefer to identify themselves as Sunnis, Hanafis, Wahabis, Qadris, Jafris, Shias, Ismailis, Bohris, Ahle-Hadis, and many other denominations. Then he poses the question, 'Is this the state that Allama Iqbal dreamt of?' He answers the question by quoting from Iqbal's *Jawab-i-Shikwa*, in which God responds to the Muslim's complaint, by declaring that Muslims have degenerated into schisms and sects, like the Syeds, the Mirzas, and the Afghans, which have obscured their sense of direction. Jafri also wonders if this was the 'Pakistan that Jinnah made', in which religion would have nothing to do with the business of the state. His lament:

The self-defeating divisive tendencies are more prominently and ominously at work in the manner religious education is now being imparted to children in Pakistan. Every sect or subsect has its own schools... (which) plant a particular angle, or call it inspiration, to the education they provide to students who are taken at a very early stage in life, which is also delicately sensitive and im-pressionable. Unlike other educational institutions, these *madaris* are not amenable to any social or state regulations or disciplines.[25]

Jafri's concern is shared by many scholars whose verdict is based on their keen perception and a deep study of the factors that brought about the decline of the Islamic society. Here is the view of Eqbal Ahmad whose ideas, based on keen observation, left a deep impact on Muslim minds:

....Our religious parties are inheritors, unfortunately, not of Islamic tradition of humanism, universalism and aesthetics as they developed over the centuries but of sectarian disputes and textual contestation. Given a chance, they shall reduce Islam to an imagined and harsh penal code.[26]

...Before the 15th Amendment is put to final vote, it may be instructive for Nawaz Sharif to at least commission a well-rounded Ulema assembly, including in it the Barelvi and the Deobandi Mashaikh, and Sipah-i-Sahaba along with the Ahle-Bait, to prepare a blueprint of institutions, laws, and codes based on the Quran and Sunnah. Such an exercise will let the public know where this amendment shall take them, or more fortuitously, of forcing the PM to look straight into the hornet's nest he is so keen to disturb.[27]

Fundamentalists, in their attempt to turn Pakistan into a mullah-dominated state, have weakened the foundations of the state. The worst victim of this interplay of divisive forces unleashed by General Ziaul Haq has been the province of Sindh, as observed by Askari:

...The most damaging legacy of Ziaul Haq's regime is the sharp divisions created along religious, ethnic, cultural and social lines which has almost irretrievably fragmented the Pakistani society. This legacy is to be seen in its grimmest form in the present day Sindh.[28]

The interplay of divisive and mutually exclusive sects and their potential to destroy the structure of the state has been best illustrated by Justice (retd.) M. Munir:

...The net result of this is that neither Shias nor Sunnis nor Deobandis nor Ahle-Hadith nor Barelvis are Muslims, and change from one view to the other must be accompanied in an Islamic state with the penalty of death if the government of the state is in the hands of the party which considers the other party to be *kafirs*. And, it does not require much imagination to judge the consequences of this doctrine when it is remembered that no two ulema have agreed before us as to the definition of a Muslim.[29]

Almost the entire educated class, having full faith in Pakistan, as conceived by Iqbal and achieved by Jinnah, and being aware of the exploitation of religion by the opportunists, joined the chorus of protests against the rise of fundamentalism and warned against the passage of the fifteenth amendment. Dr Kamal was one of them:

> The truth is that after the passage of the fifteenth amendment, giving almost unbridled power to the federal government, the country would become neither a modern, nor Islamic, nor welfare state but would turn into a repressive and totalitarian polity where the forces of religious bigotry and intolerance will rule the roost.[30]

The political role of Muslim clerics, rather than creating a positive and constructive impact on the socio-economic and political environment, has been a negative input in many ways:

(a) The clergy stand for an ideological state which can survive only under a one-party system which they seek to establish. That is ruled out in a plural society. A single-party state is a sure recipe for disintegration of the federation. The very concept of a clergy-led party is, therefore, self defeating inasmuch as it seeks to establish a unitary, dictatorial, and totalitarian form of government, which controls the print and electronic media, imposes censorship, suppresses freedom of speech, movement, association, travel, and trade, and discriminates against non-conformists.

(b) Clergy-led parties have been intolerant to dissent, and by their very nature, violent. Examples: anti-Ahmadi riots, sectarian terrorism, etc.

(c) Clergy-led parties are divisive. They split the community into sects and compartments, each sect assumes the role of a political force, and strives to win power through terrorism, sabotage, street battles, and violence.

(d) Under compulsion of public opinion and as a constitutional obligation, some clergy-led parties like the JI, the JUI, and the JUP have entered the political process which is based on a multi-party system. Since they are not likely to come into power by democratic means, they settle down to the status of junior partners, opportunists, spoilers, and pull their strings from behind the scene. Under the cover of democracy, they raise cadres of young men to practice violence and terrorism in the campuses and against their opponents. Example: the student wing of the JI.

(e) Clergy-led parties obstruct the progress of society. They obstructed population planning programmes, organ donation, and pragmatic family laws passed by Ayub Khan. They opposed the appointment of non-Muslims as judges, supported the tribal custom of 'honour killings', and opposed *ijtihad*.[31]

(f) To inflame the passions of ordinary folk, the clergy use Friday sermons as a political platform to support or denounce state policies on intricate domestic or external issues, which should only be debated with responsibility in the appropriate political and intellectual forums.[32]

(g) The clergy manipulated the state to declare the Ahmadis non-Muslims, and to enact harsh laws on blasphemy. 'In 1995, two Christians, one a mere boy, were condemned to execution by a court for insulting the Holy Prophet of Islam. Such decisions were not based on Islamic law *per se*, but reflected several traditions.'[33] In their attempt to 'purify' Islam, they reduced it to a narrow-minded code of penalties and punishments. Akhtar Hameed Khan, a great Muslim with superhuman qualities, was victimized under the cover of blasphemy laws, which is an indication that either the law is defective or its application is flawed. This incident alone created an environment which suffocated intellectual activity and suppressed rational judgement. It closes the doors of *ijtihad* and gives a free hand to the theocrats to play havoc with the people of Pakistan.

(h) A prominent cleric (Maulana Ajmal Qadri) issued a *fatwa* that those senators who voted against the fifteenth amendment introduced by Prime Minister Nawaz Sharif (1998) had committed an offence which was punishable by death. These violent passions were incited by Nawaz Sharif who let loose the clerics to intimidate the legislators in the name of an Islamic state.

The clergy got what they wanted—an Islamic state, an Islamic constitution, rule of the *sharia*, and Islamic rulers like Ziaul Haq, and Nawaz Sharif. After half a century, what is the shape of Pakistan? A model Islamic state? Let us draw a balance sheet. One hardly finds any explorers, pioneers, or innovators who brought glory to Islam, but there are many who brought glory to Europe, America, and Japan. Maybe it is too early to expect miracles. But, how does one explain the degeneration of society? A food surplus has turned into a food deficit. Poverty, illiteracy, and a poor health care system are a challenge to a civilized state. There is proliferation of dictators, fanatics, sectarian killers, ethnic terrorists, smugglers, drug pushers, gun-runners, tax-evaders, and loan defaulters. Corruption and election rigging are a way of life. Who is responsible for this downhill slide?

When the army took over on 12 October 1999, the Islamic lobby felt threatened that their hope of converting Pakistan into a theocracy under the proposed fifteenth constitutional amendment would be frustrated. Consequently, orthodox Islamic scholars closed ranks and renewed their campaign to prevent any effort to alter any religious content in the constitution or the laws of the state. Numerous letters and articles were published in newspapers. One of them emphasized the parameters of Islamic polity as follows:

...The different organs of the state...have to be built and developed in accordance with the norms of authority, liberty, equality, consultation and justice as ordained in the Holy Quran. Man is thus emancipated from all bonds and burdens that he has forged for himself...Islamic polity based on the *shura* within the framework of equality, liberty and justice is designed to liberate man from man-made bonds and burdens that imprison him. All men have been created equal...as the inheritors of the earth and are therefore entitled to participate in conducting the affairs of the state.

...The members of the parliament...will not be divided along party lines, nor would they be bound by their party whips. They would be free to vote according to their conscience...in case there arises any conflict and difference between...the parliament and an individual...the matter will have to be referred...to an independent and impartial judicial forum...This completely rules out the sovereignty of the parliament or of the people and establishes the sovereignty of Allah...

Secularism is foreign to Islam...fundamental rights guaranteed under the constitution can be suspended under certain conditions like national emergency but not so in an Islamic polity...the rights granted by Allah and his apostle can in no circumstances be suspended or abridged or modified in a modern democracy. The head of the state/government enjoys immunity from judicial accountability and can grant pardon to the doers of even the most heinous crimes. Not so in an Islamic state.[34]

The above scholarly discourse is completely at variance with the constitution and the laws of the Islamic state of Pakistan, even under the most theocratic rulers like Ziaul Haq and Nawaz Sharif. The parliament and the system of government are based on the Western model. All citizens are not treated equally. Some are more equal than others. Members are divided along party lines. According to the Fourteenth Amendment, a member can lose his seat in the assembly if he votes according to his conscience. Parliament is sovereign, and the judiciary is subjected to pressure and intimidation if it exercises its independence.[35] The head of the state is empowered to grant pardon to a convict. Fundamental rights are suspended under emergencies. The assertion that there is no room for secularism in Islam is in conflict with the interpretation by Allama Iqbal who claimed that secularism is an integral part of an Islamic state. The problem with Islamic scholars is that in one breath they emphasize the institution of *shura* (consultation and consensus), and in the same breath they deprive the *shura* of the power of rational judgement which, they assert, must be in keeping with the eternal and unalterable principles and percepts of the Holy Quran and Sunnah. As for the principles and precepts, the theocrats go by the letter and not the spirit. Thus, the views and opinions expressed by Islamic scholars have only theoretical value, without any link with the existing realities both within and outside Pakistan. Such attempts tend to confuse rather than educate. The scholars would render better service if they get together and prepare an agreed model of a modern, liberal, Muslim state, based on *ijtihad*, but which they have failed to do in more than half a century.

In refreshing contrast, Prof. Syed Jamil Wasti claims that:

> In Islam there is no church, no Pope and no theocracy of clergy and clerics. Islam has established a democratic polity based upon the consent of and consultation with the people, and upon justice and equality of all citizens. Islam is the only religion without any ordained priesthood and a clerical hierarchy, and thus it can be called a secular religion. Secularism implies and denotes a system which is anti-theocratic but not anti-religious.[36]

Prof. Wasti's view is a reflection of those of Allama Iqbal and the Quaid-i-Azam. But, such voices have been drowned in a sea of fundamentalist propaganda. The mullahs had nothing to do with the making of Pakistan, and their encroachment in its polity must be removed.

The entire confusion began by linking the two-nation theory with the partition of India. Under this theory, the Muslims of South Asia, having a common bond of religion, culture, historical experience, and aspirations were called a nation within the framework of the Muslim *ummah*. The *ummah* is indivisible, it cannot be partitioned, and it transcends national, ethnic, and linguistic barriers. It makes no distinction among Muslims, whether Arabs, South Asians, South-East Asians, Africans, Europeans, or Americans. The *ummah* is one, but it recognizes the European concept of nation-states out of necessity and pragmatism. Thus, there are fifty-six Muslim states, besides millions of Muslims living as minorities in more than a hundred countries.

The partition of India may have been inspired by this theory inasmuch as it created a Muslim state, but it did not take place in fulfilment of the aims and objects of the theory, which stood for the unity and not the partition of the *ummah*. Partition was demanded as a temporal necessity rather than for spiritual reasons. It was not demanded to rescue Islam. If Islam was in peril in a united India, it is in greater peril in a divided and residual India. Today, the Muslims in three nations, namely, Pakistan, India, and Bangladesh owe allegiance to their respective nations. Spiritually, they continue to be a part of the Muslim *ummah*, which, in the context of South Asia, became the two-nation theory.

The theory provided an ideological inspiration to the movement for Pakistan. An ideological inspiration can create a state, but the state can only be held together by territorial nationalism, since an ideological base can prove to be tenuous. A territorial base is inviolable, it is sanctified by history, international law, tradition, and conventions. By contrast, ideological orientation may change, leading to disintegration and dismemberment. A Communist Soviet Union split in 1991, and an Islamic Pakistan split in 1971. When socialism lost its credibility, Czechoslovakia, Yugoslavia, and Ethiopia split up too, each in its own way. The ideology served to strengthen the political clout of the Muslim League and established its credentials as the sole legitimate spokesman of the Indian Muslims. To give the theory a concrete shape, Jinnah demanded a specific territory, a piece of land, by dividing India. Once this point is understood, the clash with the fundamentalists, who opposed the creation of Pakistan, falls into place.

> Politics are, by and large, a secular avocation. At exceptional moments in a given history, faith intervenes, often as a motivational, mobilizing force. Faith is crucial in investing values and morality on society and individuals in it. As such, its imprint on history can be deep and lasting. But the course of history is determined by temporal realities—individual anxieties and ambitions, economic forces, national interests, ethnic or linguistic identity—not by ideological pronouncements. (Eqbal Ahmad, *Dawn*, 3 May 1992)

In opposing the creation of Pakistan, the fundamentalists were in good company, namely, the British Government, the Indian National Congress, and the Hindu Mahasabha. Each opponent had its own rationale. The Muslim religious parties argued that Islamic ideology could not be confined to a particular territory to be governed by secular elites, and furthermore, the partition of India would divide the *ummah* rather than solve the communal problem. However, both arguments were dismissed by the Indian Muslims themselves by defeating these opponents and supporting a pro-Pakistan party. After the creation of Pakistan, the religious leaders were reborn and changed their tune. They formulated a new strategy whereby they tried to transform their pre-partition defeat into post-partition victory. They have had phenomenal success, and that has created a dilemma for the people of Pakistan who are in a state of confusion.

How is Pakistan going to resolve this dilemma? Shehzad Amjad posed a valid question:

> The two-nation theory was an intellectual culmination of the man who till his last breath remained an ambassador of peace and unity. Therefore, Pakistan means peace for the whole of the subcontinent. Pakistan means unity in diversity. Pakistan means separation as a key to coexistence. Above all, Pakistan means moral and intellectual leadership in the subcontinent. Who will then write a

new script for a new subcontinent? Let Muhammad Ali Jinnah answer this question.[37]

A very valid question indeed by a thinking Pakistani whose heart bleeds at the tragic events in the subcontinent, and who is searching for a new statesman with a vision for South Asia—someone like Jinnah. But, the calibre of leadership is determined by the quality of the environment. In the first half of the twentieth century, South Asia was fertile enough to produce political stalwarts like Gandhi and Jinnah. Both stood for peace and harmony. Both agreed to the partition to achieve peace and harmony. But the subcontinent lost its bearings and went out of their control. Independence was achieved, but not without blood and tears, not without the loss of two million lives, the displacement of twelve million people, and not without countless rapes and other inhuman acts. Did India and Pakistan learn any lessons from that colossal tragedy? India has gone fanatic, and so has Pakistan. We need another Gandhi and another Jinnah.

India and Pakistan have fought three wars, and each time Indian Muslim soldiers have fought with and killed Pakistani Muslim soldiers, and vice versa. These wars were fought between the two nation-states and not between Islam and *kufr*. Similarly, Pakistani non-Muslims fought and killed Indian non-Muslims, and vice versa. The element of success or defeat of Islam against *kufr*, or vice versa, was completely absent. The question arises as to why should a non-Muslim citizen of Pakistan lay down his life for Pakistan if he is not treated as an equal citizen in all respects? And, he has no chance of being an equal citizen except in a secular state.[38]

The concept of a nation-state, having been imported from the West, was alien to most Pakistani Muslims, who were earlier misled by slogans of the rule of *sharia*. In the West itself, the concept of secularism finally came to stay after going through the trauma of conflict with the church for hundreds of years. The struggle still continues, as it did in the break-up of Yugoslavia into Bosnia, Slovenia, and Croatia, and possibly Kosovo. Similarly, pre-1947 India could have split into dozens of nation-states based on their ethnic and linguistic diversity. India should thank the British rule which encouraged the growth of the concept of Indian nationalism and built the infrastructure to sustain it. The emergence of Indian leadership of national stature owes its origin, growth, and development to that foundation. Jinnah, too, visualized Pakistan as a viable nation-state built on the same foundation, with a superstructure based on Islamic ideals, as adapted to the contemporary scene.

Both India and Pakistan were created as multi-ethnic states, and they were expected to consolidate their nationhood and achieve the goal of integration in decades, something which Europe achieved in centuries. In this endeavour, India went ahead but Pakistan lagged behind. The difference lies in that India adopted the time-tested recipe of a secular democracy while Pakistan is still experimenting with the grand ideas of an Islamic state without having a clue as to what it means, how it is to be established, and who would run it. Civilians, the army, elected leaders, and unelected dictators have all tried it, but have failed because all were clueless. Together, they have landed Pakistan in a quagmire—dismembered, corrupted, indebted, tax evasive, industrially sick, misgoverned, divided on ethnic and sectarian basis, and under the shadow of religious terrorism.[39] There have been insurgencies, revolts, and popular uprisings, but these were suppressed by brute force, which is the hallmark of dictatorships and undemocratic and fundamentalist regimes—all of whom have prevented democracy from being given a chance.[40]

An Islamic state in South Asia has either to follow a role model or evolve a model of its own. We have many models before us—the Khulafa-i-Rashidin, Ummayads, Abbasids, Fatimids, Ottomans, and the Indian Muslim rulers, who ruled India for 800 years. None of these models are relevant today. But, Islamic history in general, and the history of Muslim rule in India, have a few lessons that we could learn from. The Indian Islam has been tempered by local faiths and cultures. It has been influenced by sufism too. Those rulers who secularized their statecraft had a relatively smooth and trouble-free tenure.

Orthodox ulema invariably opposed the liberal and tolerant rulers. Had the orthodox ulema prevailed, Muslim rule in India, which has left behind some golden memories, would not have lasted more than a century.

What the orthodox school must understand is that 'since Islam claims to be a code of life for all times and in all lands, fresh and vigorous thought has to be applied to make it a faith ideally suited to the complex industrial society of today.'[41] The human race has existed on the globe for millions of years and will continue to exist for millions more. The message of Islam is barely 1500 years old, which is only a drop in the ocean. For the drop to become an ocean, and the message to reveal its timelessness, it must be liberated from the control of the fundamentalists. Let scientists, who have the vision of the universe, be the leaders of Islam.

When the government of Nawaz Sharif was overthrown by General Pervez Musharraf on 12 October 1999, the mullahs found a new opening and an opportunity created for them. The first shot was fired when they criticized General Musharraf's admiration for Turkey's Kemal Ataturk. Since the military regime which tookover in October 1999 moved on an uncharted course in this particular aspect, the Pakistani liberal intelligensia felt apprehensive about a possible showdown by the fundamentalists:

> It is not beyond the realm of possibility that the fundamentalist elements operating through the support that they have gained in the civil and military bureaucracy should want to exploit the present political vacuum and try to neutralize General Musharraf's liberalism... It may therefore be in the interest of the objectives spelled out by the military regime to give an indication of the direction in which they would want the country to move... one has to remind oneself that from time to time the fundamentalist elements indicated that they plan to convert Pakistani society into an obscurantist entity and to work for the elimination from responsible position all those whom they look upon as being in favour of some form of secular nationalism in Pakistan. What havoc such tactics can wreak upon society is evident from the sectarian and factional killing which has been going on in the

country over the last many years and which has divided society
into several antagonistic and warring camps.[42]

Can there be a fundamentalist takeover in Pakistan? The
answer is that it cannot be ruled out. Their insignificant presence
in the elected assembly is of little consequence. They do not
depend upon the ballot box anyway. They have 'other methods'
to capture power—rhetoric, slogans, militancy, terrorism, etc.
Pakistan should never forget that Zia entertained dreams of
establishing an orthodox Islamic state and ruled for eleven years,
which could have been prolonged had he not met with a
mysterious death. They should also be aware that the Taliban
raised in Pakistan captured power in Kabul, which could be a
starting point for the Talbanization of Pakistan. The constitution
made Pakistan an Islamic state. That prepared the ground for
the mullahs to make it a militant Islamic state. This
transformation took place almost as a natural consequence. The
state authority did not resist this transformation. On the contrary,
there is evidence that in some cases at least, it was facilitated.
On their part, the mullahs are fully poised to rule Pakistan
(*Dawn*, 16 June 2000). It is no longer a secret that the mullahs
have made significant ideological inroads into the officer corps.

Does Pakistan have a model of an Islamic state to follow or
does it have to evolve its own model? So far it has not been
able to do so. Ayub Khan asked his experts to study Islamic
history and the constitutions of other Muslim countries. But,
they failed to produce a model. The 1973 constitution
established an Islamic Ideology Council. Bhutto banned alcohol
and declared Friday as a holiday under pressure from the
fundamentalists. He brought certain economic reforms to
enforce what he called Islamic socialism.[43] But, these steps did
not establish an Islamic state. General Ziaul Haq ran Pakistan
as a military, theocratic state, enacted many laws affecting the
rights of women and minorities, and changed the joint electorate
system to a separate electorate system. He established the
Federal Shariat Court with powers to declare any law unislamic
if it was repugnant to the *sharia*. At the end of eleven years, he

failed to create a model Islamic state. Finally, Nawaz Sharif introduced the fifteenth constitutional amendment to make Pakistan a model Islamic state, but the amendment could not get through the senate.

There are fifty-six Muslim states in the world. They are members of the Islamic community. Together, they constitute the Muslim *ummah*. Ideally, they should join together and form one Islamic state or caliphate, and adopt an Islamic constitution. But, all the fifty-six countries will oppose such a move. Individually, they have monarchies, dictatorships, republics, secular republics, and a few are Islamic republics. There is no concept of monarchies and dictatorship in Islam. Thus, even if they may follow certain Islamic laws, their system of government is not Islamic. In Pakistan, a parliamentary form of government is considered Islamic on the basis that it incorporates the element of *shura* (consultation). So is the presidential system in Iran, although Iran's constitution gives an upper hand to the Shia clergy. In Libya, the concept of direct participation of the people through committees was introduced in 1979. Thus, each Muslim state has its own perception of an Islamic state. If the perceptions vary from state to state, depending upon varying interpretations, they also vary within a single state, like Pakistan. That explains why there has been disagreement over the content and substance of the Islamic state in Pakistan. The only way out of this confusion is to separate religion from the business of the state and let both flourish in their respective spheres.

In February 1995, BBC television in its Correspondent series interviewed the head of a religious group in Pakistan, a member of the Assembly, who openly declared that minorities like the Shia should be persecuted, threatened, and, his rhetoric suggested, eliminated. Pakistan had split into sectarian factions. Cameras showed young boys in chains, tied to iron posts, virtual prisoners of religious teachers in rural Pakistan. About the same time, the BBC programme, Travelogue, exposed the horrors of life in contemporary Pakistan. As if to confirm all this, unknown gangs in Karachi killed a record number of innocent people in bazaars and shopping malls.[44]

Our society is now distinguished by its ethnic militarism, sectarianism, and fundamentalism. All the three establishments employ terrorism as their preferred weapon to press demands, win recognition, and achieve their goals. Are these the attributes of a progressive Islamic society or a sick and degenerated society? Akbar Ahmad, Jinnah's biographer, says:

The paradox is that the world pointed a finger at Pakistan and declared that here was Islam disintegrating, an Islamic society corrupt, violent and sick. This was a paradox because the Islamic notion of a society rests on just leaders, people who heed the exhortations in the Quran to show justice, morality, piety and compassion. Pakistani society is in a state of anarchy, its old laws derived from the British decaying and falling apart. In its place, there is a hotchpotch of laws that are simultaneously Islamic, Pakistani, tribal and state laws. In the end, they often negate each other and lead to confusion and chaos.[45]

NOTES

1. Upto 1962, Pakistan was governed by the Government of India Act 1935. The first constitution was passed in 1956, but it was abrogated by Ayub Khan in 1958 before it could become effective. Ayub Khan gave the 1962 constitution which was abrogated by Yahya Khan in 1969. The 1973 constitution has been subjected to rough treatment. Bhutto amended it to concentrate power in his own hands. Zia held it in abeyance, then amended it drastically to Islamize it. Nawaz Sharif amended it for personal power. General Pervez Musharraf suspended it in 1999. But, the document is still alive.
2. This provision was made for the first time in Article 2.
3. Rafi Raza, ed., *Pakistan in Perspective 1947-97*, Oxford University Press, Karachi, 1997, p. 31.
4. Ibid.
5. Ibid., p. 36.
6. Ibid., pp. 37-8.
7. *Dawn*, 13 January 1995.

8. Colonel (retd.) Mazharul Haq, letter in *Dawn*, 22 October 1999.
9. Disclosures of corruption by General Ziaul Haq and General Akhtar Abdur Rahman quoted by Sherbaz Khan Mazari in his book *Journey to Disillusionment*, Oxford University Press, Karachi, 1999, pp. 587 and 619.
10. The list has been compiled on the basis of published information. None of these parties originated in rural Sindh.
11. Harkatul Mujahideen runs a number of guerilla training facilities inside Pakistan, near Mansehra, *Herald*, January 2000, p. 121.
12. Al-Badar is a militant Islamic jihad organization run by the Jamaat-i-Islami, with its training camps in the Hazara district of NWFP. See *Herald*, January 2000.
13. Idrees Bakhtiar and Zaffar Abbas, *Herald*, August 1994. The IJI was to be brought into power by manipulating elections. Rs 140 million were distributed among various candidates. Reference may be made to the disclosures made by General (retd.) Mirza Aslam Beg, and the complaint to the Supreme Court by Asghar Khan, which is sub judice. Also, see *Dawn*, 25 April 1994. See also *Dawn*, 17 May 1999, quoting *London Observer*, claiming that Nawaz Sharif personally received Rs 3.5 million from the secret account opened by the ISI in 1990, under presumed instructions of President Ghulam Ishaq Khan, to provide support to the IJI to defeat the PPP. The *Herald* of April 2000 (p. 27) published the list of beneficiary anti-PPP politicians and the amounts received by them from the ISI to defeat the PPP: Nawaz Sharif: Rs 3.5 million, Mir Afzal Khan: Rs 10 million, Lt. Gen. Rafaqat: Rs 5.6 million (for disbursal to the media), the Jamaat-i-Islami: Rs 5 million, Abida Hussain: Rs 1 million, Altaf Hussain Qureshi and Mustafa Sadiq: Rs 0.5 million, Ghulam Sarwar Cheema: Rs 0.55 million, Ghulam Mustafa Khar: Rs 2 million, Malik Meraj Khalid: Rs 0.2 million, Ghulam Mustafa Jatoi: Rs 5 million (on 3 October 1990), Jam Sadiq Ali: Rs 5 million (20 September 1990), Muhammad Khan Junejo: Rs 2.5 million (28 September 1990), Abdul Hafeez Pirzada: Rs 3 million (20 September 1990), Yusuf Haroon: Rs 5 million, Muzaffar Hussain Shah: Rs 0.3 million, Ali Akbar Nizamani: Rs 0.6 million, Arbab Ghulam Aftab: Rs 0.2 million, Pir Noor Muhammed Shah: Rs 0.3 million, Arbab Faiz Muhammad: Rs 0.3 million, Pir Pagara: Rs 2 million (on 9 September 1990), Ismail Rahu: Rs 0.2 million, Humayoon Khan Mari: Rs 5.4 million, Jamali: Rs 4 million, Kakar: Rs 1 million, Liaqat Baloch: Rs 1.5 million, Jam Yousuf: Rs 0.75 million, Bizenjo: Rs 0.5 million, Nadir Mengal: Rs 1 million, smaller groups in Sindh: Rs 5.4 million, miscellaneous groups: Rs 3.4 million.

General (retd.) Hamid Gul, Lieutenant-General Asad Durrani, General (retd.) Mirza Aslam Beg, and President Ghulam Ishaq Khan used these methods to defeat a secular party and bring in an Islamic rule.

14. The Barelvis do not pray with the Deobandis, and vice versa, even though both are Sunnis. Shiites: Ismailis, Bohras, Asna Ashris, pray in their respective places of worship, some of which are called mosques, while others are not. Sub-sects within a single sect carry their mutual hostility to the point of absurdity, even during a crisis. For example, during the PNA agitation in 1977, the leaders of the 9-party alliance were imprisoned at the Sihala rest-house, near Rawalpindi. During daily prayers, Maulana Noorani of the JUP refused to pray with Maulana Mufti Mahmood of the JUI. The former belonged to the Barelvi school of the Sunni sect while the latter belonged to the Deobandi school of the same sect. Sherbaz Khan Mazari, who was a member of the PNA team and held in custody at Sihala, mentions this episode in his book *Journey to Disillusionment*, OUP, Karachi, pp. 456-7. Both Mufti and Noorani were Islamic scholars, both carried their sectarian differences even to jail. While they were trusted to bring down Bhutto's government, they did not inspire enough confidence to form an effective and harmonious alternative government. Hence, their dialogue with Bhutto culminated in an army rule and a disaster for Pakistan. The PNA agitation had begun on the issue of election rigging, but it was taken over by the demand for *Nizam-i-Mustafa* (Prophet's regime), spearheaded by mullahs who were themselves divided on the basics of the religion of Islam.

15. Maulana Ubaidullah Chitrali and twelve others were killed in sectarian riots in Chitral in Sept. 1999. The riot was triggered by the welfare work done by the Aga Khan Foundation in the predominantly Ismaili areas. Rival sects resorted to killings in order to draw the attention of the Islamic state (*Herald*, October 1999, pp. 41-2). A stage has been reached where welfare work of one sect is looked upon with suspicion and jealousy by others.

16. *Dawn*, 10 October 1999.

17. Extracts from *Dawn* editorial, 27 January 2000.

18. *Dawn*, 28 January 2000.

19. The author saw this real life drama from his office window in the Foreign Office. The massive Shia protest shook Zia. Next day, I escorted the chief Libyan delegate to meet Zia, who devoted the entire discussion to finding out how Colonel Qadhafi would have handled a similar situation. The Libyan smiled and said that Qadhafi's philosophy has no place for sectarian distinctions.

20. *Dawn*, editorial, 10 October 1999.

21. K.K. Aziz, *The Making of Pakistan—A Study in Nationalism*, National Book Foundation, 1976, p. 178.

22. Ibid. Quoting Zia-ul-Hasan Farooqi, The Deoband School and the Demand for Pakistan, 1963, p. 40.

23. Amina Jilani's weekly column in *Dawn*, 17 October 1999.

24. Amina Jilani, *Dawn*, 17 October 1999.

25. A.B.S. Jafri's article, 'Is this the Pakistan that Jinnah made?', *Dawn*, 27 November 1999.

26. Eqbal Ahmad, 'Sectarianizing National Identity', *Dawn*, 18 November 1992.

27. Eqbal Ahmad, 'Turning Islam into a Liability', *Dawn*, 15 November 1999.

28. M.H. Askari, 'In the Shadow of Legacy', *Dawn*, 26 August 1992.

29. Justice Muhammad Munir, *From Jinnah to Zia*, p. 219.

30. Dr K. T. Kamal, 'Bypassing the Real Issues', *Dawn*, 7 November 1998.

31. They opposed Justice Bhagwandas's appointment as a High Court judge. They asked for the removal of Justice (retd.) Shaiq Usmani who had proposed *ijtihad* in women's property rights.

32. They demanded Foreign Minister Abdul Sattar's resignation, (for supportting to signing of the CTBT) during Friday sermons throughout Pakistan. See *Dawn*, 13 January 2000, Dr Pervez Hoodbhoy's article, 'Why CTBT is Controversial'.

33. Akbar S. Ahmad. *Jinnah, Pakistan and Islamic Identity*, p. 216.

34. Israrul Haque, 'Parameters of Islamic Polity', Friday feature in *Dawn*, Karachi, 3 December 1999.

35. In 1997, the Supreme Court was physically attacked by the party in power (the PML-N) to subdue its independence.

36. *Dawn*, 3 December 1999, letter by Prof Syed Jamil Wasti.

37. *The News* International, 18 October 1998.

38. A prominent Pakistani moved the Supreme Court against the appointment of Justice Bhagwandas, a well-known Sindhi-Hindu jurist, as a judge on the basis that he was a non-Muslim and, therefore, not qualified to interpret Islamic law. How can a non-Muslim soldier lay down his life for Pakistan if he is not treated as an equal? Non-Muslims have given their blood, tears, and talent for Pakistan. Zafarullah Khan's debates on Kashmir in the UN are unforgettable. Dr Abdus Salam, the Nobel Laureate, was a proud Pakistani. Brigadier Iftikhar Janjua was the hero of the Kutch battle with India. General Akhtar Malik pushed back India in the Akhnoor sector in 1965. Brigadier Abdul Ali frustrated the Indian advance in Chawinda in 1965. General Iftikhar Janjua laid down his life and General Nasir Chaudhry was seriously wounded in the 1971 war. Scores of others perished in the wars of 1965 and 1971. (Zafar Ahmad, *Dawn*, 4 September 2000).

39. Corruption accounts for Rs 40 billion annually, loan default Rs 211 billion, foreign loans $ 32 billion, tax evasion Rs 140 billion annually, 4000-5000 sick units.

40. In 1971, East Pakistan revolted. The army moved in to suppress it without success. In 1973, Balochistan revolted, and the army moved in to suppress it. In 1998, Sindh was placed under central control although

an elected government could have been formed. All these political issues
were capable of being solved though dialogue.

41. Kunwar Idrees, 'Pre-Conditions of an Islamic State', *Dawn*, 13 January
   1995.
42. M.H. Askari, 'Pitfalls along the Way', *Dawn*, 24 November 1999.
43. He nationalized banks, selected industries, and brought about land
   reforms.
44. Akbar S. Ahmad, *Jinnah, Pakistan and Islamic Identity—The Search
   for Saladin*, Routledge, London and New York, 1997, p. 216.
45. Ibid., p. 217.

12

RELIGION AND THE STATE – III

The thrust of Pakistani fundamentalists towards a *sharia*-based state at a time when the rest of the world has kept religion out of the business of the state has created many problems, which need to be examined in depth. On the face of it, this mindset seems to have developed as a result of religious intolerance practiced by the majority Hindu community in India. As a consequence of the Muslim rule over India for 800 years, prior to the British rule, Hindus entertained deep-rooted hatred against the Muslims. Unlike Buddhism, Jainism, and other faiths, Islam maintained its distinct identity, not only because of its foreign origin, but also because of its total rejection of the Hindu belief in idol worship, caste system, and untouchability. Despite the secularist tendencies and integrationist approaches of some Muslim rulers, like the emperors Akbar and Jehangir, Islam and Hinduism existed in the subcontinent through the centuries as two separate and parallel streams. British rule was marked by the emergence of extremist Hindu political parties with the aim of ruling India after independence as a Hindu state. The rise of the Indian National Congress as a secular party could not contain the tide of Hindu fanaticism. It was against this background that the Muslims demanded the partition of India—not to establish a fundamentalist Islamic state, but to enable the Muslims to safeguard their political and economic interests and act as a balancing factor for peace and harmony in the subcontinent.

After half a century of independence, what has been the balance sheet? Whereas in India, the rule of democracy has been sustained, a secular constitution has been preserved, and institutions have been stabilized to safeguard, nourish, and strengthen democracy and secularism, Pakistan has moved in the opposite direction. It has surrendered itself to fundamentalism, its institutions stand paralysed, its democratic culture destroyed, and Iqbal's concept of Islamic secularism trampled upon. In consequence, Pakistan, apart from posing a danger to itself and negating the basic justification for India's partition, has done a great disservice to the Indian Muslims who contributed to its creation.

India has as many Muslims as Pakistan, but their loyalty to India was suspect because of their support for partition. Their honourable existence as loyal Indian citizens is tied up with their integration in a secular and democratic India. In their attempt to do so, they have faced two obstacles: lingering suspicion of their loyalty, and discrimination by the Hindu majority in India, on the one hand, and the wave of fundamentalism engulfing Pakistan on the other. Indian Muslims rendered immense sacrifices for the creation of Pakistan. Pakistani Muslims have lived up to the expectations of their brothers by a crude display of fundamentalism, which has shaken the foundations of Pakistan and obliterated the sacrifices rendered by them.

What the Pakistani *ulema* seem to ignore is that irrespective of the nature of slogans used in favour of the partition of India, Pakistan was created in the vision of Iqbal (and not in the vision of Maulana Maudoodi), hence the shape of the constitution has to be in keeping with Iqbal's teachings and not the sermons of the *ulema*. Iqbal's concept of a modern Muslim state is unambiguous inasmuch as it has no room for theocracy.

Pakistanis have to think hard and do some soul searching to find the reasons for India's success and Pakistan's failure in influencing world opinion. Even though India is currently ruled by an extremist Hindu party (the BJP), it has been able to successfully sell its secularism to the outside world by using its diplomatic skill, its functioning democracy, and stable institutions. How is it that a fundamentalist Hindu party is able to nourish all these institutions of a secular democracy?[1] By contrast, how has Pakistan failed to prove its claim of superiority as an Islamic state, which is said to be secular in essence, when all its pretensions of democracy have been exposed, its institutions almost demolished, and its policies have encouraged terrorism, loan defaults, tax evasions, corruption, sectarianism, and ethnic violence?

A comparison between the Indian and Pakistani approaches may be in order. Hinduism has always tended to assimilate rather then exclude. During the twentieth century, it has largely assimilated the principles of equality and social justice. In the process, Hinduism has shed much that had a negative value. Though all its scriptures are held sacred, yet they are open to figurative interpretation. Unlike Islam, Hinduism has never depended on the letter of the scriptures. Thus, it has room to adapt itself to the rapidly changing conditions of the twenty-first century without formally rejecting any part of its inheritance from the past.[2] The old Hinduism still exists, but it is giving way to the new, not by a religious revolution but by a steady process of adaptation.[3]

Lord Buddha (563-483 BC) taught his own system of salvation that thoroughly rejected Brahminic Vedic authority and Brahminic pretensions to sacrosanct powers by virtue of birth. But, several centuries later, 'the Brahminic establishment proved its unique adaptability and diplomatic skills by bringing the Buddha under the infinitely expanding umbrella of Hinduism', as a re-incarnation of the god Vishnu.[4]

Take the example of Mahatma Gandhi. His attitude to caste distinctions, untouchability, and ritual pollution was hostile. He looked upon these as accretions which had corrupted the pure Hinduism of ancient days. Many of his doctrines were derived from non-Indian sources—mostly European. For example, Hinduism prescribes vegetarianism for the high castes, while non-violence applies only to the ascetics. But, he applied these concepts to all. Also, his insistence on the nobility of manual labour is attributed to the influence of Tolstoy, Ruskin, and William Morris.[5]

Hinduism has been more successful with the media than Islam. It absorbs, mimics, subverts whatever culture it comes in touch with, its philosophers and scholars are able to interact with the larger world. Muslim scholars in contrast appear inward looking and defensive in their thinking, wanting to draw up barriers, to shut out the world. (Akbar S. Ahmad, *Jinnah, Pakistan and Islamic Identity*, pp. 248-9)

Examples of Hinduism's adaptability can be multiplied. For example, why has the fanatic Bharatya Janata Party (BJP), which stands for Hindutva, implemented secularism as its state policy, convinced non-Hindus in India and abroad of its secular polity, defeated the secular Congress party more than once in the general elections, and projected India's secular image in the West? By contrast, Allama Iqbal's theory that an Islamic state and a secular state are synonymous, has been rejected in the land of his dreams.[6] World opinion is formed on the basis of actions, on performance, and not on theories which are not backed by implementation. Judging by its actions, Pakistan is being transformed into a fundamentalist state. India has used this as a propaganda weapon to tarnish the image of Pakistan by launching a psychological war.

Pakistan's weak and debt-ridden economy and signs of domestic disarray have been highlighted, together with its support to the Taliban in Afghanistan, who were allegedly believed to be behind other terrorist organizations active in Kashmir. Indeed, with Osama bin Laden, who is accused of masterminding anti-American terrorism, enjoying sanctuary in Afghanistan, India has succeeded in creating the impression that it is in the same boat as the USA in facing fundamentalists and terrorists, while Pakistan, which has recognized the Taliban, is providing them with backing and sustenance. Recently, USA and India entered into an agreement to coordinate operations and planning against terrorism in the region.[7]

Pakistan's internal situation is of its own making and has been fully exploited by India. For some time, the Western world has been in the grip of Islamophobia. There has been a sustained campaign against what has been dubbed as militant Islam. The question is: Is there militant Islam in Pakistan? The answer is yes, there is—in the religious *madressahs*, in sectarian intolerance, in ethnic terrorism, and in the cries for *jihad* by the fundamentalists. All this activity has tarnished the image of the Kashmiris' struggle for self-determination. A genuine struggle has been dubbed as Islamic terrorism and the Kashmiris are paying the price for the rhetoric of Pakistani fundamentalists:

> Would former Prime Minister Menachem Begin, President Nelson Mandela, Archbishop Makarios or President Arafat be classed as freedom fighters or terrorists? ... would our support for the KLA be classed as incitement to terrorism in Kosovo? Who determines which freedom struggle or right to self-determination campaign we can support?... I have heard references made to Islamic terrorists. No one describes the IRA as a Christian terrorist organization, or extremists in the Jewish community as Jewish terrorists, or describes any other group in that way.[8]

The misfortune of the Kashmiri freedom fighters being branded as Islamic terrorists, and not freedom fighters, at par with the Kosovars, the Irish Catholics, the Palestinians, the South Africans, and the Jews, has its origin in the seeds of Islamic terrorism, born and bred in Pakistan, as a direct result of the rise of fundamentalism, under the constitutional umbrella provided by the Islamic state. If India exploited the situation, crushed the Kashmiris, and painted a dark picture of Pakistan and isolated Pakistan in the world forums, the people of Pakistan should have opened their eyes and put their house in order.

> In India, they (the Hindus) have burned down churches and destroyed a historic mosque. In Palestine they (the Jews) describe themselves as pioneers, desecrate mosques and churches, and with state support, dispossess the Muslim and Christian inhabitants of their ancient land...In Serbia, they attempted genocide and ran rape camps...The Jewish zealots in Palestine are called 'settlers'...The Hindu militant is described as a 'nationalist', and the Christian is labeled 'right wing' or 'messianic' ...In Pakistan,

they have hit Christians, Ahmadis, Shia Muslims, and also each other. They wage holy wars, and commit atrocities...They spill blood in bazaars, homes, courts, in mosques and churches. The Western media invariably refer to them as 'Islamic fundamentalists' – an epithet reserved for the Muslim variety. Others of this ilk are assigned more neutral nouns... The bias in the use of language obscures an important reality... They are reflections of a common problem, with shared roots and similar patterns of expression... The restorationist wants to return somehow to an old way of life, re-impose the laws and customs that were, recapture lost virtues, rehabilitate what he believes to have been the golden past – Hindutva, Ramraj, Eretz Israel, Nizam-e-Mustafa...With Pakistan's exception, the secular alternative has been favoured in post-colonial South Asia...In Pakistan, on the other hand, the issue of relationship between religion and state has remained a source of confusion, instability and misuse of Islam in politics, a phenomenon which contributed greatly to the violent separation of East Pakistan in 1971...[9]

Relating the Kashmiri struggle for self-determination and the violation of human rights by India to the surge of Islamic terrorism in Pakistan and its export to Kashmir and Afghanistan has become a familiar mode of presenting a political scenario in the Western media. Islamic resurgence around the world has caused a chain reaction. Muslims will account for 30 per cent of the world population by the year 2025. The West is concerned about nuclear proliferation, immigration, oil, and the survival of Israel. India fears Pakistan and the potential alienation of over 100 million Muslims in India itself. We, in Pakistan, are dependent upon the West. Prudence demands that we trim our sails.[10] The subtle manner in which India projects Pakistan as a terrorist state may be judged from the psychological war carried out by its leading journalists and columnists who have earned recognition in Pakistan as fair and unbiased commentators:

Whether the hijackers of Indian Airlines plane were Pakistanis or Afghans, there is no doubt that they are from an Islamic militant group. They are the ones who are giving a bad name to Islam. Even the hijackers are reported to have observed that they were not bothered about Kashmir but they were concerned about the Ummah. How have they helped the Ummah by hijacking innocent men, women and children is not understandable...Since Pakistan is a member of the OIC, it should explain its conduct because the plane was taken to Lahore from Amritsar. Islamabad's hostility towards New Delhi is nothing new, but the issue was that of human rights. Instead of appreciating that point, Pakistani F.M. Abdul Sattar began abusing India when the plane was still on the Lahore airport tarmac. ..From Delhi, it looks as if Islamabad's efforts are directed towards sustaining tension in the neighbouring country by one method or another. This way, it believes, it can keep people occupied in its own country. They have been asking questions about why both military and civilian governments have failed to tackle the basic problem of want and hunger..... India has at least a democratic system which is accountable to the elected parliament. And it does not use religion to justify its existence.[11]

The rest of the world, including its electronic media, have no time to verify the truth. They go by reputation and past history. On that score, Pakistan's image has been negative and in building that image, Pakistan's own actions, whether by governments or by private agencies, have played a major part, besides providing enormous evidence to India to play up Pakistan's aggressive fundamentalism against Indian secularism. A terrorist act of plane hijacking presented yet another opportunity to whip up the prejudices against what has been dubbed as militant Islam. That the terrorists of yesterday are the heroes of today, and the terrorists of today might be the heroes of tomorrow, is not relevant when it suits the powerful to malign the weak.[12] The problem in any comparison between the two countries with regard to religious freedom is that India's manifestations of communalism are often seen as aberrations in a nation with a secular constitution. In the case of Pakistan, they are considered to be the inevitable products of the constitutionally mandated Islamic character of the state.

Pakistani rulers have cheated and lied to their people. Ayub Khan called his *coup* of 1958 a revolution. He disenfranchised the people, manipulated his election, and called it a 'democracy which people would understand'. Yahya Khan aided and abetted in the dismemberment of Pakistan. Bhutto cheated on land reforms[13] and rigged the elections of 1977. Ziaul Haq cheated on election dates, Islamization, referendum, and by appointing himself as the president. Nawaz Sharif cheated on bank loans, freezing of foreign currency deposits, the Kargil fiasco, and the rigging of elections. They cheated under the umbrella of the Islamic state, surrounded by a galaxy of *ulema*.

When Zia left the scene in 1988, he left behind a chaotic half-baked 'Islamic state', torn asunder by ethnic terrorism, sectarian extremism, intolerant fundamentalism, drug culture, gun culture, corruption, tax evasion, smuggling, loan defaults and a get-rich-quick culture.[14] When Nawaz left the scene in 1999, he left Pakistan in shambles.

Islam spread in Arabia, which had also given birth to Judaism and Christianity. The Arabs who embraced Islam retained many tradition and rituals of the two preceding faiths by designating them as *Ahle-Kitab*. On that basis, Islam encouraged co-existence with them. When the Arabs conquered Sindh, they accorded similar status to the existing faiths in Sindh, namely, Buddhism and Hinduism. Consequently, the converted Sindhi-Muslims retained many customs and traditions of their previous faiths and preserved their pre-Islamic cultural heritage.[15] Islamic beliefs in Sindh have been moulded by sufis and mystics, who preached peace, tolerance, accommodation, and a harmonious co-existence with non-Muslims on the basis of equality. Sindhis in general, and Sindhi intellectuals in particular, have a secular orientation in their political choices. Sindh-born leaders, including Jinnah, Bhutto, and G.M. Syed, were great believers in secularism. That explains why the MRD uprising of 1983 took the shape of a violent revolt in rural Sindh against the brutal and fundamentalist inspired dictatorship of General Ziaul Haq, who crushed the revolt in the most savage and ruthless manner. This exposed the real face of the fanatic ruler. The massive uprising in rural Sindh under the MRD (1983) was clear evidence that rural Sindh could not be browbeaten by a theocratic dictator who used Islam to prolong his despotic rule and crush the democratic urges of the people. The impact of this protest against the misuse of religion was widespread and far-reaching. This has been acknowledged by many politicians, scholars, intellectuals, and thinkers. Here in the verdict of veteran politician Sherbaz Khan Mazari:

> ...with the hindsight, I believe that the MRD, despite its many weaknesses, did serve its purpose by continuing the struggle for democracy during the longest period of martial law the country had ever experienced. I. A. Rahman, one of Pakistan's senior journalist, once listed the MRD's achievments:
>
> 1. It frustrated the regime's efforts to isolate the PPP and liquidate it politically.
> 2. It deprived the martial law regime of any political support that could satisfy the ruler's need for legitimacy.
> 3. In 1983, the MRD agitation exposed the soft belly of the state and forced the martial law government to compete with the political opposition on the basis of an elected parliamentary system. The August 1983 plan of phased withdrawal of martial law was the direct result of the MRD pressure.
> 4. The alliance took a correct stand on the referendum of December 1984 and elections of 1985. A decision to participate in these affairs would have nullified all the political gains the democratic forces had achieved.
> 5. Above all, the MRD has remobilized the democratic aspirations of the people and their rejection of any surrender of or encroachment upon their sovereign rights. In a country where democracy has never had a chance to form, this is an achievement of the highest order.[16]

Since no fundamentalist joined the rural Sindhis in this uprising, it became clear that rural Sindhis had a liberal and secular orientation. In 1973, G.M. Syed had openly called for a secular state of Sindhu Desh.[17]

What does prudence now demand, and how does one trim the sails? In a predominantly Muslim country, Islam faces no danger. If the people who struggled for Pakistan lacked in

Islamic content, there would have been no Pakistan. Pakistan came into being not to save Islam but to remove poverty, improve economic conditions, provide equal opportunity, banish illiteracy, spread superior education, promote science and technology, create industry and employment, establish a welfare state, provide equal treatment to all citizens without distinction of faith, caste, creed, gender, and class in the true spirit of Islam, practice freedom of speech, and compete with the advanced countries in all modern programmes, including mass communication, international affairs, diplomacy, and self-reliance.

After half a century, Pakistan is known to be corrupt, ill-governed, near bankrupt, poverty stricken, and torn by sectarian and ethnic terrorism. A stage came when Pakistan was in danger of being declared a terrorist state. It was also on the brink of being declared a bankrupt state. How has all this happened?

The religious elites found Pakistan's salvation in fundamentalism as a reaction, a safety device, against the invasion of Western influence. But, this is a poor response, being devoid of contemporary tools. The results of fighting modern warfare with obsolete weapons are there for everyone to see. Let us hear from Bhandara, who has a deep commitment to Pakistan, of Jinnah's concept:

Let us give the people of Pakistan a plain choice: do they wish Pakistan to be modelled on the principles communicated by the Quaid on 11 August 1947—or a sectarian-ridden theocratic Pakistan? Truly, we are in search of an identity. The dichotomy – or if you like, the split identity – in our nation's psyche has reached the point where it can no longer be swept under the carpet... It is a tribute to the political genius of the Quaid that he foresaw that the imprint of Islam on state religion would let loose sectarianism and divisiveness among the people – which would stymie the building of a modern democratic state... The doors of *ijtihad* have been long closed. The Shia tradition of an established ecclesiastical authority is struggling to cope with the problems of the modern state. Reformers such as Shah Waliullah and non-seminarian intellectuals such as Sir Syed Ahmed Khan and Allama Iqbal have been apostalized. The only reason that a similar fate has not befallen the Quaid is that most Muslims today in the subcontinent realize that Jinnah was all the way right on Pakistan and the seminarians who had dubbed him as the 'kafir-i-azam' were completely and totally wrong. Living in an enclosed world, they had little knowledge of the world outside.[18]

Does Islam need the crutches of state power to survive, grow, and prosper? It is the youngest religion, and it retains the vigour and resistance to withstand the stresses and strains of hostile forces. It has over one billion followers spread over in all the continents. Secularism in Europe, America, and India has not hurt either Christianity or Hinduism—both have flourished without state crutches. Seeking state patronage would amount to an admission of weakness. State patronage makes religion a handmaiden of state power and a tool in the hands of a dictator who may use religion for his personal ends.[19] In fact, much of the decline in Muslim societies can be attributed to state control and state interference exercised under the mistaken notion that there is a linkage between religion and the business of the state. Besides, much of falsehood and adverse publicity spread across the world by the anti-Islamic forces can be traced to this linkage. This linkage creates inter-dependence, whereby Islam tends to thrive on state power and the state tends to use traditional Islam to justify its dictatorship. In the process, both become vulnerable, and neither of them is able to withstand the onslaught by their adversaries. For example, in the propaganda blitz and psychological war following the hijacking of the Indian plane on 23 December 1999, both Pakistan and Islam were clubbed together as a single target and a composite villain. The mere fact that the hijackers, the freed prisoners, and the swapped hostages were all Muslims, was enough justification for the adversaries to malign Pakistan and Islam. To counter adverse propaganda, Pakistan must use the tools of science, technology, human resources, economic clout, and sophisticated methods of mass communication. It trails behind India on all these counts and takes refuge behind its Islamic credentials, thus puting

Pakistan on the defensive. Has Pakistan even paused to think that, despite tensions and insurgencies, other countries in South Asia, namely, India, Bangladesh, and Sri Lanka, are moving ahead positively in terms of growth and investment while Pakistan is stagnating? This state of affairs turns world opinion against Islam and Pakistan. For example, the nuclear bomb of the USA, the UK, and France is not a Christian bomb, the Israeli bomb is not a Jewish bomb, the Indian bomb is not a Hindu bomb, but the Pakistani bomb is dubbed as an Islamic bomb.

NOTES

1. India has been able to successfully project a secular image despite the religious and sectarian intolerance practiced in that country. Examples: Desecration of the historic Babri Mosque in Ayodhya, torching of the Hazratbal Shrine in Kashmir, storming of the Sikh Holy Golden Temple in Amritsar, killing of Sant Bhindranwalle, the rape of Christian nuns, burning of Christian churches, and frequent religious riots, etc. But, the world believes that Islamic terrorism, born in the Islamic state of Pakistan, poses the real threat to civilization. Terrorism has come to be identified with the Islamic state.

2. R.C. Zaehner, ed., *The Concise Encyclopedia of Living Faiths*, Hutchinson of London, p. 253.

3. Ibid., p. 254.

4. Stanley Wolpert, *A New History of India*, University of California Press, Berkeley, California, pp. 32-3.

5. R.C. Zaehner, ed. *The Concise Encyclopedia of Living Faiths*, Hutchinson of London, p. 251.

6. Allama Iqbal and Justice Javed Iqbal claim that an Islamic state is a truly secular state.

7. Dr Maqbool Ahmad Bhatti, 'Campaign to Analyse Pakistan', *Dawn*, 22 November 1999.

8. Lord Nazir Ahmad, member of the British Parliament's Upper House, speech in Parliament on 27 November 1999, reported in *Dawn*, Karachi, 28 January 1999.

9. Eqbal Ahmad, 'Roots of the Religious Right', *Dawn*, 24 January 1999.

10. Ardeshir Cowasjee, 'The Fault Line', *Dawn*, 26 September 1999.

11. See *Dawn*, 1 January 2000, Kuldip Nayar's letter from New Delhi. The Indian plane was hijacked in Kathmandu on 23 December 1999 and released in Kandahar on 31 December 1999. The allegation of Islamic

terrorism and the demand for Pakistan's explanation may be noted. The plane landed at Amritsar, Lahore, Dubai, and Kandahar. But, Nayar singles out Pakistan for condemnation on the assumption that Pakistan was involved in the crime.

12. How does the world judge Laila Khalid, Khudi Ram, Bhagat Singh, General Suharto, Franco, Salazar, Marcos, Pinochet, Allende, Saddam Hussain, Jomo Kenyatta, Tom Paine, Menachem Begin, David Ben Gurion, and Nathuram Godse? A.B.S. Jafri, 'Some Thoughts on Acts of Terror', *Dawn*, 2 January 2000.

13. Sherbaz Khan Mazari, *A Journey to Disillusionment*, Oxford University Press, Karachi, 1999, p. 266, states: 'In May 1971, I met Nusrat Bhutto and she confided to me that her husband had recently transferred the ownership of a large portion of his agricultural holding to the names of his farm staff. She then suggested that I do the same to forestall the impact of future land reforms. I did not follow her advice'.

14. Ibid., pp. 587, 619. The author quotes General Akhtar Abdur Rahman's son boasting that the 250 million dollars made by General Ziaul Haq were peanuts as compared to the wealth made by his father. Apparently, the American money meant for the *jihad* in Afghanistan came as a bonanza for the ruling generals; this was one of the legacies of the Islamic state established by General Zia.

15. The Arabs did not go beyond Sindh, hence the differences in the impact made by Islam on the Sindhis and the rest of the South Asian Muslims. Besides, sufis and mystics narrowed the gulf between the Muslims and non-Muslims. Hence, the Sindhis are more inclined to secularism than non-Sindhi Muslims.

16. Sherbaz Khan Mazari, op. cit., pp. 254-5. He quotes I.A. Rahman, *Pakistan Under Siege*, Rohtas Books, Lahore, 1990, p. 261.

17. In his book, *Sindhudesh—A Study in its Separate Identity Through the Ages*, G.M. Syed Academy, Karachi. Syed gives a blueprint of his proposed Sindhu Desh, as a secular state.

18. Extracts from M.P. Bhandara's article, 'As We Enter the New Millennium', *Dawn*, 1 January 2000.

19. General Ziaul Haq used Islam to justify his illegal *coup* in 1977, to rig the referendum in 1984, and prolong his dictatorship for eleven years. Similarly, Prime Minister Nawaz Sharif tried to perpetuate himself by introducing the fifteenth amendment on the basis of his heavy mandate.

13

RELIGION AND THE STATE – IV

Secularism in the European society is the end result of the Renaissance which demolished the old socio-political structure based on the supremacy of the Church and paved the way for the age of reason, enlightenment, rationalism, scientific revolution, and independent judgement. Has a similar revolution taken place in the Islamic society? If it has, where has it occurred, and what has been its impact? If it has not, what have been the factors inhibiting the change? Also, is it now possible to have a renaissance in a Muslim society, with particular reference to Pakistan?

The European society had its own traditions, values, and norms to guide its process of change, and to readjust itself. The European mould gives an insight into the dynamics of its own history. Likewise, every civilization has to adopt its own course and move ahead in the light of its own traditions.[1]

The classical ideas of Greek and Roman culture provided tools to the European society to fight against the medieval traditions... gradually. The new ideas inspired by the wisdom of the classical age over-powered the religious ones and a secular society emerged.[2]

In contrast, no such revolution took place in the Islamic society. The pre-Islamic society in Arabia was at a low level of civilization, and Islam came to civilize it. Besides, Islam was a complete code of life, for all times to come, with its message of universal brotherhood. But, Islam's dynamism lay in its teachings to explore, acquire, and learn science and knowledge from nature and from all possible sources. The early Muslims, imbued by these teachings and propelled by the spirit of inquiry, drew upon the Greek, Roman, Chinese, and Indian civilizations, and on that base, built up an edifice of a highly progressive and outward looking Islamic society with phenomenal accomplishments in many fields like science, mathematics, and philosophy.

The decline of the Islamic society began when *ijtihad* was discontinued, and with that, the process of reasoning and rational judgement came to a halt. It was argued that there was no room for reform in a religion which was a comprehensive code for all times to come. To purge the faith from new ideas, the clergy led the campaign for reverting back to classical dogmas and traditional concepts to maintain the purity of religion and to curb the tendency to re-interpret and reform. This was a defensive mechanism against what was perceived as the onslaught of European culture, as well as to purge new cults and ideas of revolt from the *ummah*. This was a triumph of fundamentalism and the beginning of the stagnation of Islam and the Muslim society.

The harm done by the stagnation has been beyond description. It has stunted the intellectual faculties of the *ummah*. It has deprived the Islamic society of dynamism, vigour, a pragmatic outlook, and a pioneering spirit. It has deprived the Muslims of the strength and the confidence to confront the advance of European culture, which is armed with new and more powerful tools. Unlike early Islam, medieval Islam withdrew into a shell and deprived itself of the gains of evolution which results from human endeavour, human progress, and the growth of society.

When the world began to shrink with the advent of rapid means of transportation and advances in methods of mass communication, the West began to move out of Europe and spread itself into the East and the West, to dominate the world politically, economically, and culturally. Evolution of a universal culture began to take shape. Human progress became a universal phenomenon. Islamic universalism, however, remained confined to theories and dogmas preserved in the minds of the *ulema*. They saw the spread of European ideas as a confrontation between Christianity and Islam, rather than in terms of domination of a backward civilization by an advanced one. Europeans did not single out Muslim lands for domination. They dominated Asia, Africa, Australia, North America, and South America, irrespective of whether Muslims, Hindus, Buddhists, animists, pagans, or aborigines lived there. Hindus and Buddhists grasped the reality and adapted themselves to join the race for progress and close the gap of past isolationism. By contrast, the Muslims persisted in their folly and lagged behind in devising an effective startegy for their progress. What is worse, instead of blaming themselves for their self-created isolationism, resulting from their stubborn adherence to antiquated dogmas and their negative attitude towards reform, they chose to scapegoat the West for the ills that befell the Muslim society.

One may ask: Is it possible to have a renaissance in Muslim society? Is it possible to reject divine intervention in human affairs and make man responsible for building his own destiny, and change society according to his need, on his own authority and will? Is it possible to build a society that would be free from all dogmatic influences and where secular values would determine human conduct in the temporal aspects of life? The picture does not appear to be bright to some thinkers:

> It appears doubtful that Islamic societies will accept this formula to get rid of fundamentalism and religious rigidity, liberate individuals from divine limits and make him independent to shape his own destiny.[3]

The answer to these questions may be found in case studies of movements started by some outstanding personalities who rose to prominence as leaders of the Indo-Muslim community. Among them were Sir Syed Ahmed Khan, Allama Muhammad Iqbal, Maulana Abul Kalam Azad, Muhammad Ali Jinnah, and a few others. Sir Syed stood for blending Western thought with Eastern ideas. He is rated as the greatest Indian-Muslim of the nineteenth century. Muslim India of the twentieth century owes its awakening, its emancipation, and its struggle for rights to the groundwork laid by him. Yet, he was condemned by the orthodox *ulema* for his endeavour to introduce the English language, and some radical ideas in religion. He set up the Aligarh College, which later became a university, producing hundreds of thousands of enlightened and talented Muslims who rose to provide leadership in various fields. His Pakistani spiritual heirs are active in the educational and cultural fields. They have established the Sir Syed University in Karachi to perpetuate his name and traditions. In the realm of bringing about reforms in orthodox Islam, and to bring it in line with contemporary ideas, as envisaged by Sir Syed himself, their contribution is through education, but which necessarily is a slow process. They have not produced a reformer to take Sir Syed's place. But, they will produce scientists and mathematicians to fulfill his dream.

We have the shining example of Shah Waliullah, who took the path of research, enquiry, and *ijtihad* on religious issues in the nineteenth century.

He established the historical basis of Islamic traditions and commended evolution, rather than closed thinking, in this sphere... He went a step further by attempting a reconciliation between the Shias, the Sunnis, the sufis, the four schools of jurisprudence and various Islamic sects. He recognized the validity of the Hindu path to knowledge, God and truth and probed into the nature of other religions of the Indian subcontinent. A number of hostile Muslim and non-Muslim opponents developed whom he combated with the force of ideas, arms and a glittering litany of followers.[4]

Similarly, Iqbal, in his lectures compiled in the shape of *Reconstruction of Religious Thought in Islam*, has emphasized the need for *ijtihad* to enable the Muslim society to come out of its centuries old stagnation and adopt intellectual tools to enable it to coexist on honourable terms with the rest of the world. Iqbal's son, Justice (retd.) Javed Iqbal, who was his spiritual heir, did not protest, as a senator, against the proposed fifteenth constitutional amendment designed to convert Pakistan into a theocratic state.[5]

As for Jinnah, he preached and practiced secularism all his life, within the framework of Islam, but he died too soon after the creation of Pakistan. His successors were swept away by the tide of fundamentalism. They frustrated Jinnah's attempt to secularize Pakistan by falling into the trap of diehard and determined mullahs who succeeded in turning away the followers of Jinnah from the course adopted by him. That was a turning point which changed the direction of the state. Once the course was changed, there was no going back.

After half a century, Pakistan is in the tight grip of the fundamentalists, who, unable to get themselves elected to the assemblies, have yet mustered enough street power and militant muscle to be able to achieve all their goals, within and outside the assemblies, by all possible means, including angry rallies, fiery speeches, provocative sermons, and the use of bullets. One of the reasons why there has been no serious and meaningful debate at the grass-root level on the implications of *sharia* rule versus liberal Islam is the language barrier. A majority of the population is illiterate, and their opinion on this issue is swayed by the mullah who preaches in the neighbourhood mosque.[6] Among the literate population, a great majority can read and write only in one language, which is their mother tongue. Secular issues are not discussed in any local language of Pakistan.[7] Most of the debate and projection of the idea of secularism is carried out in the English press whose readership is limited to a small fraction of the population, and its dissemination is confined to the drawing rooms of the elite class which is not actively involved in moulding public opinion.

Iran, Pakistan's next door neighbour, is projected as a Shia fundamentalist state, established by Ayatollah Khomeini and ruled by his devout followers. It is an interesting case study for comparison with the Pakistani brand of fundamentalism:

...how many realize that Iran has made huge strides in education, with around 700,000 students at its Universities with women to the fore (comprising 52 per cent of the Tehran University intake this year)?[8] How many have any notion of the degree of freedom of expression and open political activity that now prevails? Even the conviction of Abdullah Nauri, who was yesterday sentenced to five years in prison for 'insulting Islam' and criticizing the legacy of Ayatollah Khomeini, has a silver lining. Nauri turned the tables on his accusers, using the witness box as a pulpit to justify the campaign of his paper, *Khorad*, in favour of democratic values. Like a latter-day Luther, he berated the reactionary mullahs for misinterpreting the Quran and the meaning of the 1979 revolution... Neither his three day lecture, nor the blanket coverage it received in the press, was blocked. It was electrifying.

Iran is a country in flux, bursting with political energy, released first by the revolution and then by the liberalization astutely presided over by Muhammad Khatami, who was elected President in 1997 by 69 per cent of the votes on an 80 per cent turnout. He crushed the official candidate in a largely uncorrupt, free election.[9]

Worthy of note is the full media coverage given to the anti-fundamentalist speech delivered over a period of three days by a convict in Iran, and compare it with the news blackout of the portion of the speech delivered by the founder of Pakistan, advocating separation of religion from the state. The speech was delivered at a time when Pakistan had a liberal orientation, and the mullahs were lying low and had not yet surfaced. Also to be noted is the election of a liberal president in the mullah-dominated state of Iran in a free and fair election. In the Islamic state of Pakistan, election rigging at the highest level is a rule rather than an exception, a turnout of 25 per cent is considered adequate, and a 15 per cent vote is called a heavy mandate, and a licence to demolish state institutions.[10] Pakistanis should also ponder over the fact that Iranian President Khatami publicly upheld the right of Abdullah Nauri, convicted by the clergy-dominated court, to voice criticism freely, which was a liberal approach. He regretted the conviction because in his view it was to the detriment of the Iranian Revolution, which must have room for criticism and dissent.[11]

By contrast, the Islamization process in Pakistan has put a stop to rational thinking and progressive ideas essential to any socio-economic reform. For example, Ayub Khan initiated a process of land reform, and Bhutto carried the reforms forward. These reforms did not represent the ultimate goal, but they certainly paved the way towards the goal. There were many positive elements, including the resumption of 2 million acres which were distributed among 130,000 peasants.[12] Since then, further fragmentation has taken place under the law of inheritance. Besides, the law made many concessions to the tenants. Implementation of the reforms suffered from some impediments. Some land was hidden in the name of trusted servants. But, the greatest handicap was the judgment of the Supreme Appellate Shariat Court Bench of 1989, which stopped the takeover of two million acres resumed under the reform law because it was declared un-Islamic.[13] Implementation of this judgment would mean surrender of two million acres by the tenants, restoration of the same to the original owners, reversal of the land reforms of Bhutto and Ayub Khan, and putting the clock back by forty years. That would amount to confusion of the worst kind. This is a dilemma for which no solution has yet been found. Equally destabilizing is the judgment of the Federal Shariat Court that bank interest is un-Islamic. The government's appeal against the verdict of the Federal Shariat Court was also dismissed by the Shariat Bench of the Supreme Court on 23 December 1999.[14]

Pakistan's entire economy is based on capitalism, in line with the system prevailing in the world. Basically, it is the function of the legislators to change the economic system. Whether interest, as it is practiced today, is the same as *riba*, which was banned in Islam for being exploitative, is a separate issue. The real issue is that this is an economic problem which can best be understood in economic terms. If a country's economy is weak, as that of Pakistan, the interest is high. It was as high as 22 per cent, which was brought down to 16 per cent, not by economic forces, but by an administrative order of the State Bank. The borrowers are the industrialists and traders who use the borrowed money to make profit. In countries with a strong economy, like Japan, the interest is as low as 2 to 2½ per cent. If Pakistan's economy is not mismanaged, taxes are fully paid, corruption is controlled, leakages are plugged, smuggling is checked, the underground economy is documented, and the quality of governance is improved, the interest rates would come down. In ideal conditions, which must prevail in a truly Islamic country, the interest rate could be negligible. Pakistan should aim at improving the economic conditions to attain the goal laid down by Islam rather than relying on judicial verdicts to achieve the goals made difficult by mismanagement and poor governance. Court verdicts cannot restore the faith of Pakistanis in their own country and its economy.[15] Economic decisions must be based on the economic realities of today. The Islamic ban on *riba* must be reinterpreted within the spirit of the *sharia* to enable the *ummah* to overcome their economic problems.

Similarly, the spirit and meaning of jihad needs to be understood in the proper perspective. The best example of jihad is that conducted by Jinnah to achieve Pakistan. Presently, there is a need for jihad against all the evils that have brought Pakistan to the brink of economic, political, and spiritual bankruptcy. There is rampant corruption, enormous loan default, smuggling, drug trafficking, tax evasion, black marketing, election rigging, horse trading, use of religion for personal power, rise of fundamentalism, erosion of liberal Islamic values, rise of ethnic militarism, urban terrorism, illiteracy, poverty, and violation of human rights. A derailed Pakistan must be put back on the rails. This jihad has a much higher priority than any other jihad, whether in Afghanistan or in Kashmir.

Jihad in Afghanistan was in fact an encounter between American capitalism and Soviet Communism, using Afghan Mujahideen and Zia's Pakistan as surrogates. Victory was achieved by America, the Soviet Union disintegrated, Afghanistan was Talbanized[16], and Pakistan was devastated by the Ojri Camp disaster,[17] gun culture, drug culture, and corrupt rulers.

Likewise, the jihad in Kashmir must be seen in perspective. India has deployed half a million soldiers to crush the freedom fighters. It has flaunted UN resolutions which call for the Kashmiris to exercise their right of self determination. Yet, it has been able to successfully project an image of a secular democracy which has won credibility the world over. Even Muslim countries are not too concerned about India's role in Kashmir. By contrast, the concern shown by the people of Pakistan, and the call for jihad given by some religious parties, has been dubbed as terrorism, and such propaganda carried out by India has had sympathetic listeners in the USA and elsewhere. The United Nations has been rendered ineffective in implementing its own resolutions. If the cause of Kashmir is legitimate, there must be some basic flaw in Pakistan's approach which has rendered its diplomacy ineffective. Does this call for a reassessment of the weaknesses, revision of the strategy, and a need to redefine the parameters of jihad to suit prevailing conditions? Is the liberation of Kashmir a religious cause or a human rights problem? If it is religious, then the world is in no mood to pay any heed to it. If it involves human rights, then the talk of holy war must stop. Why is Muslim society unable to cope with ugly and unpleasant situations in the contemporary world? Because they apply primitive solutions to problems created by contemporary situations. Because they have not tuned themselves to see things in a modern perspective. Because the doors of *ijtihad* have been closed. Jinnah had opened these doors, but no sooner than he died, they were closed by the orthodox mullahs. The rhetoric of Pakistani mullahs is a negative input to the genuine jihad of the people of Kashmir and needs to be restrained.

How does one explain such extravagant undertakings by a country which is politically unstable, economically poor, and weakened by ethnic and sectarian terrorism? Does Pakistan lack a sense of priority?[18] Dr Mubarak Ali, a prominent historian writes:

...As Pakistani society becomes intellectually and creatively bankrupt, there remains only one choice: to adopt a militant and violent approach to resist and fight against modernity and globalization. This shows utter helplessness of the Muslims of Pakistan and also the Muslims in general to understand the power and energy of modernity. Hence their inability to combat it.

Creativity emerges only in a free and open society where debate and difference of opinion are tolerated. Islam cannot become a dynamic religion in a feudal, dictatorial milieu. Militancy and violence also cannot protect its values. On the contrary, this makes society backward and ignorant.[19]

Absence of rational thinking has created an intellectual vacuum which has provided an opportunity to the theocrats and their supporters. They have subjected religion to an interpretation to suit their limited vision:

There is a relatively small community of politicians, retired generals, bureaucrats, academics, media men and assorted opportunists who have gone through life without any meaningful initiative to terminate their intellectual colonial status which is reflected, above all, in their slavish semantic dependence on the West. Then, even more seriously, there are the religious bigots who have missed out on the reconstruction of Islamic thought...Their colossal ignorance, backed by armed militants...they corrupt their Quranic concept of Jihad by dressing up their ignoble sectarian prejudices and their irrational fears of progress as soldiering in the path of God.[20]

NOTES

1. Mubarak Ali, 'Is Renaissance Possible in an Islamic Society?', *Dawn*, 16 October 1999.
2. Ibid.
3. Ibid.
4. Amresh Misra, *Lucknow—Fire of Grace: The Story of Renaissance, Revolution and the Aftermath*, Harper Collins, India, 1998, p. 18.

5. *Dawn*, 1 December 1999. After the dismissal of the PML (N) government by the army on 12 October 1999, an individual member of the party (Sartaj Aziz) proposed *ijtihad* to resolve differences in the Islamic system, election, reforms, limits on private property, rights of minorities, women, and interest.

6. In rural Sindh, mosques are not used for political sermons.

7. Z.A. Bhutto became popular in Pakistan for his serious and meaningful speeches on secular issues. His followers take the same approach, G.M. Syed concentrated on secularism in his speeches and writings. The MQM leaders are totally secular in their outlook, their manifesto, and their dialogue.

8. Compare this with Pakistan's ghost schools, militant *madressahs*, and phantom teachers.

9. Andrew Philips, 'The West Must Look into Real Outwardness within Iran', *Dawn*, 29 November 1999, dateline London.

10. Elections in 1990 were rigged, and those who connived or participated in the rigging included the president, the COAS, and the ISI. In 1997, the voter turnout was 25-26 per cent only, which indicated that the remaining 75 per cent of the voters lacked confidence in the quality of the leadership. A 15 per cent vote was a heavy mandate for the ruling elite, which was misused to destabilize Pakistan.

11. Reuters report, 29 November 1999, datelined Tehran, *Dawn*, 30 November 1999.

12. Sheikh Muhammed Rashid, a federal minister in the PPP government (1972-77), distributed this land, *Dawn*, 21 December 1999.

13. See *Dawn*, 21 December 1999. Earlier, the Council of Islamic Ideology used to advise in the light of the *shariah*. Now, the *shariah* court passes verdicts which nullify the law enacted by the parliament of elected Muslims. Then who is the sovereign—the Parliament or the Court?

14. *Dawn*, 24 December 1999.

15. Pakistanis lost faith when they saw defaults on loans by a prime minister to the tune of billions, freezing of foreign currency accounts in spite of a pledge not to do so, and the leaking out of this decision to favourites who transferred million of dollars overnight to banks outside Pakistan.

16. Talibanization of Afghanistan has been variously interpreted. It is the end result of factional fighting after the Soviet withdrawal. The Taliban control 90 per cent of the country, yet their regime has not been recognized by the UN, the USA, and the rest of the world (except Pakistan, Saudi Arabia, and the UAE) because of human rights violations and the exclusion from the government of non-Pakhtun ethnic groups. Talbanization is gradually creeping into Pakistan.

17. Ojri camp is located in Islamabad, and was used as a dump for weapons and ammunition meant for use in the jihad in Afghanistan. Mismanagement of the dump triggered the bombs and missiles which exploded in all directions, killing 1000 persons and injuring 1100. Prime Minister Junejo wanted to expose the guilty, but he was dismissed and the matter hushed up.

18. Apart from other expensive adventures, Pakistan supplied arms to Sikh militants during the rule of General Ziaul Haq (Sherbaz Khan Mazari *A Journey to Disillusionment*, OUP, Karachi, 1999, p. 592).

19. Dr Mubarak Ali, 'Pakistani Islam Lacks Dynamism', *Dawn*, 17 October 1998.

20. Tanvir Ahmad Khan, 'Of Jihad and Terrorism', *Dawn*, 9 May 2000.

APPENDIX

List of judicial verdicts pertaining to political crimes in Karachi.

1. Date: 30 April 1999.
   Source: *Dawn*, 1 May 1999.
   Judge: Hakim Ali Abbasi.
   Case: Murder of Zuhair Akram Nadeem, PML-MNA.
   Accused: Dilawar Khan, Aslam Nak Chapta, Jehangir Kancha, Arif (Berger), Altaf Hussain (MQM Chief), and Syed Ayub Haider Naqvi.
   Verdict: Death sentence plus Rs 100,000 fine each to Dilawar, Jehangir, and Aslam; Arif acquitted; Altaf Hussain declared an absconder, Syed Ayub Haider Naqvi absconding, already sentenced in the murder of Ismail Memon, Chairman Board of Secondary Education.

2. Date: 18 May, 1999.
   Source: *Dawn*, 19 May 1999.
   Judge: Arshad Noor Khan.
   Case: Murder of Ismail Memon, Chairman Board of Secondary Education.
   Accused: Syed Ayub Haider, Kazi Khalid Ali, and others, (MQM-A).
   Verdict: Life term and fine of Rs 170,000 to Syed Ayub Haider, Kazi Khalid Ali, and others absconding. (Judgement later reversed)

3. Date: 18 May 1999.
   Source: *Dawn*, 1 May 1999.
   Judge: Rahmat Hussain Jaffri.
   Case: Recovery of *bhatta*.
   Accused: Mohammed Ashraf, Ghulam Ali, Murtaza, and M. Nadeem, (MQM-A).
   Verdict 7 years RI to each.

4. Date: 19 May 1999.
   Source: *Dawn*, 20 May 1999.
   Judge: Hussain Bux Khoso.
   Case: Murder of Ranger Dildar Hussain and Mumtaz.

Accused: Muhammed Faisal, Muhammed Razak, Muhammed Imran, Syed Junaid, Taha, Nadirshah, Ubaid, K2 Miru, and others, (MQM-A).

Verdict: Death Sentence + 10 years RI + Rs 10,000 fine + Rs 50,000 compensation to first four. Taha, being a minor, to be tried separately. Others absconding.

5. Date: 24 May 1999.
    Source: *Dawn*, 25 May 1999.
    Judge: Muhammad Javaid Alam.
    Case: Murder of Malik Shahid Hamid, M.D., KESC, driver Muhammad Ashraf, and gunman Khan Akbar.
    Accused: Saulat Khan alias Saulat Mirza, (MQM-A).
    Verdict: Death sentence + Fine Rs 1,00,000 + 7 years RI, Fine Rs 10,000.

6. Date: 25 May 1999.
    Source: *Dawn*, 26 May 1999.
    Judge: ATC Judge.
    Case: Murder of Constable Ghiasuddin.
    Accused: Fazal Rahim, Tahir, Nasir, Sarwar Khan, and Altaf Ahmed, (MQM-A).
    Verdict: Death to Fazal, 7 years RI to others.

7. Date: 4 June 1999.
    Source: *Dawn*, 5 June 1999.
    Judge: Dr. Qamaruddin Bohra.
    Case: Murder of Hakim Muhammad Said, Hakim A Kadir, and Wali Muhammad.
    Accused: a) Muhammad Aamirullah Suhail, Muhammad Asif, Ezazul Hasan Mohd. Zubair Hasan, Nadeem Ahmed Mota, Muhammad Shakir Langra, Mohd. Faisal, Muqarrab Ali Nazar, and Muhammad Aba Imran Pasha, (MQM-A).
    Verdict: Death sentence, + Fine Rs 1,00,000 each, + Fine Rs 10,000 + 10 years RI. Amirullah and Nadeem also awarded 7 years RI + Fine Rs 10,000.

    Note: Witness MQM ex-Senator Ishtiaq Azhar said in his statement that Hakim Said possessed some important secrets of the MQM, one of which was the transfer of Rs. 680 million from Karachi to London, and that Hakim Said had apprised him about these secrets a few days before his murder.

Accused:	b) Mohd. Naushad (Dandi), Arif Baig (Daddan), Masroor Iqbal, Rehan, Abdul Wahab, Bandhani, Shah Nawaz, Mohd. Abid, Mohd. Amin, Mohd. Ayub, Mumtaz (KK), Mohd. Asim, Arif KDA Walla, Javed Turk, (MQM-A). All declared absconding.
Accused:	c) Altaf Hussain (MQM Chief) and Zulfiqar Haider, MPA declared absconding.
Accused:	d) Saeed Bhaiji and Haji Gul turned approvers, (MQM-A).

8. Date: 15 June 1999.
   Source: *Dawn*, 16 June 1999.
   Judge: Qamaruddin Bohra.
   Case: Murder of Kashif Aziz, Rashid, Arshad Beg, and Mohd. Javed.

   Accused: a) Muhammad Waseem (Kala), Asif Jameel, Ateeq Azam, Irshad Ahmed, Bashir Ahmad, and Khurram Aziz, (MQM-A).
   Verdict: Death sentence plus fine Rs 2,00,000 each.

   Accused: b) Suhail Commando, Mobin Ahmad (Tinda), Junaid (Ponni), Nasim Abbas, Raju, Tariq Chamber, Alim Nooro, Iftikhar Fuzail, Shabbir, (Farhan), Zulfiqar Haider (MPA), and others, (MQM-A).
   Verdict: Declared absconding.

9. Date: 24 June 1999.
   Source: *Dawn*, 25 June 1999.
   Judge: Abdul Hameed Abro.
   Case: Murder of Lance Naik Fayyaz.
   Accused: Muhammad Yasin and Wasim Zaidi, (MQM-A).
   Verdict: Death sentence plus fine Rs 200,000 each plus 10 years RI plus fine Rs 50,000.

10. Date: 1 July 1999.
    Source: *Dawn*, 2 July 1999.
    Judge: Sindh High Court.
    Case: Judgement of ATC at Sr. No. 1 in murder of Zuhair Akram Nadeem.
    Verdict: Upheld.

11. Date: 3 July 1999.
    Source: *Dawn*, 4 July 1999.
    Judge: Hussain Bux Khoso.

Case:	Murder of Asim and Disher (MQM-A).	
Accused:	Zahid Hussain, Mushtaq, Tariq (MQM-H).	
Verdict:	Death sentence plus fine Rs 2,00,000 each.	

12. Date: 13 July 1999.
    Source: *Dawn*, 14 July 1999.
    Judge: Hussain Bux Khoso.
    Case: Murder of Abdul Jabbar Bengali.
    Accused: Kashif, Faisal, Afzal, (MQM-A).
    Verdict: Death sentence plus fine Rs 50,000 each.

13. Date: 28 July 1999.
    Source: *Dawn*, 29 July 1999.
    Judge: Abdul Hameed Abro.
    Case: Murder of Inspector Zafar Paracha.
    Accused: Naushad Ali Mohd. Javaid (Lamba), Shaikh Faisal (Gora), Mohd. Faisal (Chhota), Mohd. Ali (MQM-A), and Azeem (MQM-A).
    Verdict: Acquitted.

14. Date: 16 August 1999.
    Source: *Dawn*, 17 August 1999.
    Judge: Farooq Ali Channa.
    Case: Murder case of Muhammad Sabir.
    Accused: Humayun Akhtar, Syed Mohd. Ali, Muhammad Shoab, Arif, Mohd. Tariq, (MQM-A).
    Verdict: Acquitted.

15. Date: 21 August 1999.
    Source: *Dawn*, 22 September 1999.
    Judge: Hussain Bux Khoso.
    Case: Murder of four Americans and a Pakistani driver of Union Texas.
    Accused: a) Ahmad Saeed (Bharam), Mohd. Saleem (Denter) (MQM-A).
    Verdict: Death sentence plus 7 years RI, plus fine Rs 1,000,000 each.

    Accused: b) Altaf Hussain (Chief of the MQM), Nadeem Nusrat, Anis Advocate, Ajmal Pahari, Kashif David, Faisal (Lamba), Waseem (Tunda), Sajid.
    Verdict: Declared absconding.

16. Date: 25 August 1999.
    Source: *Dawn*, 26 August 1999.
    Judge: ATC No. 4.
    Case: Murder and Encounter.
    Accused: Tariq Hussain, Iran Mirza, Muhammad Imran, Naeem (Macha), Wasim (Tunda), Aslam (Tundi), Shabbir (Cheater), Wazir, Javaid (Chhota), and Javaid (Bara), (MQM-A).
    Verdict: First four acquitted, others absconding.

17. Date: 28 August 1999.
    Source: *Dawn*, 29 August 1999.
    Judge: ATC No. 5.
    Case: Murder of ASI Tariq Artaza.
    Accused: Muhammad Nadeem (Marble), Akram (Kana), and Rizwan, (MQM-A).
    Verdict: Acquitted.

18. Date: 2 September 1999.
    Source: *Dawn*, 3 September 1999.
    Judge: Abdul Hameed Abro.
    Case: Murder of Inspector Jalali.
    Accused: Kashif (MQM-H), Hamid (MQM-H).
    Verdict: Life term, 1 year RI, fine Rs 100,000 each plus fine Rs 2,00,000 each.

19. Date: 3 September 1999.
    Source: *Dawn*, 4 September 1999.
    Judge: Dr. Qamaruddin Bohra.
    Case: Murder of Constable Nazar Abbas.
    Accused: Nadeem (Machhi) Mohd. Ahmed, Abdul Fahim, Mohd Riyyaz, Danish, Mehtab, (MQM-A).
    Verdict: Acquitted, given benefit of doubt.

20. Date: 8 September 1999.
    Source: Dawn 9 September 1999.
    Judge: Sindh High Court.
    Case: Murder of Sepoy Dildar Hussain at Sr. No. 5.
    Accused: a) Muhammad Faisal, Muhammad Razzak, Muhammad Imran, (MQM-A).
    Verdict: Acquitted, appeal upheld, sentence set aside.
    Accused: b) Junaid (K-2).
    Verdict: Death sentence commuted to life.

21. Date: 15 September 1999.
    Source: *Dawn*, 16 September 1999.
    Judge: Sindh High Court.
    Case: Murder of Constable Ghausuddin.
    Accused: Fazal Rahim (MQM-A), Tahir (MQM-A), Sarwar Khan, and Altaf Ahmad.
    Verdict: Death to Fazal Rahim commuted to life. All others acquitted.

22. Date: 19 September 1999.
    Source: *Dawn*, 20 September 1999.
    Judge: Muhammad Javaid Alam.
    Case: Murder case of an American consulate officer.
    Accused: Saulat Mirza (MQM-A), Salman Haider, Arif Tutu, (MQM-A).
    Verdict: Acquitted.

23. Date: 22 September 1999.
    Source: *Dawn*, 23 September 1999.
    Judge: Muhammad Javaid Alam.
    Case: Murder of Havaldar Azizullah.
    Accused: Mubeen (Tunda) MQM-A, Javaid Michael (MQM-A), and Farooq Dada (MQM-A).
    Verdict: Death sentence to Mubeen in absentia. Others killed in encounter.

24. Date: 29 September 1999.
    Source: *Dawn*, 30 September 1999.
    Judge: Sindh High Court.
    Case: Demanding *bhatta* from Feroze Alam.
    Accused: Muhammad Ashraf (MQM-A), Ghulam Ali Murtaza, Muhammad Nadeem, (MQM-A).
    Verdict: Appeal against 7 years RI, dismissed.

25. Date: 4 October 1999.
    Source: *Dawn*, 5 October 1999.
    Judge: Arshad Noor Khan.
    Case: Attack on police party with heavy firing on 10 May 1999.
    Accused: Shahid Nisar (MQM-A), Sohail Alam, and four others, (MQM-A).
    Verdict: 21 years RI for Shahid Nisar, Suhail acquitted, four others absconding.

26. **Date:** 12 October 1999.
    Source: *Dawn*, 13 October 1999.
    Judge: Arshad Noor Khan.
    Case: Kidnapping Mohd. Javaid and demanding ransom.
    Accused: Muhammad Ali, (MQM-A).
    Verdict: Capital punishment, + 7 years RI, + fine Rs 20,000 + 7 years RI.

27. **Date:** 21 October 1999.
    Source: *Dawn*, 22 October 1999.
    Judge: Muhammad Javaid Alam.
    Case: Carjacking.
    Accused: Syed Arif (MQM-A), Imran and Obaid, Danish (MQM-A).
    Verdict: 7 years RI plus, fine Rs 5,000 each. Danish absconding.

28. **Date:** 1 November 1999.
    Source: *Dawn*, 2 November 1999.
    Judge: Dr. Qamaruddin Bohra ATC 6.
    Case: Kidnapping and killing Sirajuddin, a KESC employee,
    Accused: Asif Jameel (Papper) MQM-A, Qaiser.
    Verdict: Death sentence + Fine Rs 100,000 each.

29. **Date:** 10 November 1999.
    Source: *Dawn*, 11 November 1999.
    Judge: Rahmat Hussain Jaffery ATC 1.
    Case: Snatching a passenger coach.
    Accused: Zaheeruddin (MQM-H) (Three accomplices absconding).
    Verdict: Seven years RI plus fine Rs. 25,000 plus seven years + fine Rs 25,000 + Rs. 25,000 compensation.

30. **Date:** 2 December 1999.
    Source: *Dawn*, 3 December 1999.
    Judge: Shamshad Kazi, Additional Sessions Judge.
    Case: Firing at house of MPA Zulfiqar Hyder in 1994, and at the police.
    Accused: Mumtaz Haider, Taqi, Jamil Kazmi, Asim, Rafique, and Shakeel, MQM (H) activists.
    Verdict: Acquitted.

31. **Date:** 9 December 1999.
    Source: *Dawn*, 10 December 1999.
    Judge: Abdul Hameed Abro, ATC 2.
    Case: Killing Mohd. Ashraf, a police driver.
    Accused: Javed Murgh, Tahir Tipu, and Saeed Mamoon, (MQM-A).

Verdict: Acquitted, as no identification parade was conducted as required by law.

32. Date: 11 December 1999.
    Source: *Dawn*, 12 December 1999.
    Judge: Abdul Hameed Abro, ATC 2.
    Case: Trespass, abduction and murder of Constable Muhammad Arif and Akbar Ali.
    Accused: Farhan Hussain and six others, (MQM-A).
    Verdict: Acquitted.

33. Date: 14 December 1999.
    Source: *Dawn*, 15 December 1999.
    Judge: Arshad Noor Khan, ATC 3.
    Case: Murder of Lance Naik Ahmad Yar Khan and Sepoy Muhammad Idrees of Baloch Regiment on 27 July 1998.
    Accused: Salman Ilyas alias Waseem Raju, Suhail alias Kala, Muna, alias Faim Muna, Mohd. Adeel, Shafiq Arian, Irshad Kantap, and Abdul Famid of MQM (A).
    Verdict: Death sentence, + 7 years RI, + Rs 50,000 fine for each.

34. Date: 18 January 2000.
    Source: *Dawn*, 19 January 2000.
    Judge: Sindh High Court.
    Case: Murder of Anees Khan alias Anees Kala of MQM (H) in June 1997.
    Accused: Nadeem Shahpur alias Sharper of MQM (A), sentenced to death by Hakim Ali Abbasi, ATC 7.
    Verdict: Appeal allowed.

35. Date: 21 January 2000.
    Source: *Dawn*, 22 January 2000.
    Judge: Sindh High Court.
    Case: Murder of Malik Shahid Hamid, MD, KESC.
    Accused: MQM (A) member Saulat Mirza (Saulat Ali Khan) convicted by ATC 5, and sentenced to death.
    Verdict: Appeal rejected.

36. Date: 1 Februaryy 2000.
    Source: *Dawn*, 31 January 2000.
    Judge: Khan Pervez Chang, ATC 4.
    Case: Murder of Sepoy Deedar Hussain.
    Accused: Taha Hussain (MQM-A); co-accused acquitted in appeal by High Court vide serial No. 20.

Verdict: Convicted. Sentence to be decided by the government, as the convict is a juvenile.

37. Date: 6 May 2000.
    Source: *Dawn*, 7 May 2000.
    Judge: Additional District and Sessions Judge Karachi East, Syed Ali Bukhari.
    Case: Murder of Asif Siddiqi on 2 June 1995, employee of KSWB.
    Accused: Azam, Mahmood, and Biltees (Mutahida).
    Verdict: Acquitted, as the prosecution could not prove his guilt beyond any shadow of doubt.

38. Date: 6 May 2000.
    Source: *Dawn*, 7 May 2000.
    Judge: Additional Sessions Judge Mohd. Jamil.
    Case: Kidnapping and murder of Mohd. Hasan, owner of a cigarette kiosk.
    Accused: Tariq (MQM-H).
    Verdict: Acquitted.

39. Date: 11 May 2000.
    Source: *Dawn*, 12 May 2000.
    Judge: Akhtar Chaudhry, Additional District and Sessions Judge Karachi West.
    Case: Creating disturbance, burning tyres during strike in 1994.
    Accused: Saghir and Nadeem, (MQM-A).
    Verdict: Acquitted for want of incriminating evidence.

40. Date: 23 May 2000.
    Source: *Dawn*, 24 May 2000.
    Court: ATC Judge, Syed Jamil Raza Zaidi, Additional Distt. and Sessions Judge, Karachi East.
    Case: Shooting at Abdur Razzak, killing an unidentified passer-by.
    Accused: Zafar Ahmad Rangar (MQM-H), Muzaffar Ahmad Rangar (MQM-H), Rizwan alias Bhola.
    Verdict: Acquitted.

41. Date: 2 June 2000.
    Source: *Dawn*, 3 June 2000.
    Court: Mrs. Qaisar Iqbal, Distt. and Sessions Judge, Karachi, West.
    Case: Possessing unlicensed assault rifle AK-47 Kalashnikov.
    Accused: Muhammad Yunus alias Commando (MQM-A).
    Verdict: Sentenced to 3 years RI plus fine Rs. 5,000 or additional one year in lieu thereof.

42. Date: 27 June 2000.
    Source: *Dawn*, 28 June 2000.
    Court: ATC-1.
    Judge: Rahmat Hussain Jafferi.
    Case: Hijacking a passenger coach, opening fire on the police, possessing an unlicensed Kalashnikov assault rifle.
    Accused: Zaheer Ahmad, Nadeem Hussain, Arshad alias Fauji (MQM-H).
    Verdict: Zaheer Ahmad sentenced for hijacking the bus and possessing an unlicensed gun. But, acquitted on the charge of opening fire on the police party and attempting to kill a policemen. Nadeem Hussain acquitted. Verdict on Arshad not reported.

43. Date: 9 August 2000.
    Source: *Dawn*, 10 August 2000.
    Court: ATC 3.
    Judge: Arshad Noor Khan.
    Case: Looting of passengers of a minibus on route No. W-25 and later killing Head Constable Shamim Akhtar when a police party challenged them on 20 April 2000.
    Accused: Muhammad Yusuf and Muhammad Shahid alias Shahid Lamba (MQM-A).
    Verdict: Acquitted, given the benefit of the doubt.

44. Date: 1 September 2000.
    Source: *Dawn*, 2 September 2000.
    Court: Additional District and Sessions Judge.
    Case: Murder of Abid Ali (22), Zeeshan Ahmad (21), Muhammed Arshad (26), Shahid (21) on 9 June 1997.
    Accused: Nasir Ahmad alias Nasir Chingari, Shahzad Ahmad, Muhammed Nadeem (All MQM-H).
    Verdict: Acquitted.

45. Date: 13 September 2000.
    Source: *Dawn*, 14 September 2000.
    Judge: Jaffar Iqbal, Judicial Magistrate, Karachi East.
    Case: Possessing an unlicensed pistol.
    Accused: Muhammad Adnan (MQM).
    Verdict: Acquitted.

46. Date: 18 September 2000.
    Source: *Jang*, 19 September 2000.
    Judge: Additional District and Sessions Judge, Karachi East.

Case: Murder of two Bengali youth on 9 November 1995 in
           Korangi.
Accused: Muhammad Hussain, Abdul Aziz, and seventeen others
           (MQM-A)
Verdict: Acquitted.

47. Date: 30 September 2000.
    Source: *Dawn*, 1 October 2000.
    Judge: Additional District and Sessions Judge, Karachi Central.
    Case: Arson, creating disturbances to impose a strike on
               1 October 1995.
    Accused: Shoaib Bukhari and Vakil Jamali (MQM-A).
    Verdict: Acquitted.

48. Date: 4 November 2000.
    Source: *Dawn*, 5 November 2000.
    Judge: Arshad Noor Khan ATC 3.
    Case: Retrial of the murder of Ismail Memon, Chairman Board
               of Secondary Education, under order of Sindh High Court.
               Accused were convicted vide Sr. No. 2 above.
    Accused: Syed Ayub Haider Naqvi, Kazi Khalid, ex-minister of
               education, and others, (MQM-A).
    Verdict: Acquitted. Investigation Officer to show cause why he
               should not be punished for improper investigation.

49. Date: 14 November 2000.
    Source: *Dawn*, 15 November 2000.
    Judge: Salman Ansari, District and Sessions Judge, Karachi
               Central.
    Case: Armed encounter with police in October 1998. Accused
               were convicted vide Sr. No. 2 above.
    Accused: Ajmal Bihari, Naushad alias Major Dandi, Arif KDA Walla,
               Ijaz alias Kala alias Munna, Wahab Qandhari, Asif Burger,
               Shahid Commando, and Tariq Sukkur Wala (all MQM-A).
    Verdict: All acquitted.

50. Date: 21 November 2000.
    Source: *Dawn*, 22 November 2000.
    Judge: Riyaz Shaikh, Additional District and Sessions Judge.
    Case: Shooting encounter with police on 20 August 1998.
    Accused: Muhammad Aslam alias Chore (MQM-A), Salim alias
               Jhallo (MQM-A).
    Verdict: Acquitted.

51. Date: 24 November 2000.
    Source: *Dawn*, 25 November 2000.
    Judge: Saudagar Ali Solangi, Additional City Magistrate, Hyderabad.
    Case: Arson and violence in 1995.
    Accused: Ehteshamul Haq, Haji Yaqoob (President, Chamber of Commerce), Zakir bin Zahid (Chairman, Anjuman-i-Tajiran-i-Sindh). All MQM-A.
    Verdict: Acquitted.

52. Date: 15 December 2000.
    Source: *Dawn*, 16 December 2000.
    Judge: Riyaz Shaikh, Additional District and Sessions Judge, Karachi Central.
    Case: Attacking police party, injuring police constable Anees Ahmad.
    Accused: Shahid Faisal, Waseem, Aslam, and Shakeel (MQM-A).
    Verdict: Acquitted. Prosecution could not produce incriminating evidence.

53. Date: 19 December 2000.
    Source: *Dawn*, 20 December 2000.
    Judge: Riaz Shaikh, Additional District and Sessions Judge, Karachi West.
    Case: Murder of MQM-H workers.
    Accused: Shahid Afroze, (MQM-A).
    Verdict: Acquitted.

54. Date: 9 January 2001
    Source: *Dawn*, 10 January 2001
    Judge: Additional District and Sessions Judge, Karachi Central.
    Case: Murders.
    Accused: Shoaib Bukhari, Vakil Jamali, Mohammad Matin, Iqbal Ghauri, and Javed Pinky (MQM-A).
    Verdict: Acquitted.

55. Date: 10 January 2001.
    Source: *Dawn*, 11 January 2001.
    Judge: Riyaz Shaikh, Additional District and Sessions Judge.
    Case: Opening fire on a police party near Usman memorial chowrangi in Azizabad on 15 August 1998, and injuring constables Naseemuddin and Shoaib Ahmad.
    Accused: Shahid Afroze, Muhammad Azim, Abdul Shafiq, and Irshad Ahmad alias Munna (MQM-A).

Verdict: All above accused acquitted. Accused Atiq, Shakeel, and Asif alias Kala declared absconders. Case will remain dormant till their arrest.

56. Date: 15 January 2001.
    Source: *Dawn*, 16 January 2001.
    Judge: M. Riyaz Shaikh, Additional District and Sessions Judge, Karachi Central.
    Case: Attack on a police mobile on 15 September 1994 in Nazimabad, murdering Subedar Abdus Sattar, injuring Captain Mujib-ur-Rahman, Lance Naik M. Aslam, Sarfraz, M. Rafiq, and Shabbir Ahmad.
    Accused: Shoaib Bukhari (ex-MPA), Afzal Aver (ex-MPA), Musarat Ali Khan, and Shahid Kibriya (MQM-A).
    Verdict: Acquitted. Altaf Hussain, Chief of the MQM-A, and twenty-one others declared absconders.

57. Date: 8 February 2001.
    Source: *Dawn*, 9 February 2001.
    Judge: Muhammad Aziz Jamali, Additional District and Sessions Judge, Karachi Central.
    Case: Murder of drug addict in 1998.
    Accused: Habib, Safdar and Shahid (MQM-A).
    Verdict: Acquitted.

58. Date: 8 February 2001.
    Source: *Dawn*, 9 February 2001.
    Judge: Syed Qurban Ali Shah Lakyari, Additional District and Sessions Judge, Karachi East.
    Case: Vehicle snatched from Muhammad Ashraf on 29 June 1995.
    Accused: Ghulam Murtaza, Nadeem Chhota, and Zakir Hasan (MQM-A).
    Verdict: Acquitted.
    Accused: Ashraf alias Achhu, Zubair Chhota, Ibrahim, Tariq, and Tahir Ali alias Nadeem S.P. (MQM-A) were declared as proclaimed offenders.

59. Date: 12 February 2001.
    Source: *Dawn*, 13 February 2001.
    Judge: Ayaz Mustafa Jokhio, Judicial Magistrate, Karachi Central
    Case: Possessing an unlicensed pistol (1998).
    Accused: Muhammed Imran alias Puppu (MQM-A).
    Verdict: Sentenced to two years imprisonment and fine Rs 1000.

60. **Date:** 13 February 2001.
    Source: *Dawn,* 14 February 2001.
    Judge: Muhammad Riaz Shaikh, Additional District and Sessions Judge, Karachi Central.
    Case: Using criminal force against police during violent strike on 27 March 1994.
    Accused: Altaf Hussain, Hasan Husanna, Abdul Qadir, Kunwar Khalid Younus, and Shoaib Bukhari (MQM-A).
    Verdict: Kunwar Khalid Younus and Shoaib Bukhari acquitted, others declared absconding.

61. **Date:** 13 February 2001.
    Source: *Dawn,* 14 February 2001.
    Judge: Ms Akhtar A. Choudhry, Additional District and Sessions Judge, Karachi West.
    Case: Double murder after kidnapping Allah Wasaya and Muhammad Shafi.
    Accused: Ashfaq, Muhammad Shakil, Sanaullah, Muhammad Siddik, Muhammad Hanif, Sultan, Yusuf, Muhammad Habib, Imran Patni, Muhammad Arif, and Shaikh Ferozuddin (MQM-A).
    Verdict: Acquitted.

62. **Date:** 13 February 2001.
    Source: *Dawn,* 14 February 2001.
    Judge: Ms. Akhtar A. Choudhry, Additional District and Sessions Judge, Karachi West.
    Case: Robbery, looting Rs 32,000 and jewellery from the house of Manzoor Khan on 17 September 1996.
    Accused: Zeeshan, Sajid, Kashif, Hussain alias Papa, and Muhammad Airwali (MQM-A).
    Verdict: Acquitted. Prosecution did not produce the record.

63. **Date:** 13 February 2001.
    Source: *Dawn,* 14 February 2001.
    Judge: Ms Akhtar A. Choudhry, Additional District and Sessions Judge, Karachi West.
    Case: Attempted kidnapping of police Head Constable Nasrullah Khan Jadoon and his friend ,Nasir, on 24 April 1998.
    Accused: Shaukat alias Lala, Mujahid, Yusuf Ghanchi, Jamal Bukhari, Muhammad Ali, and Rehman alias Mola (MQM-A).
    Verdict: Acquitted.

64. Date: 13 February 2001.
    Source: *Dawn,* 14 February 2001.
    Judge: Nuzhat Ara Alvi, Additional District and Sessions Judge,
               Karachi West.
    Case: Possession of an illegal sub-machine gun.
    Accused: Yousuf Ghanchi (MQM-A).
    Verdict: Acquitted.

65. Date: 13 February 2001.
    Source: *Dawn,* 14 February 2001.
    Judge: Bashir Ahmad Khoso, Additional District and Sessions
               Judge, Karachi East.
    Case: Attacking a police party.
    Accused: Umer Farooq and Mujahid alias Pappu.
    Verdict: Acquitted.

66. Date: 17 February 2001.
    Source: *Dawn,* 18 February 2001.
    Judge: Khan Parvez Chang, ATC-4.
    Case: Anti-Pakistan activities, keeping explosive materials.
    Accused: Abdul Jabbar, Muhammad Shafiq, Haji Dogar, Hashim,
               Jumman, Maroa, and Saleh Muhammad (MQM-A).
    Verdict: Death sentence and 14 years imprisonment to Abdul Jabbar
               and Muhammad Shafiq. Remaining five accused acquitted.

67. Date: 20 February 2001.
    Source: *Dawn,* 21 February 2001.
    Judge: Muhammad Riaz Shaikh, Additional District and Sessions
               Judge, Karachi Central.
    Case: Anti-state activities and other charges under sections 147,
               148, 149, 324, 336, 335, and 120 B. Committing violence
               during party-sponsored day of mourning and setting two
               vehicles on fire.
    Accused: Kunwar Khalid Younus, Afzal Anwar, Altaf Hussain and
               eight others (MQM-A).
    Verdict: Kunwar Khalid Younus and Afzal Anwar acquitted under
               section 265 H of criminal procedure code.
    Accused: Altaf Hussain and eight others declared absconding.

68. Date: 20 February 2001.
    Source: *Dawn,* 21 February 2001
    Judge: Ahmad Nawaz Shaikh, Additional District and Sessions
               Judge, Karachi Central
    Case: Attack on a police party, attempt to kill a policeman

Accused: Kunwar Khalid Younus, Shoaib Bukhari, Vakil Jamali, Rafi Danish, Altaf Hussain, and twenty others (MQM-A).

Verdict: Kunwar Khalid Younus, Shoaib Bukhari, Vakil Ahmad, and Rafi Danish acquitted. Altaf Hussain and twenty others declared absconders.

69. Date: 1 March 2001.

Source: *Dawn,* 2 March 2001.

Judge: Justice Ghulam Nabi Soomro and Justice Ataur Rahman of Sindh High Court.

Case: Appeal against conviction by ATC to 10 and 20 years RI for hijacking a taxi on 15 March 2000, near Hasan Square.

Accused: Ghazanfarali and Muhammad Amir (MQM-A).

Verdict: Acquitted.

70. Date: 3 March 2001.

Source: *Dawn,* 4 March 2001.

Judge: Roohullah Chaglah, S.T.A Court Judge, Hyderabad.

Case: Murder of the uncle, mother, and servant of Mir Amir Khan on 30 September 1988 in Latifabad.

Accused: Nadeem Omar and Fakhr Ayub (MQM-A).

Verdict: Acquitted.

71. Date: 16 March 2001.

Source: *Dawn,* 17 March 2001.

Judge: Nouman Memon, Additional District and Sessions Judge, Karachi Central.

Case: Violence and arson during party-sponsored strike in May 1994.

Accused: Kunwar Khalid Younus, and twelve others (MQM-A).

Verdict: Kunwar Khalid Younus acquitted. Twelve others declared absconding.

72. Date: 24 March 2001.

Source: *Dawn,* 25 March 2001.

Judge: Syed Zakir Hussain, ATC-I.

Case: Killing a constable and injuring another.

Accused: Muhammad Hussain ex-MPA, Ijaz Ahmad, Zahiruddin alias Babar, Shadab Ahmad, and six others (MQM-A).

Verdict: Acquitted due to improper investigation.

73. Date: 27 March 2001.

Source: *Dawn,* 28 March 2001.

Judge: Ahmad Nawaz Shaikh, Additional District and Sessions Judge.
Case: Firing, arson, and looting on the day of mourning called by the party.
Accused: Kunwar Khalid Younus, ex-MNA, Wakil Ahmad Jamali, ex-MPA, Shoaib Bukhari, Syed Javed, and Rafi Javed (MQM-A).
Verdict: Acquitted.

74. Date: 12 May 2001.
Source: *Dawn,* 13 May 2001.
Judge: Zafar Ahmad Khan, District and Sessions Judge, Karachi Central.
Case: Possession of unlicensed weapons.
Accused: Maqsoodali Qureshi (MQM-A).
Verdict: Acquitted as the prosecution could not produce incriminating evidence.

75. Date: 19 May 2001.
Source: *Dawn,* 20 May 2001.
Judge: Sarwat Sultana, Judicial Magistrage, Karachi Central.
Case: Burning of a truck of KESC during MQM-sponsored strike on 2 May 1994.
Accused: Kunwar Khalid Younus and others (MQM-A).
Verdict: Acquitted.
Note: This was the sixtieth acquittal of the accused. There are still thirty-three cases pending against him.

76. Date: 24 May 2001.
Source: *Dawn,* 25 May 2001.
Judge: Ahmad Nawaz Shaikh, Additional District and Sessions Judge, Karachi Central.
Case: Creating disturbance and police encounter.
Accused: Rana Safdar Ali, ex-MPA, Asad Javed, Ashraf, and Muhammad Aamir (MQM-A).
Verdict: Acquitted. Police could not bring on record the incriminating evidence.

77. Date: 31 May 2001.
Source: *Dawn,* 1 June 2001.
Judge: Sindh High Court.
Case: Murder of Hakim Said and others.

Accused: Shaikh Muhammad Amirullah, Muhammad Shakir alias
           Shakir Langra, Muhammad Nadeem alias Nadeem Mota,
           Muhammad Faisal, Muhammad Zubair, Abu Imran Pasha,
           Nazar alias Muqarrib, and Ezazul Hasan.
Verdict: Conviction set aside. All accused sentenced to death by
           ATC on 4 June 1994 (vide Sr. no. 7 above) acquitted.

GLOSSARY
(Local terms, abbreviations, and acronyms)

Aalmi Majlis Tahaffuz Khatam-e-Nabuwwat: International Association for the Protection of the Concept of the Finalty of Prophethood. This party has links with the Jamiat-ul-Ulema-i-Islam and the Taliban.

Ahimsa: A doctrine of Buddhism and Jainism, meaning respect for life, both plant and animal. It enjoins vegetarianism, belief in the unity of life, and non-violence.

Ahle-Kitab: People of the Book. Muslims accord this status both to the Jews and Christians. When the Arabs conquered Sindh, they accorded similar status to the Hindus, Buddhists, and Jains. This was done mainly for administrative reasons and for the payment of taxes.

Ahmadis: Followers of Mirza Ghulam Ahmad of Qadian. The Ahmadis were originally regarded as a sect of Islam. Subsequently, they were declared non-Muslims in Pakistan.

Al-Badar: An organization of holy warriors formed in 1971 with the help of the Jamaat-i-Islami to fight against the Mukti Bahini in East Pakistan. Now trained by the JI for a holy war in Kashmir.

Al-Shams: Organization of holy warriors formed in the former East Pakistan in 1971 to fight against the Mukti Bahini.

ANP: Awami National Party. *Awami* means the people.

APMSO: All Pakistan Muhajir Students Organization.

Awami Tehrik: A political party founded by Rasool Bakhsh Palijo in Sindh. The name translates as the People's Movement.

ATC: Anti-Terrorist Court.

Banh Beli: An NGO working in Sindh. The name literally translates as 'A Helping Hand to a Friend in Need'.

bhatta: Extortion, protection money, donation made under duress.

BNP: Balochistan National Party.

Bohra: A sub-sect of the Shias.

CP: A province of India, earlier called the Central Provinces and now renamed Madhya Pradesh.

crore: Ten million.

CTBT: Comprehensive Test Ban Treaty.

fatwa: Verdict, religious edict.

Hadith: Any of a number of collections of traditions rendering the sayings of the Prophet (PBUH) which, with accounts of his daily practices (Sunnah), constitute the major source of guidance for Muslims after the Quran.

Harkat-ul-Jihad-i-Islami: Movement for an Islamic Holy War.

Hizb-i-Jihad: Party of the Holy Warriors.

IJI: Islami Jamhoor Ittehad or the Islamic Democratic Union. A temporary alliance formed in 1989 by the Pakistan Muslim League(N), Jaamat-i-Islami, and other political parties and groups. The Alliance contested the elections against the PPP in 1988 and 1990, and governed from 1990-1992 before disbanding.

Ijtihad: Rational judgement.

Islami Jamiat-ul-Tulaba (IJT): The student wing of the Jaamat-i-Islami. Literally, the Party of Islamic Students.

Ismailis: Followers of the Aga Khan. The Ismailis are a sub-sect of the Shia Islam.

Isna Ashris: Followers of the Twelve (infallible) Imams. This is the largest of the sub-sects of Shia Islam.

Jag-Punjabi-Jag: Arise, O people of the Punjab. A slogan coined by the Pakistan Muslim League (N) after losing the national elections in 1988. The slogan worked, and in the provincial elections held three days later, the PML(N) won a majority in the Punjab.

Jam: Title of a chief of a Sindhi clan.

Jamaat-i-Ahle-Hadith (JAH): Party of the Followers of the Prophet's Tradition.

Jamiat-ul-Mujahideen: Party of Holy Warriors.

Jiye-Sindh Quomi Movement (JSQM): Long Live Sindh National Movement.

Jamaat-i-Islami (JI): Literally, Party of Islam. Founded by Maulana Abul Ala Maudoodi. It opposed the creation of Pakistan.

Jinnahpur: A hypothetical Muhajir territory proposed to be carved out of Sindh.

Jiye-Sindh: Literally, Long Live Sindh. Name of a political party.

Jiye-Sindh Mahaz (JSM): Literally, The Vanguard of the Long Live Sindh Movement. Name of a political party.

Jiye-Sindh Taraqi Pasand (JSTP):	Literally, The Progressive Front for the Long Live Sindh Movement. Name of a political party.
Jamiat-ul-Ulema-i-Islam (JUI):	The Party of Islamic Scholars.
Jamiat-ul-Ulema-i-Pakistan (JUP):	Party of Islamic Scholars of Pakistan.
Katchi abadis:	Temporary dwellings, slums, clusters of squatters.
kafir, kuffar:	Unbelievers, heathens, idolaters, pagans.
Khaksar Tahrik:	Political party founded by Allama Inayatullah Mashriqi. It opposed the creation of Pakistan. A member of the party made an assassination attempt on Jinnah in Bombay.
Khulafa-i-Rashdin:	The first four caliphs of Islam. Literally, the rightly guided caliphs.
KLA:	Kosovo Liberation Army.
KPT:	Karachi Port Trust.
Kufr:	Heathenism, idolatry, lack of (Islamic) belief, paganism.
lakh:	A hundred thousand.
Lashkar-i-Taiba:	Holy Regiment. Their training centres are located in many places including Muridke—near Lahore. In 1999, they shifted their base of operations from Afghanistan to Kashmir.
madressah:	An institution for imparting religious education.
Majlis-e-Tahaffuz-e-Khatm-e-Nabuwat:	Party for the Protection of the Concept of the Finality of Prophethood after Muhammad (PBUH).

Markazi-Jamiat-i-Ahle-Hadith (MJAH):	Central Party of the People of the Prophet's Tradition.
Markazi-i-Dawa:	Centre for the Propogation of Islam.
Markazul Dawat Wal Irshad:	Centre for the propogation of Islam and for Guidance.
mazar:	Grave, tomb, mausoleum.
masjid:	Mosque.
Maulana:	A Muslim religious scholar.
millat:	Nation. Muslims use this term to include the world Muslim brotherhood.
Muhajir:	Immigrant.
Muhajir Ittehad Tehrik (MIT):	Movement for Unity of Immigrants.
Muhajir-Punjabi-Pakhtun Mutahida Mahaz (MPPMM):	United Front for the Muhajirs, Punjabis, and Pakhtuns.
Mukti Bahini:	Liberation Army. The militant wing of the Awami League formed to fight for the liberation of the former East Pakistan.
Muhajir Qoumi Movement (MQM):	Translated as Immigrant National Movement. A political party, which came into existence in urban Sindh in 1984. In 1992, the party split in two, the breakaway faction calling itself the MQM-Haqiqi, or the real MQM. The parent body became known as the MQM (Altaf), named after its leader Altaf Hussain. Later, it was renamed the Mutahida Quomi Movement (MQM) which translates into the United National Movement.
MRD:	Movement for the Restoration of Democracy, formed in 1983 to confront

President Ziaul Haq's military dictatorship. In 1983, the MRD posed a serious
challenge in Sindh to the military regime.

Mutahida Jamiat-i-
Ahle-Hadith (MJAH):   United Party of the People of the
                          Prophet's Tradition.

Mutahida Ulema
Council: United Council of Islamic Scholars.

Mutahida Ulema Front: United Front of Islamic Scholars.

NDP: National Democratic Party.

Nizam-i-Mustafa: Literally, The Prophet's System of
                          Governance. This was the call given by
                          the Pakistan National Alliance (PNA) in
                          1977 when it agitated for the cancelling
                          of the allegedly rigged elections held
                          under Z.A. Bhutto, and for the holding of
                          fresh election.

no-go areas: Areas of MQM(A) influence allegedly
                          occupied by the MQM(H). MQM(A)
                          leaders were banned from entering these
                          areas.

Pagaro: Literally, the wearer of a turban or a head
                          gear. This hereditary title is used for the
                          head of the house of saints of Kingri
                          town—the Pir Pagaro.

pandit: Literally, Hindu religious authority; is
                          also used as a surname.

phatak: Gate, railway crossing.

riba: Usury. The Federal Shariat Court has
                          included commercial bank interest in its
                          defination of *riba*.

pir: Saint. In Sindh, descendants of saints are
                          also called *pir*. It is thus also a surname,
                          the bearer of which may possess no
                          attributes of a saint.

Pirzado:	Literally, descendant of a *pir*. Used as a hereditary family name.
PML:	Pakistan Muslim League. This party is divided into many factions, each faction named after the person heading it. Thus, PML(N) Nawaz Group, PML (Chattha) Chattha Group, PML(F) Functional Muslim League (led by Pir Pagaro), and PML(Q) Qaiyyum League.
PPP:	Pakistan People's Party, founded by Z.A. Bhutto in 1967.
PPP (SB):	Pakistan People's Party (Shaheed Bhutto). This was the breakaway faction of the PPP formed by Z. A. Bhutto's son, Murtaza Bhutto.
pushto:	Language spoken by the Pathans.
Qadianis:	*see,* Ahmadis.
Rabita Alam Al Islami:	Mecca-based World Islamic Coordination Council.
ram raj:	Supremacy of the god Rama; rule of Hinduism.
RAW:	Research and Analysis Wing (Indian Intelligence).
Sayed, Sayyid	Arabic word, used to denote respect as in Mister or Sir. In Sindh, the word is used to denote descent from Prophet Muhammad (PBUH).
shah:	Literally, king. Used as a suffix by Syeds.
Shah-jo-Risalo:	Complete works of the mystic Sindhi poet Shah Abdul Latif of Bhitai.
Sharea, Shariat:	Islamic law.
Shia, Shiite:	A sect in Islam, believing that Caliph Ali was the rightful successor to Prophet Muhammad (PBUH).
Sindhi Hari Tehrik:	Sindhi Peasant Movement.

Sindhu Desh:	The land of the Indus and its tributaries which corresponds to present-day Pakistan as defined by G.M. Syed in 1943; in 1972, Syed changed his definition to restrict the territory to the province of Sindh only and called for its independence.
Sindhi-Muhajir bhai bhai:	A slogan expressing brotherhood between the Sindhis and the Muhajirs.
Sipah-i-Sahaba-i-Pakistan (SSP):	Soldiers of the Prophet's Companions.
Sipah-i-Muhammad Pakistan:	Soldiers of Muhammad (PBUH).
suba:	Province.
SNA:	Sind National Alliance.
Sufi-Sufism:	Mystic, Mysticism.
Sunnah, Sunnat:	A traditional portion of Muslim law based on the Prophet's words or acts accepted as authoritative by many Muslims.
Tahrik-i-Jafria Pakistan (TJP):	Literally, movement for the Jafria school of jurisprudence.
Tahrik-i-Nifaz-i-Fiqh-Jafria (TNFJ):	Movement for the Introduction of Jafria (Shia) School of Jurisprudence.
Tahrik-i-Ittehad:	Movement for Unity.
Tehrik-i-Nifaz-i-Shariat-i-Muhammad (TNSM):	Movement for Introduction of Muhammad's (PBUH) Law.

Tahrik-i-Tahaffuz-i-Namoos-i-Risalat (TTNR):	Movement for Preservation of the Prophet's Pre-eminence. This is an alliance of about three dozen politico-religious parties.
Taliban:	Literally, students. Name of the student militia which captured Kabul, occupied 90 per cent of Afghanistan, and formed the government there.
Tanzim-ul-Akhwan:	Party of Brothers (in religion).
Tanzeemul Mashaikh Pakistan:	Party of Scholars.
Taqseem:	Division.
UDI:	Unilateral Declaration of Independence.
ummah:	People, community, nation; used to denote world Muslim brotherhood.
UP:	A province of India, earlier called the United Provinces now renamed as Uttar Pradesh.
zakat:	Obligatory annual religious tax a Muslim has to pay for charitable purposes, equivalent to 2.5 per cent of his moveable assets.
zimmis:	Non-Muslims who are guaranteed protection in an Islamic state.

BIBLIOGRAPHY

Ahmed, Akbar S., *Jinnah, Pakistan and Islamic Identity, The Search for Saladin*, Routledge, London 1997.

Ahmed, Manzooruddin, ed., *Contemporary Pakistan—Politics, Economy, and Society*, Royal Book Company, Karachi, 1980.

Ahmad, Zaheer, *Sindh Mein Quom Parasti Ke Nae Aur Purane Ruhjanat* (Urdu), Naya Daur Publications, Hyderabad, 1987.

————, *Jamhoori Daur Ka Naraz Sindh* (Urdu), Shambal Publications. Karachi, 1980.

Ali, Chaudhry Muhammad, *The Emergence of Pakistan*, Research Society of Pakistan, Lahore, 1973. [1964]

Ali, Dr Mubarak, *Sindh-Khamoshi Ki Awaz* (Urdu), Progressive Publishers, Lahore, 1992.

Ali, S. Ameer, *The Spirit of Islam*, Pakistan Publishing House, Karachi, reprint 1968.

Amin, Tahir, *Ethno-National Movements of Pakistan, Domestic and International Factors*, Institute of Policy Studies, Islamabad, 1993.

Aqil, Mukhtar, *Sindh Card*, Shabl Publications (Pvt.) Ltd., Karachi, 1990.

Aziz, Dr K.K., *The Making of Pakistan—A Study in Nationalism*, National Book Foundation, Islamabad, 1976. [1967]

Baloch, Justice Mir Khuda Bakhsh Marri, *Search Lights on Baloches and Balochistan*, Royal Book Company, Karachi.

Baluch, Muhammad Sardar Khan, *History of the Baloch Race and Balochistan*, 1958.

Basham, A.L., *Hinduism – The Concise Encyclopaedia of Living Faiths*, ed. R.C. Zaehner, Hutchinson, London.

Burton, Richard F., *Sindh and the Races that Inhabit the Valley of the Indus*, OUP Karachi, 1973.

Chandio, Maula Baksh, *Zikr Zindan Jo*, (Sindhi), Mehran Publications.

Durant, Will and Ariel, *The Story of Civilization. Part VII*, 'The Age of Reason Begins, The Islamic Challenge', New York.

Gauhar, Altaf, *Ayub Khan, Pakistan's First Military Ruler*, Sang-i-Meel Publications, Lahore, 1993.

Haq, Ziaul, 'Islamic Process – Realities and Trends', *South Asia Bulletin*, Vol. VIII, 1988.

Iqbal, Javed, *Ideology of Pakistan*, Ferozesons Ltd. Karachi.

Iqbal, Muhammad, *Reconstruction of Religious Thought in Islam*, Muhammad Ashraf, Lahore, reprint 1977.

Jafri, Aqil Abbas, *Pakistan Ke Siyasi Wadere*, Frontier Post Publications, 1993.

Jahandad, Lieutenant. General, *Pakistan – Leadership Challenges*, OUP, Karachi, 1999.

Jalibi, Dr Jameel and Kazi Quadir (eds.), *The Identity of Pakistan Culture*, Royal Book Co., Karachi, 1984.

James, Sir Morrice, *Pakistan Chronicle*, OUP, Karachi, 1993.

Jansen, G.H., *Militant Islam*, Pan Books, London and Sydney, 1979.

Khairi, Saad R., *Jinnah Reinterpreted*, OUP, Karachi, 1995.

Kamrani, Shahid, *Sindh Ka Manzarnama* (Urdu), Maktaba Fikr-o-Danish, Karachi.

Khan, Shafiq Ali, *Two-Nation Theory—as a Concept, Strategy and Ideology*.

Korejo, M.S., *G.M. Syed—An Analysis of His Political Perspectives*, OUP, Karachi, 1999.

Low, D.A., ed., *The Political Inheritance of Pakistan*, Cambridge Commonwealth Series, Macmillan, London, 1991.

Mahmood, Suhail, *The Sindh Report—A Province in Turmoil*, Classic, Lahore.

Manzar, Shahzad, *Sindh Ke Nasli Masail* (Urdu), Fiction House, Lahore, 1994.

Mazari, Sherbaz Khan, *A Journey to Disillusionment*, OUP, Karachi, 1999.

Mirza, Mahmood, *Aj Ka Sindh* (Urdu), Progressive Publishers, Lahore, 1986.

Misra, Amaresh, *Lucknow – Fire of Grace. The Story of Renaissance, Revolution and the Aftermath*, Harper Collins, India, 1998.

Mujahid, Sharif-ul, *Ideological Orientation of Pakistan*, National Book Foundation, Karachi, 1976.

Muhajid, Sharif-ul, *Jinnah-Studies in Interpretation*, Quaid-i-Azam Academy, Karachi, 1981.

Munir, Justice Muhammad, *From Jinnah to Zia*, Vanguard Books Ltd., Lahore, 1979.

Peerbhoy, Akbar A., *Jinnah Faces an Assassin*, East and West Publishing Company, Karachi, 1986 (originally published in Bombay, 1943).

Rahman, Mushtaq-ur, *Land and Life in Sindh, Pakistan*, Ferozesons Ltd., Karachi.

Raza, Rafi, ed., *Pakistan In Perspective 1947-1997*, OUP, Karachi, 1997.

Read, Anthony and Fisher, David, *The Proudest Day – India's Long Road to Independence*, W.W. Norton and Company, New York and London, 1998.

Salim, Ahmad, *Sulagta Hua Sindh* (Urdu), Jang Publishers, 1990.

Soomro, Khadim Hussain, *G.M. Syed – Adrshi Insan se Awtar tak*, (Urdu) Sain Publishers, Sehwan Sharif, 1999.

Syed, G.M., *Sindhu Desh – A Study in its Separate Identity Through the Ages*, G.M. Syed Academy, Karachi.

Syed, G.M., *Struggle for New Sindh*, Sain Publishers, Sehwan Sharif, 1949.

Wolpert, Stanley, *Jinnah of Pakistan*, OUP, Karachi, 1989.

———, *A New History of India*, University of California Press, Berkeley, Los Angeles, 1991.

Zaehner, R.C., ed., *The Concise Encyclopaedia of Living Faiths*, Hutchinson of London.

Zaheer, Hasan, *The Separation of East Pakistan – The Rise and Realization of Bengali Muslim Nationalism*, OUP, Karachi.

Zaidi, Akbar S., *Sindhi v/s Muhajir in Pakistan – Contradictions, Conflict, Compromise*, Economic and Political Weekly, 18 May 1991.